BLITZKRIEG

BLITZKRIEG

HITLER'S MASTERPLAN FOR THE CONQUEST OF EUROPE

NIGEL CAWTHORNE

CHARTWELL
BOOKS, INC.

This edition printed in 2012 by

CHARTWELL BOOKS, INC.
A Division of BOOK SALES, INC.
276 Fifth Avenue Suite 206
New York, New York 10001 USA

Copyright © 2012 Arcturus Publishing Limited
26/27 Bickels Yard, 151–153 Bermondsey Street,
London SE1 3HA

ISBN: 978-0-7858-2943-0
AD002097EN

Printed in China

CONTENTS

INTRODUCTION

A parade of Sherman M4 tanks at Fort Knox in the USA – nearly 50,000 M4s were built

Based on speed and surprise, Blitzkrieg (literally 'lightning war') involved light tank units, supported by aircraft and infantrymen, punching holes through enemy lines and racing on to secure their objectives before the enemy had time to rally. After seeing the success of British tanks in the First World War, the Germans decided that the future of warfare lay in the *Panzerkampfwagen* – or armoured fighting vehicle – later simply known as the Panzer.

But Panzer meant more than just a tank. There were *Panzergruppen* and *Panzertruppen* – Panzer groups and Panzer troops, and there was the Panzer Corps. Panzer was the name taken by this elite branch of the German army, its formations and a new type of warfare.

During the 1920s, British and German military theorists saw how deploying tanks at divisional strength could completely revolutionize war.

When Hitler came to power in 1933, he quickly saw how such Panzer formations could defeat Germany's traditional enemies and allow him to build the European empire he craved. Tank production was stepped up and the Panzer Corps became the German army's new vanguard. In ten months, they overran most of continental Europe, destroying armies more than twice their size on the way.

But with this initial success came their ultimate failure. The German High Command clung to the belief that they had discovered the all-conquering weapon. Yet the Panzers could not handle the snows of Russia, and in the deserts of North Africa, the British learnt that you could halt the Panzers' lightning advances with screens of dedicated anti-tank guns – which were much cheaper and easier to produce than new tanks.

The Russians and Americans took on the Panzers head to head and simply out-produced German tank manufacturers. Large, relatively slow-moving Panzers were also vulnerable to air attack. The build-up of the Royal Air Force and the US Army Air Force meant that, after D-Day, German Panzers could not risk moving during daylight and were even open to attack during the night, when the skies were lit with flares.

The Tiger I factory in Kassel, 1943, owned by Henschel & Sohn

The Panzers had one last day of glory in the winter of 1944 with the Battle of the Bulge when poor weather grounded the Allied air forces. However, the chronic German shortage of petrol for the thirsty Tiger tanks meant that the Panzers had to depend on captured US gasoline to fuel their advance. When this was denied them, and the weather cleared, the Panzers were sitting ducks again.

Hitler hoped until the last that new and better Panzers would crush his enemies. But although German manufacturers finally managed to match the Soviets' superb T-34 technically, they could never produce anything like the numbers that rolled out of Russian factories. Hitler and his henchmen were hoist with their own petard, crushed under the tracks of the Panzer war they had unleashed.

This book is the story of the development of the Panzer concept, and the building and deployment of the Corps, how it formed the spearhead of the world's most efficient military machines, and how it came to ultimate defeat. It looks at Panzer warfare through the eyes of those who fought it and put this deadliest of weapons into Hitler's unworthy hands.

Russia's T-34 which was able to outperform all German tanks until the Tiger I, with its 88mm gun and reinforced armour, appeared

1. THE PLAINS OF POLAND

The Second World War began with a terrific gamble. At dawn on 1 September 1939, a huge German army rolled across the 1,250-mile (2,000-km) Polish border. The attack was spearheaded by Panzers, seven divisions of them. No one had tried such a strategy before. It was not one of the terror tactics the Germans had perfected during the Spanish Civil War that had raged for the previous three years. The deployment of Panzers in Spain was considered largely a failure. When German tanks rolled over the border into Austria in 1938, at least 30 per cent had broken down before they reached Vienna. Things went little smoother during the occupation of Czechoslovakia the following year. The crews lacked the experience to fix mechanical problems on the spot and a tank broken down on a bridge or a narrow road could hold up a whole brigade. They also destroyed the surface of the roads they used, slowing those who followed. Fuel was another problem. The Wehrmacht, the German army, quickly realized that there was more to tanks than guns and armour. They were

going to have to learn a whole new discipline – the art of mechanized warfare.

However, there were a handful of men who believed that tank warfare would work on the plains of Poland. Hitler was among them. The proper use of the Panzer, he believed, was something that would have to be learnt in war itself.

Case for the defence

The first lesson, it was believed, should be easy. The Poles had just one armoured brigade, 660 tanks in all, versus Germany's 2,100. Although the Polish army would outnumber the attacking Germans once it had all been mustered, the Poles started out with 17 ill-equipped infantry divisions, three infantry brigades and six cavalry brigades – real cavalry brigades with horses, not the armoured units cavalry later became. However, the German High Command was not 100 per cent confident of victory. Orders issued in Berlin in 1939 stated:

No tanks must fall into enemy hands without the crew and the crews of neighbouring tanks

Left: German armour rolls across the Polish border, September 1939

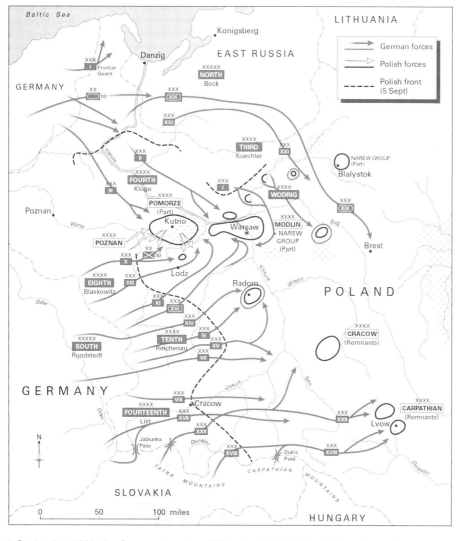

1 September 1939: the German invasion of Poland – the battle lasted for six weeks

doing their utmost to rescue or destroy it. A crew may abandon an immobilized tank only if they have run out of ammunition or can no longer fire, and if other vehicles cannot be expected to save it… If there is a risk that the tank may fall into enemy hands, it should be destroyed. Waste wool, combustible material, ammunition, etc. inside the vehicle should be soaked with fuel (possibly by ripping out the fuel pipe) and the vehicle is to be set on fire.

The German Panzer spearhead would be followed by four motorized infantry divisions,

four light divisions and forty regular infantry divisions. The Germans also had overwhelming superiority in the air. The Polish air force had just 842 obsolescent planes, while the Luftwaffe, the German air force, could put 4,700 modern aircraft in the air. One tactic the Germans had perfected during the Spanish Civil War was the terror bombing of civilian targets, including, infamously, the Basque market town of Guernica.

The Poles also believed that the French would attack Germany in the rear, across Germany's western frontier. When they finally did, they sent insufficient forces and it was too late.

The Soviet Union – Russia and its communist satellites – would be no help. It had signed the German–Soviet Non-Aggression Pact of August 1939, which publicly guaranteed that the two nations would not attack each other and privately divided Poland between them. Poland was on its own and its cavalry lances would be matched against the monstrous new machines of war: the Panzers.

Assault from the air

The Luftwaffe wiped out the Polish air force in the first two days. This left the sky clear for German Stukas to dive-bomb Polish columns which did more to dent the morale of raw Polish recruits than inflict physical damage. What tanks the Polish did possess were dispersed throughout the army, which itself made the fatal mistake of trying to defend the entire length of the border. The Panzers concentrated on weak points and broke through. They penetrated deep into the country, then fanned out, isolating and encircling Polish units.

When they came across Polish strongpoints, they simply bypassed them and allowed the bombers to take care of them later. And if they could not simply outflank a heavily fortified Polish position, they waited for the infantry and artillery to catch up, then launched a conventional assault on the stronghold.

The Poles did not grasp the full extent of the threat posed by the German armour and believed that, once they had fallen back to a defensive line, they could hold it. But the speed and depth of the Panzers' thrusts caused confusion and the dive-bombing of undefended towns choked the roads with refugees.

This was all part of Panzer theory. The idea was to prevent the enemy from using the road network to bring up reinforcements or regroup its forces. After all, civilians on the roads were no hindrance to the advancing Panzers. The refugees were simply machine-gunned from the air, producing further panic – and further obstacles to advancing Polish forces.

After the First World War, Poland had been recreated with two million Germans living within its borders. Some were involved in active sabotage. Others spread rumours of German victories, the inevitability of Polish defeat and the cowardice and deceit of Poland's leaders. This

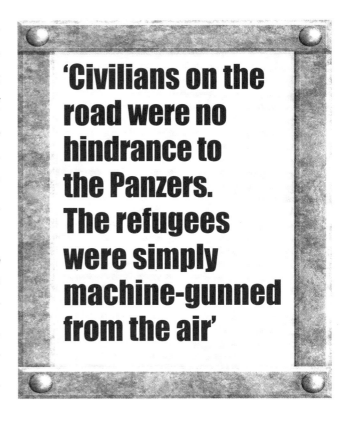

'Civilians on the road were no hindrance to the Panzers. The refugees were simply machine-gunned from the air'

tactic, known as *Schrecklichkeit*, 'frightfulness', again sapped morale.

The invasion begins

The Panzers led four deep thrusts into Poland. Two came directly from the German Reich itself, led by the XIX Panzer Corps and the XVI Panzer Corps heading for Warsaw, via Bydgoszcz and Lodz respectively. A southern thrust from Slovakia, led by the 2nd and 5th Panzer Divisions, headed through Chelm to Brest-Litovsk, where they were to meet up with the Third Army, led by elements of XIX Panzer Corps. This came via East Prussia, a part of Germany separated from the Reich by the 'Polish Corridor' which, under the Treaty of Versailles, gave Poland access to the Baltic. The Southern Army Group was under the command of General Karl von Rundstedt, whose chief of staff was General Erich von Manstein. The Northern Army Group was commanded by General Fedor von Bock.

The attack began at 0445 on Friday 1 September when the German naval training ship *Schleswig Holstein* began bombarding the Polish Corridor. The Luftwaffe then bombed the Polish airfields. At 0800 a large formation of tanks from the German 4th Panzer Division arrived at the positions held by the Polish cavalry brigade Wolynska Brygada Kawalerii. They came under fire from machine guns and anti-tank weapons, and retreated to the village of Wilkowiecko.

The Polish cavalry were then dive-bombed, which caused the horses to stampede. A swarm of Panzers left Wilkowiecko to attack the Polish 21st Lancers, who were fighting on foot along the edge of Mokra Wood, but they were forced to withdraw, leaving four burning tanks behind them. Renewed Stuka attacks and an artillery barrage left the villages of Mokra I, II and III in flames. Polish casualties were high. Nevertheless, when the Panzers went in again, several were hit and caught fire, and escaping crews were captured by the lancers.

The Germans aimed their main attack at the 4th Troop of the 21st Lancers. But at 1100 hrs, shortly before they reached the lancers' position, the Polish Armoured Platoon arrived and began bombarding them with 10cm howitzers and 7.5cm field guns. The Germans retreated behind Wilkowiecko, leaving crews behind on the battlefield in their wrecked tanks to be captured by the Poles. This was going to be no pushover.

Around this time the Reich press chief, Otto Dietrich, issued an edict that the word 'war' was to be avoided in press reports at all costs, stressing that the Polish ambassador was still in Berlin. Even the Polish News Agency said that the fighting was 'confined to border zones'. But the German First Lieutenant W. Reibel took part in the attack and described the scene:

The bow waves crashed around the tanks, spraying a cool shower over many a driver who crosses the river too fast. To our left is

SS troops advance into the 'free city' of Danzig behind an ADGZ armoured car, 1939 – many of the SS men came from the city itself

a blown-up railway bridge, at the edge of the road is a dead Polish soldier. It really is a strange feeling to know that now we have left Germany and are standing on Polish soil. Far away we hear the weak barking of a machine gun. Somewhere there is a hollow thunder of cannon – the first signs of war. Ahead of us lies a village. According to the map it must be Mokra III. The name means nothing to us yet. It's just a village like any other. But what would we have done if we had known? There! Arriving at the last houses in the village we hear rifle and machine gun fire, then comes the order: 'Prepare for combat.' The shooting steps up… projectiles strike the tank with a bright clang. Trenches crisscross our attack zone, marshy meadows impair our progress. Yet we roll on relentlessly… Slowly we reach the edge of the wood and push into a forest lane, my company ahead of me. All hell has broken loose here. Ahead of us is an embankment with an underpass. Bullets are cracking and roaring like mad… A lot of vehicles from 2nd Company and our company are now standing in the forest lane. Suddenly a tank that had already pushed through the underpass goes up in flames. Damn the lot of them. It's an anti-tank force… Many a dear comrade was missing when we assembled. Their tanks turned into iron graves. Our company too has suffered its first deaths… A short time later our company too marched back to the resting area… The burning villages lit the horizon with a red glow. Then came a sudden cry: 'Polish cavalry approaching to the left' and we seized our weapons again. But it was a false alarm. Herds of riderless horses were searching for human beings.

Nevertheless, the Wolynska cavalry brigade succeeded in holding up the advance of the German 4th Panzer Division for a whole day. Official sources in Germany told a different story. After reporting 'an almost grotesque attack on some of our tanks by a Polish lancer regiment with what annihilating consequences one can easily imagine', the army propaganda sheet *Die Wehrmacht* went on to say:

Even the anti-tank guns which the Poles believed could easily halt the advance of our tanks were soon revealed as too weak. In one battle a single German heavy tank annihilated two gun crews with a single shot and then crushed the guns themselves under its heavy track chains. Incidentally, the tank driver, a very young second lieutenant, shortly afterwards stopped a railroad train loaded with Polish reservists, forced them to climb out and herded them along – 400 men in all – in the van of his tank.

Pushed back

On 2 September, the Polish army was forced to retreat under intense pressure from the XV Panzer Corps under General Hoth and the XVI Panzer Corps under General Hoepner who threatened to encircle it from the south. Meanwhile at the head of the XIX Panzer Corps, the armoured spearhead of the Northern Army Groups, was General Heinz Guderian, the great theorist of Panzer warfare. Now, at last, he

German–Soviet negotiations over the demarcation line in Poland: General Guderian can be seen second from the right

could see his theories being put into practice. He believed that it was essential for a Panzer commander to be at the forefront of the action with his men. Reporting the situation back to an HQ in the rear then waiting for orders to be sent forward again would slow progress.

The fast-moving nature of this new type of mechanized warfare meant that troops were liable to shoot first and ask questions later. Consequently, Germans ended up firing on other Germans who had turned up in unexpected places. Nevertheless Guderian soon proved the worth of his 'command from forward' system. All the armoured unit commanders were kept as far forward as possible, allowing them to issue commands by radio direct to the Panzers and infantry troops following. This meant they could take rapid advantage of any situation. However, stationing the commander forward when the lines are fluid had its own dangers. Guderian found himself under shellfire from his own artillery who were firing haphazardly through the mist and was lucky to escape with

his life. The Luftwaffe general in charge of close air support was also fired on by his own troops, even though his plane clearly carried German markings.

The Poles also claimed some initial successes. On 5 September, their news agency reported: 'A successful Polish counter-attack has been reported against motorized divisions advancing towards Bieradz in southern Poland. The enemy abandoned considerable numbers of assault vehicles and motor cars whose occupants were taken prisoner. There were many captives.'

There were other setbacks. Panzers outran their fuel supplies, blocking the roads when they ran out of petrol. Again there was a high level of breakdowns. No less than a quarter of the tanks were out of action at any one time. This was an improvement on the 30 per cent breakdown rate they had experienced before, though all the vehicles needed an overhaul by the end of the campaign. However, the Panzers played a decisive role in the remarkable success of the Polish campaign. The Wehrmacht, under

> **'Guderian's XIX Panzer Corps was allowed to leave the Third Army behind and race south-east to take Brest-Litovsk'**

another important advocate of the Panzer, General Walther von Reichenau, covered the 140 miles (225 km) to the outskirts of Warsaw in just seven days. Guderian made even more ground in lightning thrusts with two Panzer divisions and two motorized divisions moulded into a single corps. His XIX Corps covered 200 miles (320 km) in ten days, cutting through the Narev Operational Group and destroying the Polish Eighteenth Army for the loss of only 4 per cent of its strength: 650 killed and 1,586 wounded and missing. And General Wilhelm Ritter von Thoma, Panzer commander in Spain, managed to infiltrate 50 miles though thick, though undefended, woods to turn the Polish flank at the Jablunka pass.

But the Panzers acted as a cutting edge rather than as an independent force. Their six armoured divisions comprised just 11 per cent of the Wehrmacht's strength and they were given strict orders not to outpace the infantry. The Panzers were still strictly under the command of their larger army groups. Training regulations maintained that tanks were only allowed to open fire independently 'when breaching the enemy or to ward off impending attack'.

It was only on 8 September, when it became clear that the Southern Army Group had not managed to occupy Warsaw, that Guderian's XIX Panzer Corps were allowed to leave the Third Army behind and race south-eastwards to take Brest-Litovsk, a hundred miles beyond the Polish capital to the east. But Guderian's success, according to von Manstein, was due to Germany's success in the air, rather than the Panzers themselves.

'What decided the battles,' he wrote, 'was the almost complete elimination of the enemy's air force and the crippling of his staff communications and transport network by the effective attacks of our Luftwaffe.'

But *Die Wehrmacht* lauded the success of the 15th and 16th Panzers, who had fought their way through to the outskirts of Warsaw on 6 September: 'Our spearhead rapidly reached the hills on the side of the river. The enemy artillery fired but our tanks rolled undeterred towards their targets along roundabout routes, under cover of farmsteads and underbrush. As the sun sank towards the west, our tanks penetrated the city under their protective fire, German combat engineers crossed the river so as to get behind and destroy the enemy still resisting in the city. While the armoured spearhead was still securing the river crossing, the second wave of tanks was already rolling up. It was led by a general travelling in a command tank studded with anti-aircraft machine guns. Reinforcement Panzer units and mobile divisions rolled up in an irresistible train over twelve miles (19 km) long.'

Last stand

A defence of the city had been hastily prepared. But by 8 September, Panzers had entered Warsaw. However, the 4th Panzer Division met dogged resistance in the city and 57 of the 120 attacking tanks were lost in just three hours. On the 11th, there was a report of a Polish counter-attack which claimed to have smashed 18 tanks. Although the Poles claimed on 14 September to have set more tanks on fire, and captured several anti-tank guns in skirmishes in the capital, the German thrust into Poland had been so swift that it was impossible for the Poles to pull back enough of their army to mount a concerted defence of the city.

While resistance inside the capital continued, the Polish cavalry took on the Panzers, according to Guderian. The British advocate of mechanized warfare Basil Liddell Hart also wrote of 'gallant but fantastic charges with sword and lance'. However, it is probably a myth. Denis Hills, a Briton who was in Poland at the time, dismissed this 'Balaclava stuff' as 'a bit of fantasy'. Though the Polish lancers would have come up against Nazi Panzers, they were far more effective against infantry battalions. At dawn on 9 September, the 3rd Light Horse Regiment of the Suwalki Cavalry Brigade charged a column of transport trucks just north of the Zambrow Forest, but only after they had been softened up by machine-gun fire from men hidden in the woods.

'The command "Draw sabres, gallop, march!" flew down the lines,' according to platoon commander M. Kamil Dziewanowski. 'Reins were gripped tighter. The riders bent forward in the saddles and they rushed forward like a mad whirlwind.'

This, the last cavalry charge in history, turned the Germans into 'a frantic mob' who were quickly overrun with negligible Polish losses.

'The morning sun was high when our bugler

8 September 1939: streetfighting in the Praga district of Warsaw as the 18th Infantry Division advances with Panzer II tanks in support

blew assembly,' Dziewanowski went on. 'We came up slowly, driving our prisoners ahead of us. We took about two hundred men, most of them insane from fright.'

Dziewanowski said that, although his proud cavalry brigade did turn themselves into 'an outfit of tank hunters' that autumn, they had more sense than to attack them with sabres. Instead, daredevils among them crept up on the German tanks at night and threw Molotov cocktails at them, or blew their tracks off with hand grenades.

After this one last charge, the cavalry's horses were too hungry and exhausted to mount anything like it again. However, the myth of the Polish cavalry taking on the Panzers persists. The reason may be that Poles, like the British, love stories of heroic defeat. After years of suffering under Nazi, then Soviet, tyranny, they have clutched on to the romantic idea of gallant Polish cavalry officers digging their spurs into their horses' flanks and galloping heroically at the invading Nazi divisions. In fact, the origin of the story probably lies in Nazi propaganda – Germany, a great 20th-century power, was crushing primitive Poland, stuck in the 18th.

On 17 September, Soviet forces entered Poland from the east. The country was divided between Germany and Russia along the lines of the secret protocol that accompanied the Non-Aggression Pact. On the morning of 18 September, the Polish government and high command crossed the Romanian frontier into exile and formal resistance was over. The Warsaw garrison held out against the Germans until 28 September, while terror-bombings and artillery barrages reduced parts of the city to rubble and the civilian population were starved and denied water. The last serious body of the Polish army held out until 5 October, though some guerrilla fighting went on into the winter. By then Poland as an independent state had been removed from the maps.

However, while the Poles were ill equipped and unsupported, the invasion of Poland was not the bloodless victory that the Germans had expected, or the Panzers had hoped for. The Germans lost 10,572 killed in action. Another 5,029 were listed as 'missing', but as the country was completely overrun it can be assumed that they were not taken prisoner. And 30,332 Germans were wounded.

Heavy losses

Of the 2,100 tanks that took part in the attack on Poland, 218 were destroyed. Fifty-seven of those were lost in heavy fighting in the streets of Warsaw. Tanks are not well suited to fighting in the confined conditions of city streets, where they are vulnerable to attack from the side and above. Against such a weak enemy a 10 per cent loss was considered high. Few faced anti-tank guns. When they did it was discovered that the smaller Panzer Is and IIs had neither the strength nor the firepower required for all-out mechanized warfare. It was found that the four divisions of light tanks were of little use, even in the ideal conditions of Poland. As a result four more Panzer divisions were created, bringing the total to ten and each was assigned its own Luftwaffe unit. From now on, armour and air power would work hand in hand.

The campaign had also shown up problems with the motorized infantry troops assigned

the rear and the Poles were too disorganized to mass their forces on the far bank. The Germans also learnt that the Soviet tanks had thin, outdated armour, and that their crews were often undisciplined. When the Soviets attacked Finland on 30 November 1939, their tanks could not overcome the Finnish tank hurdles and fell victim to anti-tank guns bought in Sweden. They could not cross rocky terrain. Traps were laid using felled trees and huge boulders, and slit trenches were used to conceal a soldier. When a tank appeared the man would toss a hand grenade under its gears to put it out of action. By 29 December, the Finns had destroyed 271 Russian tanks.

The commander of a Panzer I during a brief lull in fighting, 1939

to Panzer divisions. They had been carried in trucks, aptly known as 'soft-skinned vehicles', which presented easy targets to the enemy. This made the drivers cautious and large gaps opened up between them and the Panzer spearhead. Meanwhile, the infantry itself, which was on foot, was left far behind, along with the horse-drawn transports that the Germans used throughout the war.

During the Polish campaign, the rivers did not present the obstacles that the Panzer commanders had feared. Although none of the 1939 generation of tanks was amphibious, mobile bridging units were brought up rapidly from

However, the Western Allies learnt little from the Polish campaign. They dismissed many of the reports they received of lightning thrusts by armoured columns as the ravings of a demoralized people reeling under the shock of defeat. Allied strategists also failed to pick up the fact that the Panzers had not confined themselves to the wide open plains of Poland that would normally be considered perfect tank country, but had also pushed through heavily-wooded areas and over hills. Just eight months later the Western Allies would be surprised when the Panzers attacked through the heavily-wooded Ardennes, an area they would break through again in 1944 during the Battle of the Bulge.

In 1939 though, British and French military thinking was still mired in the mud of the First World War. Although forward-thinking strategists had developed the theory of mechanized warfare, those in command had turned a deaf ear and for the next three years the Panzer would reign supreme.

2. TANKS AND TANK TACTICS

Tanks were an invention born of the senseless carnage of the trenches of the First World War. At the beginning of the war in 1914, all combatants already had armoured cars and in the Tannenberg campaign in northern Poland the Germans successfully integrated them into their cavalry divisions, creating a 'supercavalry' that sent the Russians reeling. British armoured cars had had similar successes in defending Antwerp and Dunkirk.

Before the war even began, Lieutenant Colonel Gunther Burstyn, a railway officer in the Austrian army, had actually produced a prototype of his so-called *Motorgeschütz* ('motorized gun') which had caterpillar tracks and a gun on a revolving turret, a tank in all but name. This advance was ignored. Around the same time an Australian named L.E. de Mole, later a corporal in the Australian infantry, sent the British War Office his own design of a tracked armoured vehicle. It was duly filed.

After the war, a Royal Commission on Awards to Inventors fished it out and declared that de Mole's design was actually superior to the tanks that had been developed by that time.

However, the man credited with being the father of the modern tank was Lieutenant Colonel Ernest Swinton who, as the official British war correspondent in France, had seen in October 1914 the establishment of a line of fortified trenches running from the Swiss frontier to the North Sea. These were defended by artillery, barbed wire and machine guns, and it seemed to Swinton that they were unlikely to be breached by infantry or cavalry. Something new had to be tried.

Brainwave

Swinton put his mind to how to break the deadlock. Probably inspired by the H.G. Wells story 'The Land Ironclads' published in *Strand* magazine in 1903, Swinton said, 'I pictured to myself some form of armoured vehicle immune to bullets which should be capable of destroying machine guns and of ploughing through wire.' He soon realized that it would also have to function

Left: Benjamin Holt meets Ernest Swinton in Stockton, California, 1918

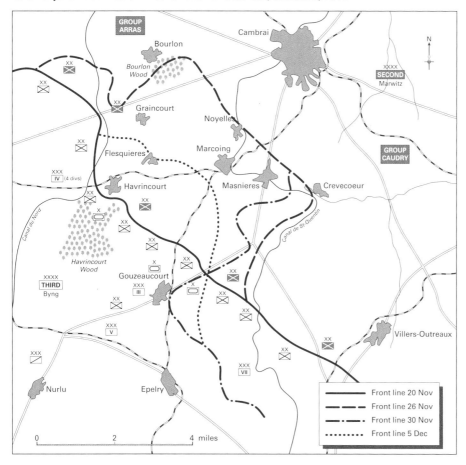

The Battle of Cambrai, 20 November–3 December 1917, where tanks showed their worth

Maurice Hankey. Hankey presented it to Lord Kitchener, the Secretary of War, who dismissed the proposal, saying that 'the armoured caterpillar would be shot up by guns'. But Hankey persisted. He drew up a long memorandum, developing the idea. He made particular reference to historical machines of war, especially the *testudo*, the Roman armoured tortoise whose shell was made by the legionnaires overlapping shields. The memo came to the attention of Winston Churchill, who liked new inventions.

in the muddy terrain of northern France, cross trenches and climb earthworks.

On 19 October, Swinton was driving past the lighthouse at Calais when he suddenly recalled reading about a new invention that had been shown at an exhibition in Belgium.

'Like a beam from the lighthouse the idea flashed across my brain,' he wrote, 'the American Caterpillar Tractor at Antwerp. I recalled its reputed performance… The key to the problem lay in the caterpillar track.'

By this time the Holt tractor was widely used as an agricultural vehicle. Its caterpillar tracks were designed to spread the weight of the vehicle over a greater area than wheels, so it could travel easily over soft ground.

Swinton took his idea to Lieutenant Colonel

Churchill, then at the Admiralty, wrote to the Prime Minister Herbert Asquith on 5 January 1915, saying, 'Forty or fifty of these engines, prepared secretly and brought to positions at nightfall, could advance quite certainly into the enemy's trenches, smashing away all the obstructions and sweeping the trenches with their machine-gun fire, and with grenades thrown out of the top. They would make so many *points d'appui* [base of operations] for the British supporting infantry to rush forward and rally on them. They can then move forward to attack the second line of trenches.'

The result was the establishment of the Landship Committee. Tests were made with the Holt tractor, but most members of the committee thought that the war would be over

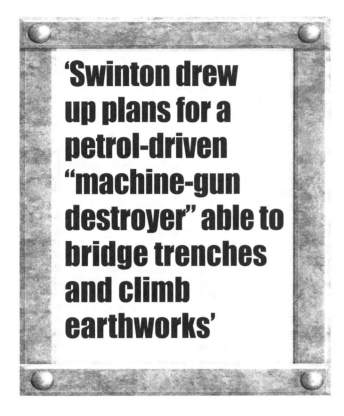

'Swinton drew up plans for a petrol-driven "machine-gun destroyer" able to bridge trenches and climb earthworks'

before anything useful could be developed. However, by June 1915, when it was clear that the war was going to drag on and hundreds of thousands of men had been killed, Swinton drew up plans for a petrol-driven 'machine-gun destroyer', armoured with hardened steel, able to bridge trenches and climb earthworks, make 90-degree turns and move back and forward over soft ground with a top speed of four miles an hour. He named experimental models 'tanks' for security reasons. The name stuck.

By September 1915, the first tank, 'Little Willie', had been built. A second model, called 'Big Willie', designed to cross wide trenches, quickly followed. This design was accepted by the British army, who ordered a hundred tanks of this type, designated the Mark I, in February 1916. Tanks would be made in two types: the 'male' tank carrying a six-pounder gun and the 'female' armed with machine guns.

Swinton not only designed tanks but became

the first great theorist of their use. In February 1916, he produced 'Notes on the Employment of Tanks'. This foresaw them rolling over and crushing machine-gun emplacements and pouring shells on to the enemy at point blank range. However, he did not envisage tank units being the kind of self-contained assault units that Panzer divisions became. He thought they should be used in combined operations.

'They must be counted as infantry and in an operation be under the same command,' he wrote. He also thought that one in ten should carry a radio so they could receive their orders from the rear. Their job would be to make a breach in the enemy's defences. Once that was achieved, they would be withdrawn and the cavalry would be brought in to exploit it.

The tank's best attribute, he thought, was novelty. It would give them the element of surprise. As this would quickly wear off, he urged that the army should wait until they had amassed a large number of tanks before deploying them.

'These machines,' he said, 'should not be used in driblets.'

First bow

On 15 August 1916, tanks went into combat for the first time at the first Battle of the Somme, where they did little to stem the 420,000 British casualties. Nevertheless, more tanks were built and the design gradually refined. In 1917, the Mark IV arrived. This was considerably heavier than earlier versions with armour plating around the petrol tank and other vulnerable parts. Gone were the tail wheels that had been used to steer

Right: British Mark I tank in Chimpanzee Valley, the Somme, 1916

The three tank brigades were then formed into a Tank Corps. It comprised nine battalions, each with three companies. These were divided into four four-tank platoons. The corps commander was Brigadier Hugh Elles. His chief of staff and one of the most influential pioneers of tank warfare was Lieutenant Colonel John Frederick Charles 'Boney' Fuller.

'Little Willie', the first prototype 'landship' to be built, in September 1915

earlier tanks, but had proved virtually useless. Instead a system of electric lights co-ordinated the steering between the driver and gearsmen who controlled the thrust going to the tracks, and the long-barrelled naval guns that had buried themselves in the mud on steep descents and were easily bent when they hit a tree or house were replaced by shorter cannon.

Even though the corps had been formed, the battle of the acceptance of the tank had yet to be won. They were heavy and made slow progress over muddy or heavily shelled ground, perhaps as little as 10 yards a minute or a third of a mile an hour. The driver's limited field of vision made it difficult to steer them in the right direction. And the heat inside and the difficulty of driving quickly exhausted the crew. But worse, at Passchendaele, the disastrous British offensive started in July 1917, tanks simply sank into the

Brigadier General Sir Hugh Elles, commander of the Tank Corps, and George V (right) watch tanks manoeuvring at Sautricourt, 1918

mud, leading to heavy losses. In all, the British lost 325,000 men during that campaign and the infantry began to see the tank as a failure. Even the crews began losing their morale, seeing their tanks wasted in small-scale attacks using only a handful of tanks.

Fuller met the situation head on. He searched his map of the Western Front for a place suitable for a large-scale attack by tanks. Between St Quentin and Cambrai there was rolling chalk downland, terrain that was especially suitable for the movement of tanks. The area had been quiet for some time, so it was relatively free of the shell craters that were the tank's greatest hazard.

Fuller came up with a plan that would prove the worth of tanks once and for all: a lightning attack on St Quentin. Elles changed the objective to Cambrai and the plan was presented to General Sir Julian Byng, commanding officer of the Third Army that held the sector. Byng liked what he saw and seized the opportunity

to make an all-out offensive in his sector. While Fuller's plan called for six battalions of tanks, Byng called for all nine. In all, 19 British divisions were assembled for the offensive, supported by five horsed cavalry divisions.

For the initial attack, eight British divisions were launched against three German divisions. Three lines of German trenches had to be breached. Even though the improved Mark IV tanks were 26 feet (8m) long, they would have some difficulty crossing some of the wider sections, so Fuller attached fascines – bundles of sticks bound together with rope – on the front of his tanks. These were held by a quick-release mechanism that dropped them into the trench to create a makeshift bridge. This technique would be used again to breach the defences of the Atlantic Wall on D-Day.

Fuller formed his tanks into sections of three: one male 'advance' tank with a 6-pounder gun and two female machine-gun-carrying 'main body' tanks to protect the male from infantry attack. A male would advance, flattening the wire for the infantry. Then it would turn to the left in front of the first trench, firing its gun to suppress the defenders. Then its two females would advance. The first would drop its fascine into the trench, cross it, then turn left and work its way down the far side of the trench, machine-gunning the occupants as it went. The second would cross the same fascine, then drop its own fascine into the second trench, cross it and machine-gun its way down the far side. The advance tank would then cross the two fascines and drop its own fascine in the third trench and cross it, hopefully with infantry still close behind.

'Other things being equal, the most mobile side must win,' said Fuller.

Surprise attack

Some 474 British tanks were secretly brought up to the front. Then at 0620 on 20 November 1917, they appeared out of the early morning mist, taking the Germans by complete surprise. Elles himself led the attack with his head sticking up out of the hatch for better visibility. The ground was dry and they made good speed. The barbed wire, which shellfire routinely failed to destroy, was crossed without incident. The fascines were dropped. The tanks crossed the trenches and raked them with fire.

Previous assaults had used just a handful of tanks. Here the Germans were confronted with long lines of them. Armour-piercing bullets, which had been effective against early models, bounced off. Faced with this mechanized onslaught, the Germans threw down their weapons and surrendered or tried to flee. Some 7,500 prisoners were taken at the cost of a few

casualties. By 0720 hours, the British had ripped a hole 6 miles wide and 3 miles (10 km by 5 km) deep through the Hindenburg Line. The infantry poured through it and, by 1000, brigade headquarters had to move forward to keep up

Light British 'Whippet' tank and crew pose for a photograph

with the advance. After three years of stalemate no one was prepared for the speed of the breakthrough. Objective after objective fell and reports coming back from the front read, according to Fuller, 'more like a railway timetable than a series of battle reports'.

However, not everything went according to plan. Ignoring Fuller's carefully thought-out strategy, General G.M. Harper, attacking the village of Flesquières near the middle of the line, kept his infantry well back and sent the tanks in in a line abreast. The German artillery on a ridge behind the village knocked out 16 tanks. According to the despatch written by the Commander in Chief, Field Marshal Sir Douglas Haig, a single German officer was responsible for destroying all 16 after all his men had been killed or had fled.

However, the following day, the attack began to run out of steam. Battlefield intelligence could not keep up with the fast pace of this new type of warfare. There were gaps in the German defences that could have been penetrated, but recognizing and exploiting them was impossible. The Germans established a new defensive line around the salient. This spread out the British tanks along a longer line and they could launch only limited strikes involving forty or fifty at a time. Tanks began to break down. German artillery fire accounted for others. The initial success of the tanks had also taken the British commanders so much by surprise that they failed to take advantage of the situation by bringing up adequate infantry reinforcements.

Bad weather prevented the cavalry exploiting the breakthrough. They stayed some 6 miles (10 km) behind the front throughout the battle and took no part in it, marking what Fuller called 'the end of an epoch'. The reason the cavalry 'did nothing but wait and wait,' Fuller said, was 'because they were commanded not from the front, but from the rear.'

Shock tactic

By 27 November the offensive had been halted after an advance of some 6 miles. The tanks were withdrawn and the British began putting up barbed wire in front of their new positions.

What happened next was almost as crucial in the development of the new type of warfare that would be perfected by the Panzers. The Germans counter-attacked using the new *Stosstruppen* (shock troop) tactics – yet to be seen on the Western Front, but only a month before they had been used to deadly effect to all but destroy the Italian army (Italy was on the Allied side

throughout the First World War) at Caporetto in October 1917. The Germans abandoned the linear tactics that they had employed for the first three years of the war. They broke up their combat units into small independent squads each with a range of weapons: artillery, machine guns and flame-throwers. These units were to advance individually, making no effort to stay in contact with the units on either flank. They were to advance as rapidly as possible, bypassing enemy strongpoints which would be dealt with by troops following behind. Everything was done to maintain the momentum of the attack. This tactic required the complete decentralization of command. While officers drew up overall

The German A7V was remarkably slow and cumbersome

objectives, how they were to be achieved was left to each squad, each fire team and, ultimately, each individual soldier.

On 30 November the Germans counter-attacked with 20 divisions. After a short and furious bombardment – compared with the lengthy barrages that had been used hitherto – the *Stosstruppen* attacked. High explosives, gas and smoke left the British bewildered. The Germans fell on them, concentrating their efforts on communications facilities and headquarters units to leave the enemy even more disoriented. They took advantage of gullies and dead spots in the terrain, co-ordinating artillery and machine-gun fire to deadly effect. They quickly overwhelmed the new British trenches and, by noon, had advanced 5 miles (8 km). And by 5 December the British had been driven back almost to their original positions. Casualties on both sides were about equal, some 45,000 each.

Although no ground had been gained, it was recognized that tanks had their first decisive role at the Battle of Cambrai. Analyzing the Allies' failure to hold on to their gains Fuller said, 'The battle came to a halt because there was not a single tank or a single infantry unit in reserve. Though planned as a decisive attack, the battle was in reality no more than a raid – for without reserves, what else could it be?'

The Germans agreed.

'By neglecting to support a brilliant initial success,' wrote the German commander of all land forces, Field Marshal Paul von Hindenburg, 'they had let victory be snatched from them, and indeed by troops which were far inferior to their own, both in numbers and quality.'

Despite the British failure to exploit the initial success of their tanks, the battle showed that armour was the key to victory on the Western Front. The French and Americans (who had joined the war in April 1917) also saw the potential of these new machines of war and tanks were used in increasing numbers by all the Allies.

The bigger, the better

The Germans were convinced too and, despite being starved of raw materials, they began building

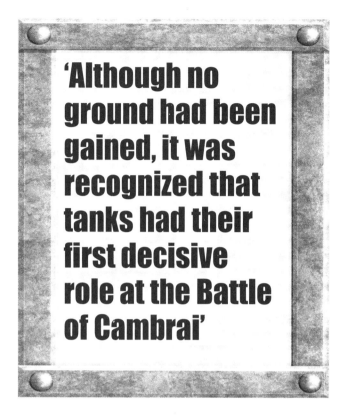

'Although no ground had been gained, it was recognized that tanks had their first decisive role at the Battle of Cambrai'

tanks of their own. Hindenburg's chief aide Major General Erich Ludendorff saw tanks as a 'terror weapon'. Consequently, bigger was better. The first German tank, the A7V *Sturmpanzerwagen*, weighed 30 tonnes and carried a crew of 18. Twin water-cooled Daimler engines gave it a top speed of 4 mph (6 kph) across country and 8 mph (13 kph) on roads. Its frontal armour was 30mm thick and it was armed with six Spandau machine guns and one 57mm gun. However, its sheer size made it difficult to handle.

The A7V first went into action during the German spring offensive of 1918. The first tank-versus-tank battle took place on 24 April 1918 outside the village of Villers-Bretonneux when three A7Vs met three Mark IVs from the 1st Battalion, Tank Corps. The Germans claimed that their superior weapon drove off the Mark IVs. The British say that two of their tanks were female and did, indeed, retire with shell holes in their sides. But the lead British tank, a male,

An A7V in Roye, France during 1918, one of only 21 ever delivered to the front – it was nicknamed the 'Moving Fortress' by the British

scored three direct hits on the lead A7V, which fell over on its side. However, a later investigation revealed that the German tank had actually tipped over while trying to climb a steep bank. The other two A7Vs fled, but the British male tank was hit by German artillery and was unable to give chase.

By 1918, the Allied blockade of Germany was biting deep, so the A7V never went into full production. Only about 15 were available for the last offensive of the war and they were outnumbered in the German lines by captured Allied tanks. However, plans were laid to make a new version better able to negotiate obstacles, the A7V-U. On the grounds that even bigger was even better, a 'K' supergiant was designed that would weigh 150 tonnes and carry seven

machine guns and four 77mm guns, but due to the end of the war, it never went into production.

Although the *Stosstruppen* were effective it was impossible to keep the momentum of the German offensive going with men on foot. By this time, Germany was starving and German soldiers would often stop to gorge themselves in captured dugouts. Nevertheless, by June 1918, the Germans were approaching the River Marne and were, once again, threatening Paris. On 15 July, they attempted to cross the river and were halted by French and fresh US forces in the Second Battle of the Marne.

With the Germans' momentum lost, the Allies counter-attacked. On the morning of 18 July, French and American forces, spearheaded by 490 tanks, hit the western flank of the Germans

at Soissons. With no initial artillery barrage to warn the defenders, the tanks penetrated 4 miles (6.5 km), inflicting heavy casualties on the German infantry. But the slow speed of the French tanks prevented a complete breakthrough.

Then on 8 August, the British Fourth Army, including the Canadian and Australian Corps, attacked at Amiens. The entire Tank Corps was there, fielding nearly 600 armoured vehicles. At 0420, 324 heavy tanks and 96 lighter, faster 'Whippet' Medium A tanks moved out through the darkness and mist behind a creeping barrage. After dawn 500 aircraft joined the fray. In front of them were seven divisions that were understrength and exhausted by a month's fighting. Surprise was total. The demoralized German troops dropped their weapons and surrendered. On the first day, a hole 11 miles (18 km) wide was punched in the German front line. The German 225 Division alone lost its entire artillery. There was nothing left of the front line units and the rest were thrown into action piecemeal. According to Hindenburg, the new faster British tanks caught divisional staff unawares in their headquarters and tore up their phone lines, isolating the troops at the front from their commanders.

'The wildest rumours began to spread in our lines,' wrote Hindenburg. 'It was said that masses of English cavalry were already far in rear of the foremost German infantry positions. Some of the men lost their nerve, left positions from which they had only just beaten off strong enemy attacks, and tried to get in touch with the rear again. Imagination conjured up all kinds of phantoms and turned them into real dangers.'

Transport columns bringing up fresh troops were ambushed and corps headquarters overrun. One tank battalion found itself so far behind German lines that it turned back, only to run into thousands of fleeing Germans. Some 40,000 were captured during the first three days.

The Allied victory was not complete and the Germans managed to reform their lines, but their morale had been badly dented. Fuller said that Amiens was 'the strategical end of the war, a second Waterloo; the rest was minor tactics'.

Ludendorff also said that 8 August 1918 was a black day for the Germany army. When the tanks suddenly appeared behind them, he said, his troops 'lost all cohesion'.

But the German author Erich Maria Remarque expressed most eloquently the effect the tanks

An English Mark IV tank marooned near Amiens, 1918

26 March 1918: the 'Whippet' tanks of 3 Battalion advance through Mailly-Maillet, supported by a New Zealand infantry division

had on the German troops in his famous novel *All Quiet on the Western Front*.

'From a mockery, the tanks have become a terrible weapon,' he wrote. 'Armoured they come rolling on in long lines, more than anything else they embody for us the horror of war.' The soldiers in the trenches did not see the guns that bombarded them. And the enemy infantry attacking were men like them. 'But these tanks are machines, their caterpillars run on as endless as the war... they roll on without feeling... invulnerable beasts squashing the dead and the wounded – we shrivel up in our thin skin before them, against their colossal weight our arms are sticks of straw, and our hand-grenades matches.'

Not surprisingly *All Quiet on the Western Front* was quickly banned in Germany when Hitler came to power in 1933. Remarque had left Germany in 1932 to live in Switzerland, where he died in 1970.

On 12 September 1918, American tank crews went into action for the first time. Two battalions of 174 Renault FT-17s, under Colonel George S. Patton, attacked at St Miheil with some success, though there was a notable logistics failure when traffic jams prevented fuel reaching the tanks. By then, the Germans would surrender to a tank without a shot being fired.

'Their sense of duty is sufficient to make them fight against infantry,' wrote one officer, 'but when the tanks appear many feel they are justified in surrendering.'

Peace breaks out

The Germans then had no option but to sue for peace and the fighting ended with an armistice on 11 November. If the war had gone on for another year, Fuller had a plan which he believed would give Allied tanks a decisive victory. His 'Plan 1919' called for an expansion of the Tanks

Corps from 17,000 to 35,000 men. They would man 5,000 new Medium D tanks that would attack without warning across a front 90 miles (145 km) wide. They would head directly to the German headquarters which would be marked by coloured smoke or flares dropped by aircraft. Bombers would attack crossroads and supply lines. However, lines of communications should be left intact so that terror and confusion could spread. The frontline troops would panic. Orders and counter orders flying about would leave them in no position to resist a second carefully co-ordinated attack using artillery, tanks and infantry. The object of this would be to take the enemy's guns and in the process occupy the Germans' 'secondary tactical zone some 10,000 yards deep'. The thing to note about Fuller's

plan was that it left no role for the cavalry.

Even though this plan was never put into operation, it pointed the way ahead for warfare. The Panzers would use the same critical co-ordination of tanks and aircraft in their *Blitzkrieg*.

'It was not the genius of Marshal Foch [commander of the Allied forces in the closing months of the war] that defeated us,' declared the German General A.W.H. von Zwehl, 'but General Tank.'

When the First World War ended in 1918, France had produced 3,870 tanks and Britain 2,636. Germany had built just 20.

The Americans had ridden to war in French FT-17s – which they hoped to build under licence in the US – and British Mark Vs. They were also involved in a joint US–UK project to produce

The US Signal Corps in their Renault FT-17 tanks, which the US government was planning to build under licence in the USA

the Mark VIII 'International' tank. An order had been placed for 15,000 two-man tanks powered by twin Model T engines with the Ford Motor Company, but only 15 were ever made and none made it to the war. It was, however, clear that all the belligerents realized just how important the tank would be in any future war.

The first result of this was that, under the Treaty of Versailles signed on 28 June 1919 concluding the war, Germany was forbidden to build or import tanks. Aircraft were also forbidden. Its army was limited to 100,000 men. Germany was shorn of its colonies. Its borders were redrawn and it was forced to pay $33 billion in reparations.

While the Germans' efforts to develop the tank were inhibited, the British threw away the advantage they had. This was partially because, after the mechanized horrors of the First World War, a body of influential officers longed to 'get back to real soldiering'. But also the senseless slaughter of the Western Front had produced a pacifist backlash and the economic climate after the beginning of the Great Depression in 1929 meant that military budgets were cut. Nevertheless the Tank Corps became the Royal Tank Corps in 1923 and formed its Experimental Mechanized Force in 1927.

Fuller was still at the forefront of mechanized thinking. Throughout the interwar period, Fuller wrote voluminously, starting with *Tanks in the Great War*, which was published in 1920. In an award-winning essay in the Royal United Service

The Renault factory with FT-17 light tanks under construction – first used in conflict in 1918, these tanks had the first fully rotating turret

Institution *Journal* that year he pointed out that warfare was 'a matter of tools' and the side with 'the highest mechanical weapon nearly always wins'. He pointed out that, with one company of machine guns, Napoleon would have won at Waterloo and that, if the British had had tanks in 1914, the war would have been over by autumn. But there were those in the army who maintained that nothing could replace a man and his horse. Typically Fuller took on his critics in a series of articles for the *Cavalry Journal* entitled 'The Influence of Tanks on Cavalry Tactics'. He was arguing, he said, not for the abolition of the cavalry, merely replacing its horses with tanks. He accused cavalry officers of 'mental lethargy' and maintained that fast-moving modern tanks would capture the 'true cavalry spirit'.

Rewriting the rules

In 1923, he became chief instructor at the Army's Staff College at Camberley. His first act was to have the head clerk burn all the lectures and manuals. Then he proceeded to write over a hundred new lectures and devised a series of new exercises. He wanted his work published but was refused permission by the Chief of the Imperial General Staff Lord Cavan. However, he had completed a book before he had taken the appointment at Camberley. It appeared as *The Reformation of War* in 1923. In his chapter on 'The Future of Land Warfare', he said that cavalry, infantry and artillery were all redundant. What was needed were two types of tank: heavy battle tanks with a top speed of 15 mph (24 kph), and light scout tanks which could travel at up to 30 mph (48 kph). With tanks travelling at these speeds, the gunners would quickly be

too far behind to offer effective support in any advance and the infantry would not be able to keep up. In a retreat, both the artillery and infantry would be quickly overrun by the enemy and captured. As only other tanks would be able to pursue the fleeing tanks, if the artillery and infantry were to have any further role, they would have to mechanize. Likewise, the cavalry would have to swap the horses for light scout tanks that could cover 150 miles (240 km) a day over any terrain and even tackle obstacles that would stop a horse. Mechanized cavalry could carry food with them and hide out in enemy territory if necessary. They could travel at twice the speed of a horse and operate at night with the aid of headlights.

He envisaged tanks that were gas-proofed and carried anti-aircraft machine guns. They would pack the punch of a field gun and, in effect, be a mobile fortress. Their tracks also liberated them from the roads and he developed 'roadless tactics', envisaging huge fleets of tanks moving across country shrouded by great clouds of smoke.

Fuller published *On Future Warfare* in 1928, but his manner became increasingly combative, and the insults he hurled at his opponents did not help his arguments. He retired from the army in 1933 to devote himself to writing, serving as a reporter during the Italian invasion of Ethiopia in 1935 and the Spanish Civil War (1936–39), and he was the only foreigner present at Nazi Germany's first armed manoeuvres in 1935. His autobiography *Memoirs of an Unconventional Soldier* was published in 1936. However, by this time, his flirtation with the British Union of Fascists meant that few people in Britain would tolerate his views. But abroad they were listened to, and his lectures – published as *Field Service Regulations III* in 1937 – were adopted for study by army general staffs in Germany, the Soviet Union and Czechoslovakia.

Think tank

The First World War threw up another great British advocate of the tank: Basil Liddell Hart. As a young infantry officer in 1916, he was gassed near Mametz Wood in the First Battle of the Somme. After the war he sat down to rewrite the army's official Infantry Training Manual, published in 1920. In it, he outlined his 'expanding torrent' method of attack. This maintained that reserves should be thrown into battle where the greatest gains had already been made, not to reinforce areas where difficulties had been encountered. It was adopted by the German advocates of mechanized warfare and became the basis of the *Blitzkrieg*.

Two articles on tactics published in the *National Review* led him into a lively correspondence with Fuller, who quickly converted him to the new gospel of armour. However, he did not follow Fuller's arguments that the infantry was now redundant. Instead, as tanks were landships, the infantry would become 'tank marines', transported about the battlefield on armoured, tracked vehicles. This was another idea adopted by the Panzer divisions.

In 1924, Liddell Hart was invalided out of the service and became the military correspondent of the *Daily Telegraph* from 1925 to 1935, then military adviser to *The Times* from 1935 to 1939. Throughout 1937 and 1938 he served as personal adviser to Secretary of War Leslie Hore-Belisha and saw many of his advocated reforms implemented. However, his efforts to completely mechanize the army with tank and anti-aircraft forces were resisted by most professional officers and his writings were more influential in Germany than in France or England.

Another of his ideas that found favour with the Germans was his concept of the 'indirect approach'. In his 1925 book, *Paris, or the Future of War*, he attacked the Allies' strategy in the First World War which, he said, was based on the ideas of the Prussian general and military theorist Carl von Clausewitz. They had sought to destroy the enemy's armed forces in the main theatre of war which had led to the trenches of the Western Front and the senseless slaughter.

What the Allies should have done, he said, was find the enemy's weakest point and attack him there, like Paris shooting his arrow into Achilles' heel, hence the title. This, Liddell Hart maintained,

The British Mark V tank was steered by the driver alone and could reach 5 mph (8 kph)

was not the enemy's army, but his willingness to fight. With people and industry packed together into cities, modern society was very vulnerable to dislocation. Aircraft dropping poison gas into the cities would paralyze any country.

Liddell Hart wrote:

> *Imagine for a moment London, Manchester, Birmingham, and half a dozen other great centres simultaneously attacked, the business localities and Fleet Street [then the London home of Britain's national newspapers] wrecked, Whitehall a heap of ruins, the slum districts maddened into the impulse to break loose and maraud, the railways cut, factories destroyed. Would not the general will to resist vanish, and what use would be the still determined fractions of the nation, without organisation and central direction?*

Similarly, the army should aim to break the enemy's will rather than take on their armed forces. The way to do that, he said, was to employ tanks – 'the modern form of heavy cavalry' – to make hundred-mile-a-day (160-km) advances into enemy territory. They should be used en masse to attack the enemy's communication and command centres, paralyzing its nervous system.

The key to victory

This theory was spelt out in great detail in *The Decisive Wars of History* in 1929 where he analyzed some 240 military campaigns stretching from ancient Greece to 1918. He concluded that only a handful had been won by a direct approach and an attacker should only take on an opponent directly if he had a decisive

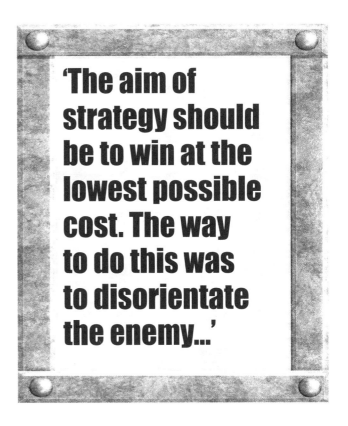

'The aim of strategy should be to win at the lowest possible cost. The way to do this was to disorientate the enemy...'

superiority in material strength. Even then the cost would be high and the aim of strategy should be to win at the lowest possible cost. The way to do this was to disorientate the enemy with a series of rapid thrusts. Nothing unbalances a fighting force so much as suddenly finding the enemy at its rear. This was the key to victory and mechanized forces had the means of doing this more effectively than any army in history.

Success lay, he said, 'partly in the tactical combination of tanks and aircraft, partly in the unexpectedness of the stroke in direction and time, but above all in the "follow through" – the way that a breakthrough (the tactical penetration of the front) is exploited by a deep strategic penetration, carried out by armoured forces racing on ahead of the main army, and operating independently.'

Not only were the British theorists giving the Germans, through their publications, everything they would need to dominate the continent of

A Mark VIII Liberty tank built as part of the Anglo-American agreement is put into service promoting US war bonds, 1918

Europe, they were also laying the foundation of a strategic system that was still in use in Operation *Desert Storm* in 1991.

So why did the British lose the lead in the 1930s? While the Great Depression sapped military budgets in Britain, Liddell Hart began to back away from his former position.

The British Way in Warfare, published in 1932, pointed out that Britain had built its empire by avoiding land wars and relying instead on its sea power.

The First World War was an aberration, which demonstrated how costly it was when Britain tried to emulate the great land powers. If land forces were needed at all, they should be small, light and highly mobile. He now became a passionate advocate of air power. Bombing alone, he argued, would be enough to bring any enemy to its knees. This seemed to be borne out in the Spanish Civil War, where tanks were easily knocked out by a new generation of anti-tank weapons. But in Spain, the effectiveness of tanks, especially large tanks, was blunted because the bridges could not take their weight.

Liddell Hart was enormously influential. In the run-up to the Second World War the British government put just six divisions into France. Their job was to defend the air bases in the Low Countries and the British army was largely equipped with fast, light, two-man tanks. When the shooting started, it was found that they were no match for the Panzers.

3. THE MAKING OF THE CORPS

After losing the First World War, what remained of the German army, the *Reichswehr*, had to go about a painful reassessment of its strategy and tactics. In terms of manpower, its position seemed impossible. Its limit of 100,000 men faced a standing army of a million conscripts in France, while to the east a reborn Poland boasted thirty infantry divisions and ten cavalry divisions.

However, a small army had its advantages. It was unencumbered by a hidebound general staff, ageing equipment or a great mass of conscripts. Its band of officers was small and tight-knit, whose one aim was to circumvent the restrictions placed on them by the Treaty of Versailles. Soon there grew up a nucleus of young strategists who believed that the slow and costly methods employed in the First World War could be replaced with faster, cheaper and more exciting types of warfare.

In 1920 the *Reichswehr* came under the command of General Hans von Seeckt. He had fought on the Eastern Front during the First World War and knew nothing of the static trench warfare fought in the west. He still believed that battles could be won by manoeuvre and encirclement, rather than attrition. He was an admirer of the Prussian cavalry commander Friedrich von Seydlitz, victor of a series of battles during the Seven Years War (1756-63) using surprise, speed, encircling movements and flank attacks. Von Seeckt even saw the advantage in keeping the army small.

'The mass cannot manoeuvre,' he said, 'therefore it cannot win.'

Small is beautiful

An army only needed to be big enough to fight off a surprise attack, he thought. Strength lay in mobility. A small, highly mobile army could manoeuvre a larger, more cumbersome army into a *Vernichtungsschlacht*, a decisive battle of annihilation. Von Seeckt still believed that there was a role for cavalry. Others thought

Top: General Hans von Seeckt and his men in Thüringen, 1925

German expansion under Hitler, 1936–1939: the occupation of Czechoslovakia brought Britain into the war

Brauchitsch began to experiment with co-ordinating motorized ground units and air forces. Present was a 34-year-old infantry officer named Captain Heinz Guderian, who had recently been seconded to the Motorized Transport Department of the Inspectorate of Transport Troops in Berlin. Born in Kulm, East Prussia on 17 June 1888, Guderian had joined the German army on 28 February 1907. During the First World War, he served with the 10th Jäger Battalion on the Western Front, ending the war as a captain. He remained with the infantry and, in 1922, he was attached to the 7th Motorized Transport Battalion. Two months later, he was posted to the inspectorate in Berlin, where his commanding officer was General von Tschischwitz, one of the new generation of military thinkers who believed that the German army could compensate for its numerical inferiority with mobility, surprise and the concentration of strength.

Von Tschischwitz ordered Guderian to make a study of the possibilities of moving large bodies of troops by motor vehicle. Guderian was reluctant to accept the posting, and requested a return to his infantry company. This was refused

that mobility meant armour and von Seeckt encouraged them on the grounds that building tanks was forbidden by the Versailles Treaty. He sought co-operation with the Swedes, who had bought Germany's old tanks, and with the Russians. This led to German officers getting hands-on training at the Tank School at Kazan, deep inside the Soviet Union.

Cardboard cutouts

As early as October 1921, motorized manoeuvres were being held in the Harz Mountains. Mock tanks were built with cardboard superstructures. Ridiculous though this looked to foreign observers, it taught useful lessons in inter-unit co-operation. Then, in the winter of 1923–24, manoeuvres under *Oberstleutnant* Walter von

General 'Fast Heinz' Guderian, who revolutionized the tactics of tank warfare

and so Guderian had to just get on with the job.

He soon found that infantry on trucks would need to be accompanied by artillery and engineers in a fully motorized formation which also employed tanks. Soon he was tracking down German tank veterans and publishing articles about tanks in *Militär-Wochenblatt* (Military Weekly) and later in non-military publications including the *Berlin Stock Exchange Journal*. He also read anything on the subject he could get his hands on, including the works of Swinton, Fuller, Liddell Hart and an obscure French officer named Charles de Gaulle who later wrote a study on military theory called *Vers l'armée de métier* (The Army of the Future). Published in 1934 it defended the idea of a small professional army, highly mechanized and mobile, in preference to the static theories exemplified by the Maginot Line, built in the 1930s to protect France against German attack.

Guderian organized exercises with the clumsy 'armoured troop carriers', which were all the German army was allowed to keep under the

Versailles Treaty. However, von Tschischwitz was succeeded by Colonel von Natzmer as inspector and, when Guderian said that he was involved in turning the motorized units from supply troops into combat troops, von Natzmer said, 'To hell with combat. They're supposed to carry flour.'

But Guderian's exercises had come to the attention of the Army Training Department. He became an instructor in military history and tactics and was posted to the 2nd Division at Stettin, which was now under the command of his old boss von Tschischwitz. In his lectures on military history, Guderian concentrated on Napoleon's 1806 campaign. In September 1806 Prussia had entered the war against France and Guderian felt that this campaign had not received the attention it deserved because it had ended with the defeat of the Prussian armies at Jena and at Auerstädt on 14 October.

In his lectures on tactics, he concentrated on mobile warfare, discussing at first the cavalry tactics employed by the Germans and French in the autumn of 1914. But then he began to elucidate his theories on motorized warfare. In 1928, he was invited to teach a course on tank tactics. Guderian had never seen the inside of a tank, but with the help of the latest British handbook, which had been translated into German, he set about a series of exercises, at first with canvas dummies pushed about by his men. He complained that schoolchildren used to push pencils through the canvas to see what was inside. These were later replaced by motorized dummies made of sheet metal. But systematically Guderian and his colleagues began exploring the possibilities of the use of tank units – studying first the tank platoon, then the tank company, then the tank battalion. Although Guderian was already regarded as an expert, it was only in 1929 that he encountered real tanks for the first time. On a visit to Sweden with his wife, a Swedish tank battalion taught him to drive one of their M21 tanks. These were a version of the old German tanks sold to Sweden at the end of the First World War and were, by then, obsolete.

'In this year, 1929, I became convinced that tanks working on their own or in conjunction with infantry could never achieve decisive importance,' he wrote. 'Rather what was needed were armoured divisions which would include all the supporting arms needed to allow the tanks to fight to full effect.' And during summer field exercises that year, he experimented with the deployment of armoured divisions.

The exercise was a success and Guderian was convinced that this was the way to deploy armour. But his new boss General Otto von Stülpnagel was deeply opposed. He 'forbade the theoretical employment of tanks in units greater

An M21-29 tank rebuilt from the original M21 and in use by the Swedish army up until the outbreak of the Second World War

than regimental strength' and dismissed Panzer divisions as a utopian dream.

'Neither of us will ever see German tanks in operation in our lifetime,' von Stülpnagel said.

First steps

However, von Stülpnagel's chief of staff, Guderian's old friend Colonel Oswald Lutz, invited him to take command of the 3rd (Prussian) Motor Transport Battalion, which was equipped with real armoured cars and motorcycles, along with dummy tanks and anti-tank guns. Guderian trained them as a motorized combat unit and, in exercises, showed that such a motorized unit could be of real use to the rest of the army.

In 1931, von Stülpnagel retired and was replaced by Lutz, now a lieutenant general. Guderian became his chief of staff. Together they began trying to convince the rest of the army of the need for Panzer divisions and later a Panzer Corps. They still faced opposition from the older arms of the military. The infantry found their manoeuvres with dummy tanks ridiculous. Almost out of pity they conceded that the tank might make an effective infantry support weapon, but would not agree to a tank corps becoming a new branch of the service.

Stouter opposition came from the Inspectorate of Cavalry. So Lutz enquired whether the cavalry saw its future role as a reconnaissance wing for the infantry or as heavy cavalry that would fight battles on its own. When the Inspector of Cavalry, General von Hirschberg, said that he envisaged heavy cavalry units, Lutz offered to take over the reconnaissance role. Lutz and Guderian then began training Panzer Reconnaissance Battalions. But when General Knochenhauer

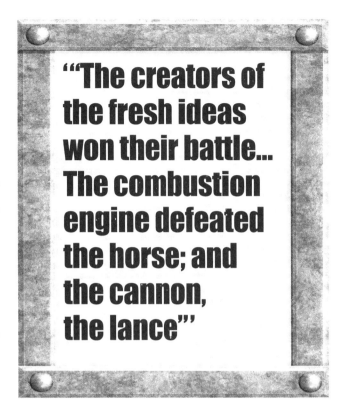

'"The creators of the fresh ideas won their battle... The combustion engine defeated the horse; and the cannon, the lance"'

took over from von Hirschberg, he tried to claw back the reconnaissance role for the cavalry. As a result, a lot of young cavalry officers were posted to the Panzer Reconnaissance Battalions. Soon the arguments over the future of the units became heated.

'But finally the creators of the fresh ideas won their battle against the reactionaries,' said Guderian. 'The combustion engine defeated the horse; and the cannon, the lance.'

Keep it simple

The Panzer's large-scale exercises in 1932, using armoured cars built by mounting steel armour plate on the chassis of a six-wheeled lorry, even fired the imagination of the ageing Field Marshal von Hindenburg, who was then the president of Germany. Afterwards, Hindenburg gave a speech to the cavalry officers who had been using the opportunity to criticize the Panzers.

'In war only what is simple can succeed,' he

Preparations for war – a column of scout cars belonging to the German Sixth Army Corps traverses the Lüneburg Heath, 1935

said. 'I visited the staff of the Cavalry Corps. What I saw there was not simple.'

Soon younger cavalry officers began to come over to the side of the Panzers.

By this time the Army Ordnance Office had produced two types of medium tanks and three types of light tanks. Two of each had been made, so the German army now had ten tanks. They had a top speed of 12 mph (19 kph), but were built out of mild steel rather than armour plate. Although they were gas-proofed, manoeuvrable and had all-round fields of fire for both turret guns and machine guns, the tank commander had to sit next to the driver giving him no rear vision and limited vision to the sides, and these tanks were not equipped with radio.

But Lutz and Guderian had their own requirements. They thought that their new Panzer divisions would require two types of tank: a medium tank with a large-calibre gun

and a light tank with an armour-piercing gun. Both should have two machine guns, one in the turret and one in the body. They fell out with the Inspector of Artillery and the Chief of the Ordnance Office who thought a 37mm gun would be sufficient for the light tank. Guderian wanted a 50mm weapon as he expected a new generation of foreign tanks to use heavier armour plate. But Lutz and Guderian had to give in as the infantry were already being provided with a 37mm anti-tank gun and it was easier to produce only one calibre of gun and one kind of shell.

Vision of the future

It was agreed that the medium tank would carry a 75mm gun and its weight would not exceed 24 tonnes – the limiting factor being the load-bearing capacity of German road bridges. Top speed was set at 25 mph (40 kph). It would carry a crew of

Left above: the Panzer I, a prototype light tank with a crew of two. Right: the unwieldy Panzer II with its 20mm machine guns

five. Each tank would be equipped with a radio, and the radio operator and the driver would sit in the body of the tank. The gunner and loader would sit in the turret, while the commander sat in a small command turret above them. This would give him all-round vision and he would issue orders through a larynx microphone.

The firms Rheinmetall and Krupp secretly produced five of these *Neubaufahrzeuge* (Nb Fz)

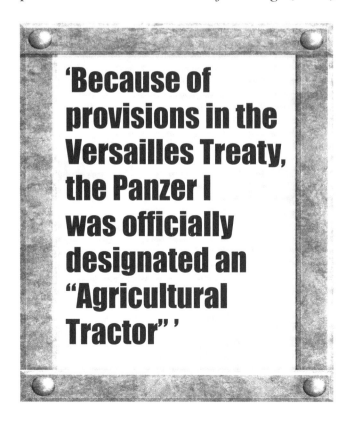

'Because of provisions in the Versailles Treaty, the Panzer I was officially designated an "Agricultural Tractor"'

or 'New Model Vehicles'. These were 23-tonne medium tanks with a 75mm gun. However, building them was a time-consuming process and it was decided, in the meantime, to produce a training tank. This was based on the chassis of the Carden-Lloyd 20mm anti-aircraft gun carrier they bought in England and could carry nothing larger than a machine gun in its turret. The result was Krupp's nine-tonne *Panzerkampfwagen* or 'armoured fighting vehicle', the Pzkw or Panzer I. Though it carried two machine guns and carried a crew of two, because of the provisions of the Versailles Treaty, it was officially designated an 'Agricultural Tractor'. No one ever imagined that, one day, the German army would go into action in these vehicles. A second tank, manufactured by the MAN company and carrying a 20mm gun, the three-man Panzer II, was also ordered.

In 1933, Hitler and his Nazi Party came to power. The new Reich chancellor was committed to the creation of a *Grossdeutschland*, a 'Greater Germany'. To do this, he said he was willing to wage a series of small wars, though he did not envisage the drawn-out total war that would later engulf the Reich. What he needed was

a highly mobile, flexible force that could wage a short, decisive campaign, ending with the total defeat of the enemy. Hitler ended the collaboration with the Soviet Union and pulled out of the League of Nations and its Disarmament Conference in Geneva. And in November 1933, Panzer School I was established in the garrison area of Wünsdorf-Zossen, thirty miles (48 km) south of Berlin, the first of many established over the following 14 years. Tank gunnery was taught at a separate training facility at Putlos in Holstein on the Baltic coast north of Hamburg.

In early 1934, Hitler saw a demonstration by a motorized unit comprising the basic elements that would later make up the Panzer divisions.

'That's what I need,' said Hitler. 'That's what I'm going to have.'

Guderian now had friends in high places. General Werner von Blomberg was minister of war and General Walter von Reichenau was chief of the Reichwehr Ministerial Office.

'Both these generals favoured modern ideas,' said Guderian, 'so I now found considerable sympathy for the ideas of the armoured force at least at the highest level of the Wehrmacht.'

General Freiherr von Fritsch was appointed Commander in Chief of the army. Guderian found him to be a

Parade of the Panzer Is, Nuremberg, 1935

man 'always ready to try out new ideas without prejudice and, if they seemed good to him, to adopt them. As a result, my dealings with him concerning the development of the armoured force were easier than with any other member of the Army High Command,' Guderian said.

From 1 July 1934, Lutz and Guderian headed the new Armoured Troops Command. In October, they formed the first proper Panzer unit at Ohrdruf. It was called the 'Motorized Instruction Commando' – later Panzer Battalion I. This was the largest Panzer unit the new chief of general staff General Ludwig Beck would allow. It was commanded by General Ritter von Thoma.

'It was the grandmother of all the others,' von Thoma told Liddell Hart in 1945. 'It was subsequently expanded into a regiment of two battalions, while two more were established at Zossen.'

When Hitler repudiated the Treaty of Versailles, Panzer IIs began rolling off the production lines in ever-increasing numbers. In March 1935, Germany admitted the existence of the Luftwaffe, a new general staff was assembled and military conscription was reintroduced.

'Meanwhile our organization was growing,' said von Thoma. 'In 1935 two tank brigades were formed – one for each of the two armoured divisions that were then created.'

Winning the argument

In July 1935 a highly successful exercise took place at Münsterlager with an improvised Panzer division which showed that large numbers of tanks could be manoeuvred and controlled in the field. But Guderian was still pressing for the use of radio communications below company level, as the situation stood then. Each tank should have a set of its own, he maintained. This would allow an attacking formation to be commanded from the front. Beck dismissed this as nonsense. 'A divisional commander sits back with maps and a telephone,' he said. 'Anything else is Utopian.'

But Beck eventually agreed to the publication of training manuals for armoured troops and the establishment of two Panzer divisions. Guderian insisted on three and, on 15 October 1935, the first three Panzer divisions came into existence. These were to have artillery and infantry carried in trucks to support the tanks. At this point, von Fritsch scrapped Beck's tactic of the 'delaying defence' which had been in the manuals since before the First World War. However, Guderian was removed from his post as chief of staff and given command of the 2nd Panzer Division. This effectively removed him from the centre of policy-making. But Lutz ordered Guderian to write the book *Achtung – Panzer!* ('Warning – Panzer!') which he did over a few months in the winter of 1936–37. This aimed to draw the maximum possible attention to the Panzers and win them the maximum resources.

Guderian argued for larger heavy tanks to assault permanent fortifications or fortified field positions. These would carry guns with calibres up to 150mm. They would weigh between 70 and 100 tonnes, but they proved too expensive to manufacture and field engineers' bridges limited the weight to 24 tonnes. The Panzer Corps had to settle for smaller faster tanks – the three-man Panzer II with its 20mm gun and top speed of 25 mph (40 kph) and the 18-tonne medium tank, the Panzer IV. This number-jumping occurred

A Panzer III, with Panzergrenadier support, goes into action on the Russian Front

because the Panzer III had been ordered – and christened – in 1936. Designed by Krupp, the Panzer IV became the backbone of the Panzer force. It weighed 17.3 tonnes and had a top speed of 18.5 mph (30 kph). With a crew of five, the Panzer IV carried two machine guns and a fairly inaccurate 75mm gun, which was not powerful enough to take the French 2C on in tank-to-tank combat. Neither of these tanks, to start with, had armour thicker than 30mm, which was enough to stop small arms fire and shell fragments, but offered little protection against a direct hit by field artillery or the anti-tank guns already in service.

Better late than never

In 1937, the Daimler-Benz Panzer III made its debut. Weighing 15 tonnes, (heavy for a 'light' tank) it carried a five-man crew. In size and appearance it was much like the Panzer IV. The main difference was in the armaments. It carried three 7.92mm machine guns – one in the hull, two in the turrent – and a 37mm gun. This was later replaced by a 50mm gun, which could be mounted without major structural modifications.

In *Achtung – Panzer!* Guderian also outlined

all that he had learnt about the use of tanks and it served as a work of theory that would prepare Germany for a new kind of war. What is most remarkable about the book is that it was published at all. It lavished praise on Hitler, but while Hitler and the Nazis blamed Germany's defeat on the Jews and socialists on the home front, Guderian makes it clear that the German army was defeated decisively on the Western Front by British tanks. He also praised Hitler's arch-enemy Winston Churchill for his part in the tank's development.

Guderian also issued a dire warning. The Soviet Union, he said, possessed the strongest army in the world, both in terms of numbers and equipment, which included, he reckoned, 10,000 tanks. It also had ample raw materials at its disposal that could supply a huge armaments industry in the depths of its vast empire. While Hitler saw Slavs as subhumans fit only to be enslaved, Guderian said, 'The time has passed when the Russians had no feeling for technology. We will have to reckon on the Russians being able to master and build their own machines, and with the fact that such a transformation in the Russians' fundamental mentality presents us with the Eastern Question in a form more serious than ever before in history.'

But no one was listening. Guderian later said that he sent a memorandum to the High Command opposing Operation *Barbarossa*, the German invasion of the Soviet Union and the one act that guaranteed the destruction of Hitler's 'Thousand-Year Reich'.

While no one heeded Guderian's warning, they

did buy his book. *Achtung – Panzer!* became a pre-war bestseller and Guderian bought his first car with the royalties. But while Guderian cites Swinton, Fuller, Liddell Hart and Lieutenant Giffard le Quesne Martel, a British pioneer who built his own one-man tank, they did not pay him a similar compliment. Guderian's book was not published in Britain and an English language edition only appeared in 1992, 38 years after the author's death.

Untimely setbacks

But 1937 was not a good year for the tank. The Japanese tried them in their war against the Chinese in the Far East, with limited success. Italian light tanks had made a poor showing against lightly armed tribesmen in Abyssinia two years earlier and the Panzer Is deployed in Spain under Major Ritter von Thoma performed poorly. Von Thoma himself was no fan, dismissing the

deployment of tanks as a failure and saying that there was no need for them to carry radio sets.

But Guderian defended his Panzers stoutly, even to the British officers he frequently met in Berlin, maintaining that 'neither the war in Abyssinia nor the civil war in Spain can be regarded, in our opinion, as a sort of "dress rehearsal" with regard to the effectiveness of the armoured fighting vehicle.' But for the dive-bombers, Spain was considered a very effective dress rehearsal indeed.

The three Panzer divisions were formed into XVI Corps under Group Command 4, with all the other motorized divisions of the German army, commanded by General Walter von Brauchitsch. When Lutz retired in February 1938, Guderian became corps commander. On 4 February 1938, von Brauchitsch became Commander in Chief of the army and von Reichenau replaced him.

Early in 1938, there were Panzer training

Italian light tanks performed badly in Abyssinia against poorly armed tribesmen because they weren't prepared for the heat or terrain

exercises which, due to muddled orders, turned into a disaster. Hitler witnessed this fiasco and was furious. Guderian posted several of his senior officers and junior officers were hauled over the coals. Nevertheless, when Hitler decided to annex Austria in March 1938, it was Guderian General Beck called for.

He was told to reassume command of the 2nd Panzer Division, which was put under the control of the Waffen-SS Division *SS-Leibstandarte Adolf Hitler* – Hitler's personal guard. Before they set out, Guderian heard that the *Leibstandarte*'s commander Sepp Dietrich was going to see Hitler one last time. It seemed to Guderian that the Anschluss, the 'union' of Austria and Germany, was going to be achieved without a shot being fired, so he asked Dietrich to ask Hitler if, to show their friendly feeling, they could deck their Panzers with flags and greenery. Hitler agreed.

The 2nd Panzer Division moved up to Passau on the Austrian border, arriving there at 2000 on 11 March. Their orders were to cross the border at 0800 the following morning. At around midnight, General Veiel arrived to head the column. He had neither maps of Austria nor fuel for the advance; Guderian gave him an ordinary Baedeker's tourists' guide in place of a map. Fuel was more of a problem. Although there was a fuel depot at Passau it was earmarked for the troops deployed in the defence of the West Wall – the so-called Siegfried Line, the German line of fortifications that faced the Maginot Line – and could only be issued in the event of a general mobilization. Even then it had to be issued by ranking officers, who had not been informed of the operation and could not be contacted in the middle of the night. In the event, Guderian

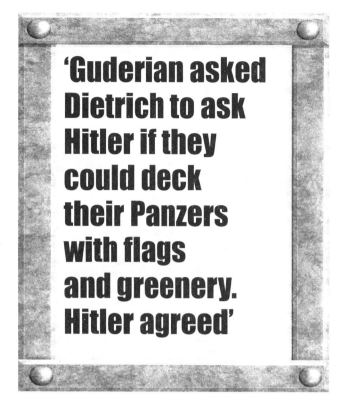

'Guderian asked Dietrich to ask Hitler if they could deck their Panzers with flags and greenery. Hitler agreed'

threatened the man in charge of the depot with the use of force and he got his fuel. The mayor of Passau then allowed Guderian the use of a number of lorries as a makeshift mobile supply line. Even so, a request had to be sent to the petrol stations along the route to stay open.

At 0900 the frontier barriers were raised and the Wehrmacht drove into Austria with the 2nd Panzer Division and Heinz Guderian at its head.

'At every halt the tanks were decked with flowers and food was pressed on the soldiers,' wrote Guderian. 'Their hands were shaken, they were kissed, and there were tears of joy. No untoward incident marred the occasion that had for so many years been longed for by both sides, the much postponed Anschluss. Children of one nation, split by unfortunate politics into two during so many decades, were now happily united at last.'

They reached Linz at midday where Guderian had lunch with the local bigwigs. He was about

Crowds of locals gather as motorized German troops cross the border at a customs post in Upper Austria, 13 March 1938

to move on when SS leader Heinrich Himmler informed him that Hitler was due to arrive at Linz at 1500 and Guderian was to supply troops to close off the road and guard the marketplace where Hitler was going to make a speech. This delayed the advance and Guderian only arrived in Vienna in a snowstorm around 0100 the following morning. There he met with generals of the Austrian army and was taken on a tour of their mechanized units. These would be incorporated into the Germany army and Guderian invited a number of officers to visit him in his garrison town, Würzburg.

The Panzers came in for considerable criticism for the high level of breakdowns during the march on Vienna. Guderian defended his unit stoutly, pointing out that his division had covered 420 miles (675 km) in 48 hours. Since the manoeuvres in March 1938 he had been warning that he had insufficient maintenance facilities.

This was soon rectified. Fuel supply was another problem that would have to be looked into, but generally, Guderian maintained, the Anschluss had proved 'that our theoretical belief concerning the operational possibilities of Panzer divisions was justified'.

He went on to say: 'The march had taught us that it was possible without difficulty to move more than one motorized division along one road… the German armoured troops were on the right course.'

Winston Churchill disagreed. In *The Gathering Storm*, he wrote:

The German war machine had lumbered

falteringly over the frontier and come to a standstill near Linz. In spite of perfect weather and road conditions the majority of the tanks broke down. Defects appeared in the motorized heavy artillery. The road from Linz to Vienna was blocked with heavy vehicles at a standstill… Hitler himself, motoring through Linz, saw the traffic jam, and was infuriated. The light tanks were disengaged from the confusion and straggled into Vienna in the early hours of Sunday morning. The armoured vehicles and motorized heavy artillery were loaded on to the railway trucks, and only thus arrived in time for the ceremony.

After the war Guderian ridiculed this account. The weather was bad, he said, with rain in the afternoon, a snowstorm that night. The convoy was only held up at Linz for Hitler's reception. Hitler, when Guderian met him in Linz, was

'Tears of joy ran down Hitler's cheeks as he addressed the crowd from the balcony of the town hall in Linz'

not infuriated. Indeed, tears of joy ran down his cheeks as he addressed the crowd from the balcony of the town hall. The road from Linz to Vienna was being re-laid, so conditions were poor. There were no defects with the heavy artillery as they had no heavy artillery with them.

The road was never blocked. They had no heavy tanks with them, so they could not have been loaded on to railway trucks – and the railroad was not running that day anyway. Churchill, Guderian said, was merely trying to demonstrate that if the Allies had gone to war in 1938, as he had urged, they would have had a good chance of winning.

Green light for the tank corps

After the Anschluss the 2nd Panzer Division remained in Austria. Meanwhile the headquarters staff of XVI Army Corps moved to Berlin and two more Panzer divisions – the 4th and 5th – along with a light division were formed in Würzburg. In addition, Panzer Corps was now given a command structure to put it on equal footing with the infantry and artillery.

On 30 September 1938, the Munich Agreement dismembered Czechoslovakia and gave the Sudetenland to Germany. The 1st Panzer Division, along with the 13th and 20th (Motorized) Infantry Divisions under the command of Guderian and XVI Corps, were chosen to lead the march into the Sudetenland. This would begin on 3 October. On 4 October the 1st Panzer Division entered the principal city, Carlsbad, again with the tanks bedecked with greenery. There Guderian was joined by his eldest son Heinz Günter, who was now Adjutant of 1st Battalion, 1st Panzer Regiment.

The following day all three divisions moved up to the new frontier.

Hitler spent the first two days of the occupation with XVI Corps. Guderian took him to one of their field kitchens where the men were enjoying regular field rations. But when the vegetarian Hitler realized they were eating a thick stew with pork in it, he had to make do with a few apples.

At the end of the month, Commander in Chief of the Army General Brauchitsch offered Guderian the newly created post of chief of mobile troops, making him titular head of all Germany's mechanized troops, as well as the cavalry. But Guderian noted that the position had no command powers, no control over the writing or publication of services manuals and no authority over personnel or the organization of units. He turned the job down. He was then told the idea of the promotion had come from Hitler himself, not Brauchitsch, and it would not be wise to refuse it. But again Guderian turned down the post, saying that he would be happy to explain his reasons to Hitler.

Bending Hitler's ear

A few days later Hitler called for him. He explained that in his present position as commander of the Panzer Corps, he was in a better position to influence the development of the armoured wing than in the new position he was being offered. He also explained that he knew that there was a powerful group in the Army High Command who still wanted to subdivide the armoured divisions among the infantry. As chief of mobile troops, he would be powerless to counter that. He would also have

insufficient powers to bring what he thought were much-needed reforms to the cavalry.

Hitler let him talk for about 20 minutes, then promised Guderian the necessary authority to develop the mechanized troops and cavalry in the way he saw fit and said that, if Guderian felt he was hindered in any way in making the necessary changes, he was to report directly back to him.

'Together we'll see that the necessary modernization is carried out,' said Hitler. 'I therefore order you to accept this new appointment.'

Hitler arrives in Vienna in his armoured Mercedes as the citizens enthusiastically proclaim a Greater German Reich, March 1938

Guderian's first task in his new post was to produce training manuals for the Panzers. Drafts had to be submitted to the Army Training Department which, at that point, did not contain a single tank officer. Guderian's draft was returned with a note that read: 'The subject matter is not arranged according to the pattern adopted by the infantry manuals. The draft is therefore unacceptable.'

Guderian's plan for the cavalry, which involved the purchase of 2,000 new horses, was similarly refused. This robbed the cavalry of the reconnaissance role Guderian had planned for it and left it no role when war came.

Guderian also noticed that his orders said, in event of mobilization, he was to take command of a Reserve Infantry Corps. It took considerable effort to get this changed to give him the command of armoured troops.

General Hoepner, Guderian's successor at XVI Corps, was at the head of the Panzers when they rolled into what remained of Czechoslovakia in March 1939. But Guderian went to collect first-hand information from the armoured units. He also examined Czech armoured equipment which was seized by the Wehrmacht and used in Poland and France.

Then came the real test of Guderian's ideas. On 22 August 1939, he was given command of XIX Army Corps. This new unit was responsible for the fortifications along the German border. Under its command was the 3rd Panzer Division, along with the 2nd and 20th (Motorized) Infantry Divisions. The 3rd Panzer Division was reinforced by the Panzer Demonstration Battalion equipped with the new Panzer IIIs and Panzer IVs.

Also attached to the corps were reconnaissance and demonstration units from the Panzer training schools. To his left, to the north, were frontier defence units under General Kaupisch; to his right was General Strauss's II Corps. These units were in position to defend the frontier in the event of a Polish attack. And if hostilities broke out, they were to be reinforced by the 10th Panzer Division, which was currently occupying Prague.

After a meeting between Hitler and his army commanders, Guderian discovered what their real mission was. They were being deployed to make a pre-emptive strike against Poland. The XIX Army Corps was to be part of the Fourth Army under General von Kluge. Guderian's men were to cross the border then make a dash for the Vistula, cutting off all the Polish forces in the Polish Corridor. Guderian said he was not eager to go to war, especially as his youngest son, Kurt, was a second lieutenant in the 3rd Armoured Reconnaissance Battalion of the 3rd

Panzer Division and was consequently under his command.

The attack was set for the night of 25 August, but was postponed. Then on the night of 31 August, there was a new alert. The 2nd (Motorized) Infantry Division under General Bader was to break through the Polish frontier defences and take the town of Tuchel.

The 3rd Panzer Division under General Freiherr Geyr von Schweppenburg was to head straight for the Vistula, followed by corps troops and the 23rd Infantry Division from the Army Reserve, while the 20th (Motorized) Infantry Division under General Wiktorin was to advance across Tuchel Heath and take the towns of

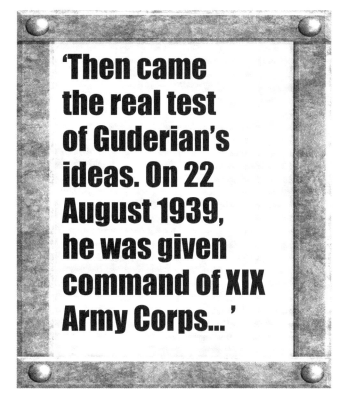

'Then came the real test of Guderian's ideas. On 22 August 1939, he was given command of XIX Army Corps...'

Osche and Graudenz.

At 0445 on the morning of 1 September 1945, the whole corps moved over the border simultaneously. Guderian was with the 3rd Panzer Division in the first wave. They met resistance north of Zempelburg where Guderian's family had once owned an estate. His father had been born there and it was the site of his grandfather's grave. Guderian claimed the distinction of being the first corps commander to accompany his tanks on to the battlefield and he first saw the family estate from his command vehicle, an armoured half-track. It was then that the division's heavy artillery started firing into the mist, despite having orders not to do so. One shell landed 50 yards (45 m) ahead of Guderian's command vehicle; a second 50 yards behind. Convinced that the next would hit home, Guderian ordered his driver to turn around. In panic, the man drove full tilt into a ditch, bending the steering mechanism and putting the half-track out of action. This was a rather ignominious end to Guderian's first foray as a wartime Panzer commander. He made his way back to the corps command post on foot, stopping to have a quiet word with his artillery men on the way.

As all Guderian's tanks were now equipped with radios, it was possible for him to keep in constant contact with the divisions under his command from the rear. But he commandeered another vehicle and rejoined the 3rd Panzer Division. By this time the mists had lifted and the lead tanks found themselves confronted with Polish defensive positions.

The Polish anti-tank gunners quickly found their mark, killing one officer, one officer cadet and eight other ranks.

When Guderian caught up, he found that the division had stopped for a rest as the divisional commander General von Bock had been called for by von Kluge. A young lieutenant told him that Polish forces on the other side of the River Brahe – their objective for that day – were light

and, although they had set light to the bridge at Hammermühle, he had put the fire out and the bridge was crossable.

Leading from the front

'The advance has only stopped because there's no one to lead it,' said the lieutenant. 'You must go there yourself, sir.'

Guderian headed off down a sandy track through the woods and arrived at Hammermühle soon after 1600, where he found the tank guns of the 6th Panzer Regiment and the rifles of the 3rd Rifle Regiment blazing away at the enemy concealed in trenches on the far bank. He ordered his men to cease fire. He then sent men from a motorcycle battalion across the river in a rubber dinghy to assess the situation and to engage the Polish bicycle company on the far bank, while the tanks crossed the bridge. The bicycle company were quickly rounded up at the cost of few German casualties.

The corps quickly built up a bridgehead on the far side of the Brahe and the whole corps was across the river by 1800. Meanwhile the 3rd Armoured Reconnaissance Battalion was on its way to the Vistula and, that night, the 3rd Panzer Division took its objective, the town of Sviekatovo. Before nightfall Guderian headed back to his corps headquarters at Zahn where he found his staff wearing steel helmets, hastily setting up an anti-tank gun. They told him that the Polish cavalry was expected any minute. Guderian disabused them. On his way back, the roads had been deserted.

The advanced troops were also nervous. The 20th (Motorized) Infantry Division had taken its objective, the town of Konitz, with some difficulty and had not advanced beyond it, while the 2nd (Motorized) Division had been halted by Polish wire entanglements. They radioed back that they were being forced to retreat by Polish cavalry. Guderian got on the radio and asked the divisional commander if he had ever heard of Pomeranian grenadiers being broken by enemy cavalry. He said he had not and promised to hold his position. The next morning, Guderian led the 2nd forward and it advanced rapidly.

With the 3rd Armoured Reconnaissance Battalion on the Vistula, the 3rd Panzer Division were straddling the Brahe when the Poles attacked along the eastern bank. At midday, the 3rd Panzer Division counter-attacked, pushing the Poles back into a wood.

The next day, the 3rd Panzer Division were on the Vistula, overrunning a retreating Polish artillery regiment and destroying it. The Panzers' advance had been so rapid that the 23rd Infantry could only keep up with forced marches. It is here that Guderian claimed that the Polish Pomorska Cavalry Brigade 'in ignorance of the nature of our tanks, charged them with swords and lances and suffered tremendous losses'. In fact, the 20th (Motorized) Division succeeded in encircling the enemy, who put up some stout resistance against the 23rd Infantry. But a regiment detached from the 32nd Infantry Division from General Strauss's Corps put an end to that and the battle for the Polish Corridor was won.

The casualties were light, but the loss of officers was disproportionately high. Two of Guderian's fellow generals had lost sons, though Guderian was reassured to see his own son alive and unscathed when he reached the Vistula. Across the river, Guderian could see his birthplace, Kulm.

The 3rd Panzers then turned back westwards to mop up any pockets of resistance. It was then that they heard that France and Britain had declared war on Germany – something they had hoped would not happen.

The next day Hitler visited XIX Corps. Seeing the remains of the artillery regiment that they had destroyed, Hitler asked, 'Did our dive bombers do that?'

'No,' said Guderian, 'it was our Panzers.'

'He was plainly astonished,' wrote Guderian in his memoir *Panzer Leader*.

Life-savers

Hitler also asked about casualties. Guderian supplied the latest figures: 150 dead, 700 wounded. Hitler was amazed that they were so light, saying that in the First World War his old regiment had lost 2,000 on the first day of battle alone. Guderian told him that the fact that the casualties were minimal was due to the use of Panzers.

'Tanks are a life-saving weapon,' said Guderian: life-saving for the Germans perhaps. One Polish cavalry brigade and two or three infantry divisions had been completely destroyed with hundreds of guns and thousands of men falling into German hands in the battle for the Polish Corridor alone.

Guderian used the opportunity to ask Hitler for more Panzer IIIs and Panzer IVs. They were fast enough, he said, but he recommended that they needed heavier armour, particularly at the front. They also needed more powerful guns with a longer range. The barrels needed extending so that the shells could be given a heavier charge. The same applied to their anti-tank guns.

On 6 September, an advance guard crossed the

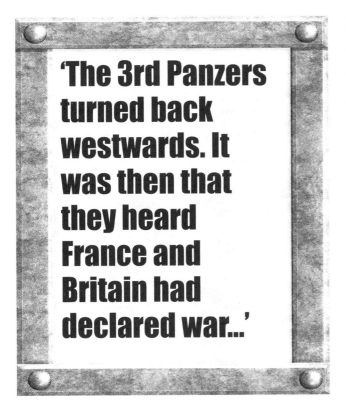

'The 3rd Panzers turned back westwards. It was then that they heard France and Britain had declared war...'

Vistula to East Prussia and set up headquarters in the castle at Finkenstein, which Napoleon had used as his headquarters on two occasions. Guderian slept in the room where Napoleon had enjoyed a few weeks with the beautiful Countess Walewska before his disastrous attack on Russia in 1812, and, while the rest of the corps crossed the river, he went hunting for deer.

Guderian's XIX Corps was then attached to General von Küchler's Third Army and was to guard its left flank. But Guderian complained that working in such close co-operation with the infantry did not make full use of the potential of his Panzer divisions. It would slow their advance and allow the Poles to pull back and establish a new defensive line along the River Bug. To counter this he suggested that his Panzer Corps be allowed to sweep around along the eastern bank of the Bug and take Brest-Litovsk at the rear of the Poles. His plans were approved.

However, he lost the 2nd (Motorized) Infantry

Division, which went to the reserve, but was given command of the 10th Panzer Division along with the Fortress Infantry Brigade *Lötzen*, comprising largely older men. The 10th Panzers' infantry and the *Lötzen* Brigade had previously moved out of East Prussia and were already involved in confused fighting around Vizna on the River Narev, a tributary of the Bug. So Guderian moved his headquarters forward to Vizna and began ferrying his Panzers across the Narev. While this was going on, the 20th (Motorized) Infantry Division was engaged in heavy fighting 15 miles (24 km) beyond at Zambrov. But ahead of them were the Reconnaissance Demonstration Battalion who were encountering no resistance. Avoiding Zambrov, the 10th Panzer Division pushed forward to Bransk, while Guderian followed to the left with the 3rd whose progress was only halted when they could not make their way through a burning village.

The 20th (Motorized) Infantry at Zambrov now encountered Polish forces withdrawing from Lomsha to the north and were in difficulties. They countered by heading back in an attempt to encircle the oncoming troops. Guderian sent some of the 10th Panzer Division to help. The following day, they succeeded in surrounding the Poles who surrendered on 12 September. Meanwhile the 3rd Panzers pushed on to Bielsk. Command of the 2nd (Motorized) Infantry Division was returned to Guderian who ordered them to advance through Lomsha to Bielsk with their divisional commander General Bader at their head. Bader arrived at Bielsk the next day, accompanied only by a wireless truck. They had been held up for a couple of hours by some Poles who had escaped the encirclement. But their wireless officer got through to Guderian, who sent Panzers. While this was going on, the 3rd Panzer had advanced another 40 miles (64 km) to Kaminiec-Litovsk and had reconnoitred as far as Brest-Litovsk some 20 miles (32 km) beyond that.

Guderian knew that the Polish forces had withdrawn into the forest of Bielovieza. But this was not good tank country, so he left troops along the edge of the forest as observers and pushed on. On 14 September, elements of the 10th Panzers had broken through the line of fortifications outside Brest-Litovsk. The corps was then ordered to descend on the city at top speed.

Faltering progress

The following day Brest-Litovsk was surrounded. But a surprise tank attack failed to take it. The Poles had parked an old Renault tank across the entrance to the citadel and the Panzers could not force their way past it. The following day an attack by the 20th (Motorized) Infantry and the 10th Panzers faltered when the infantry regiment with the 10th failed to advance behind a creeping barrage. When they did go in, they found themselves under fire from their own units in the rear and a Polish sniper on top of the ramparts hit Guderian's adjutant and killed him. The following day, while the 3rd Panzer Division skirted the city to the east, the citadel was taken by a German infantry division which advanced over the Bug from the west at the very moment the hapless defenders were trying to break out.

Von Kluge's Fourth Army caught up with Guderian at Brest-Litovsk, consolidating all the ground they had covered behind. He then planned to move the XIX Corps forward with one Panzer division going to the north-east, the other

The Panzer IV was fitted with armoured skirts and 75mm guns

south. But before they could do that the Russians arrived. It was then that Guderian learnt of the secret protocol dividing Poland between Nazi Germany and the Soviet Union. The German forces, he was told, were to withdraw from Brest-Litovsk as the border between the German and Soviet zones was to be the River Bug. Guderian complained that they were given so little time to withdraw that they could not even move their wounded or recover their damaged tanks.

'It seems unlikely that any soldier was present when the agreement about the demarcation line and the cease fire was drawn up,' he wrote.

As Guderian's Panzers pulled back into East Prussia, his corps was disbanded. After a short holiday in East Prussia, spent visiting relatives and his birthplace, he was summoned to the Chancellery in Berlin where he was decorated with the Knight's Cross of the Iron Cross. At the luncheon afterwards, he was sitting next to Hitler, who asked him how the army had reacted to the pact with the Soviet Union. Guderian said that he and his men had been relieved to hear of it as fighting on two fronts had led to disaster in the previous war. Guderian got the impression that this was not what Hitler wanted to hear.

4. THE END OF THE PHONEY WAR

There now came the period Churchill called the *drôle de guerre* – also known as the Phoney War or, sardonically, the 'Sitzkrieg'. For months after the declaration of war, the Western Allies did nothing, hoping against hope to avoid the carnage of the First World War.

The Germans used this time to evaluate what they had learned in Poland. It was decided that the light divisions, with their anomalous mixture of vehicles and troops, did not work. These would be reorganized into proper Panzer divisions. However, the supply of Panzer IIIs and IVs was slow due to the constraints at the tank factories. Guderian also complained of the 'tendency by the Army High Command to hoard the new tanks'. It was also decided that the motorized infantry divisions were too large and unwieldy. They were reduced by stripping each division of an infantry regiment.

Erich von Manstein initiated the invasion of France in 1940

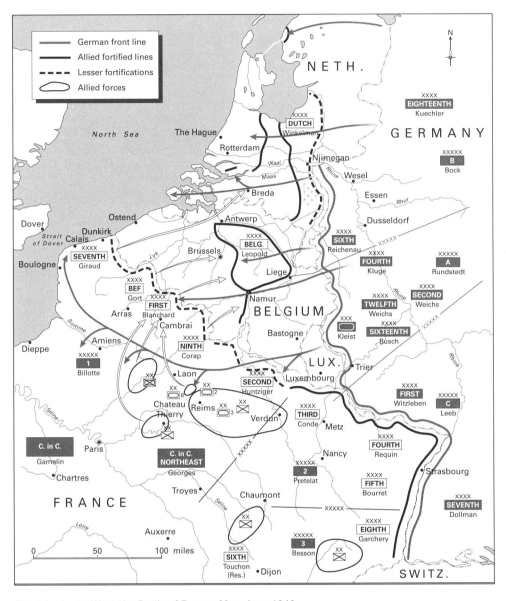

Blitzkrieg in the West: the Battle of France, May–June 1940

Hitler was eager to attack France to redress the German defeat of 1918 and the Army High Command dusted off the 'Schlieffen Plan' they had used in 1914. Devised by the Prussian General Alfred Graf von Schlieffen, who died in 1913 before seeing his plan being put into operation, it called for a rapid sweep through Belgium. It had, of course, failed to win a decisive victory in 1914 and, as it had been used before, it was hardly likely to take the Western Allies by surprise. So other alternatives were studied.

In November General von Manstein went to see Guderian. German intelligence had succeeded in breaking French military codes and, listening in on radio traffic, they had discovered a weak point between two second-rank divisions at Sedan, the very place the Germans had won their decisive victory in the Franco-Prussian War of 1870. An attack there would skirt the northern end of the Maginot Line and split the Western Front in two. Von Manstein asked Guderian to examine his plan from the point of view of the Panzers. Guderian had been in the Ardennes during the First World War and knew the terrain. He studied the maps and the Allied dispositions. From his experience in the First World War, he also understood the enemy's psychology.

The opposition forces

In 1940, the French had the largest land army in Western Europe with the strongest tank force. Not only did they have more tanks, the French tanks were superior to the Germans' in both firepower and armour. Between them, the Anglo-French forces in Northern France had 4,000

French tanks, Hotchkiss H35s, on exercise in 1940 before the German invasion – many were captured and taken over by the enemy

armoured vehicles. The Germans had 2,800, including armoured reconnaissance cars, only 2,200 of which were available for action.

While the Maginot Line stretched along the border between France and Germany, the fortifications from Sedan along the Belgian border to the sea were considerably weaker. However, the mass of the French army and the British Expeditionary Force was in Flanders, facing north-east, while the Belgian and Dutch forces massed on their borders, ready for an attack from the east. It was clear that they were expecting the Schlieffen Plan to be used once more. And Guderian saw another cause for optimism. Although the French had fought tenaciously to defend their country in the First World War, he did not expect them to put up a similar resistance this time. If they had been determined to fight to win, they would have made an all-out attack on Germany while the

bulk of her army was engaged in the fighting for Poland. The French, he believed, were hoping that a serious clash of arms could be avoided.

The building of the Maginot Line itself indicated to Guderian that the French were still committed to the old position warfare of the First World War. The proposed reforms of de Gaulle and other tank men had been ignored and the tanks had been assigned to infantry divisions, rather than being kept together in one armoured force. Guderian decided that the organization of the Panzer Corps gave the German army the advantage and reported that von Manstein's plan would work, provided that it was made with a great enough concentration of armoured and motorized divisions. If possible, Guderian said, all of them should be used.

Manstein, with the approval of von Rundstedt, his commanding officer, submitted his plan to the High Command. However, the conservatives

General von Rundstedt asked for a pause to allow the infantry to catch up with the tanks, enabling the British to evacuate Dunkirk

in the High Command wanted to stick with the Schlieffen Plan and send, perhaps, just one or two Panzer divisions through the Ardennes. In Guderian's opinion, this would have been pointless.

'Any subdivision of our already weak tank force would have been the greatest mistake we could have made,' he said.

Manstein's plan was rejected and he was sent to command an infantry corps, rather than a Panzer corps as he had requested. But as luck would have it, the Schlieffen Plan soon had to be abandoned anyway. Against orders, a Luftwaffe courier had been carrying important papers on a night flight when his plane was forced to put down in Belgium. Among the papers were proposals to attack France through Belgium using the Schlieffen Plan. It was not known if he had destroyed the papers, but it had to be assumed that they had fallen into Belgian hands and, consequently, Britain and France knew all about them.

Strategic discussions

On assuming his new command, von Manstein had to report to Hitler and took the opportunity to outline his plan. Hitler was impressed. On 7 February it was tested in a war game at Koblenz. Guderian was present and proposed that, on the fifth day of the campaign, armoured and motorized forces should cross the Meuse at Sedan, expanding its breakthrough towards Amiens. General Franz Halder, chief of the army general staff, dismissed the idea as 'senseless'. He said that the armour should wait on the Meuse until the infantry caught up on the ninth or tenth day of the campaign so they could stage 'a

'On assuming his new command, von Manstein took the opportunity to outline his plan to Hitler. He was impressed'

properly marshalled attack en masse'. Guderian disagreed vehemently.

He insisted that they mass their limited armour to make one surprise attack at one decisive point, then drive forward so wide and deep that they did not have to worry about their flanks. The Panzers, he said, must be free to exploit any gains without waiting for the infantry.

The point came up for discussion again at another war game at Mayen on 14 February. Guderian grew concerned that not even von Rundstedt appreciated the full potential of the Panzers. However, it was finally decided that the Panzer Corps should lead the attack through the Ardennes. But erring on the side of caution, von Kleist, a general not known for his enthusiasm for armour, was put in command.

Guderian was given command of the 1st, 2nd and 10th Panzer Divisions, the *Grossdeutschland* infantry and some corps troops, including a mortar battalion, forming a new XIX Corps. Along with the other army commanders, Guderian was summoned to the Chancellery to see Hitler.

Each was to spell out his duties and how he intended to carry them out. Guderian was the last to speak. He explained that he was to advance through Luxembourg, reaching the Belgian frontier and breaking through their border defences on the first day. The second day he intended to reach Neufchâteau. On the third day he would cross the Semois at Bouillon. On the fourth, he would reach the Meuse. And on the fifth he would cross it and establish a bridgehead on the far bank. Hitler then asked, 'And what are you going to do then?'

This was the $64,000 question – the question no one had thought to ask him right up until this point.

'Unless I receive orders to the contrary,' said Guderian, 'I intend to continue my advance westwards the next day. The supreme leadership must decide whether my objective is to be Amiens or Paris. In my opinion, the correct course is to drive past Amiens and on to the English Channel.'

Hitler nodded. The rest of the army commanders were taken by surprise. General Busch, an infantry officer who was to command the Sixteenth Army to Guderian's left, said sneeringly, 'I don't think you will cross the river in the first place.'

Hitler waited for Guderian's reply. It was dismissive.

'In any case, there's no need for you to do so,' he told Busch.

As it was, Guderian never in fact received any orders telling him what to do once he had crossed the Meuse. All the decisions taken on his push to the sea he took on his own authority.

In preparation for the attack, Guderian liaised with the Luftwaffe. Again they discussed the crossing of the Meuse. Close ground support would be needed. The Luftwaffe's job was to attack the French batteries while the Panzers crossed the river. The head of the Luftwaffe, Hermann Göring, also made plans for a battalion of the *Grossdeutschland* to be airlifted to Wirty, behind the Belgian lines.

Guderian drew up in corps with 2nd Panzer Division under General Veiel on the right; the 10th Panzer Division under General Schaal on the left with the *Grossdeutschland*; and the 1st Panzer Division under General Kirchner in the centre with the corps headquarters, artillery and anti-aircraft guns behind it. Guderian knew his generals well and, with the exception of the *Grossdeutschland*, had worked with all his men in peacetime.

On the move

The corps went on the alert at 1330 on 9 May 1940. The troops were drawn up in order along the border between Echternach and Vianden. At 0530 the following morning they crossed into Luxembourg. By evening, advance elements of the 1st Panzer Division had reached the Belgian frontier. The 2nd Panzer Division was fighting near Strainchamps and the 10th Panzer Division had made contact with French cavalry and Colonial infantry divisions, while the *Grossdeutschland* had been held up by demolition work along the road which could not be cleared until that night. Unable to keep up with the Panzers, the *Grossdeutschland* were soon called back into the reserve.

German forces push past a destroyed Renault tank, May 1940

The following morning the border minefield and demolition work were cleared and the 1st Panzer Division drove on to Neufchâteau. After a short skirmish with French and Belgian forces, the city was taken. By dusk the 1st Panzer Division had reached Bouillon, which the French managed to hold on to that night. The 2nd Panzer Division had taken Libramont against light opposition. That night von Kleist asked for the 10th Panzer Division to change direction towards Longwy where French cavalry had been reported. Guderian asked for the orders to be cancelled. Cavalry posed no danger to tanks and the loss of the 10th would endanger his Meuse crossing. Knowing that von Kleist was of the old

school and would take some convincing that cavalry posed no threat, Guderian pretended to obey the order and moved the 10th to the left, but kept it on a parallel course. Eventually he got the orders countermanded and the French cavalry failed to appear.

Bouillon fell on 12 May. The French had blown the bridges over the Semois, but the Panzers could ford the river in some places. Once work had started on a bridge, Guderian went forward, but was forced to turn back when it was found that the road was mined. He arrived back at Bouillon just as an Allied air strike came in. It failed to hit the new bridge, but set a few houses on fire.

Guderian then went with the 10th Panzer Division through the woods, arriving at the French frontier in time to see a reconnaissance battalion overcome the border defences. He moved his headquarters to Bouillon where they came under air attack again. Belgian planes also bombed the Panzers' bivouacs, but caused few casualties.

Flown back to von Kleist's headquarters, Guderian was told to cross the Meuse at 1600 hours the next day, 13 May. Guderian reported that, although the 1st and 10th Panzer Divisions would be in position by that time, the 2nd had run into problems on the Semois and would not be ready. Although this would weaken his attacking force, Guderian admitted that there was an advantage in keeping up the momentum. However, instead of using the Luftwaffe to bomb the batteries and make the gunners keep their heads down while the Panzers crossed the Meuse, von Kleist's plan ordered an all-out air attack beforehand. Guderian objected, fearing that the bombing would not neutralize the guns and they would be left without air support during the crossing. He was overruled.

On the way back to his headquarters his plane strayed over French lines, but he arrived back at Bouillon unscathed. There was little time to issue orders, so he took the ones that he had used in the war game at Koblenz and changed the dates and times.

By the evening of 12 May, the 1st and 10th Panzer Divisions were drawn up on the north bank of the Meuse, overlooking the fortress of Sedan. During the night the artillery was brought up. Guderian toured his divisional headquarters and, by 1530, he was with the 10th Panzer Division awaiting the Luftwaffe. But when the planes came, he saw, not the massed ranks of heavy bombers von Kleist had promised, but squadrons of bombers and Stukas with fighter escorts in the formation that he had worked out with the Luftwaffe beforehand. Von Kleist's new orders had plainly not got through in time.

Riflemen were already crossing the river and Guderian went across on the first assault boat. The landing was practically unopposed as the bombers and dive-bombers attacked the French artillery. By midnight, the whole of the 1st Panzer Division's rifle brigade had crossed the river and the tanks were awaiting the completion of a bridge.

The 10th Panzer Division had crossed the river without artillery support and had established a small bridgehead on the other side. However, they were coming under heavy flanking fire from the north end of the Maginot Line. But in the morning, the 2nd Panzer Division arrived, along with the corps' heavy anti-aircraft guns.

Consolidation

Now that the Panzers were firmly established on the other side of the Meuse, Guderian sent a telegram to Busch, who had said that he would not be able to cross the river. He received a guarded though cordial reply. By this time, the 1st Panzer Division had stormed on as far as Chémery.

Thousands of prisoners had been taken. Then the 1st Panzer Division heard that French armour was moving up, so the tanks set off to meet them. Guderian then ordered the 2nd Panzers to cross the river and went after them.

In the confusion, the German Stukas mistakenly attacked Chémery, causing heavy German casualties. The French and British pilots did not do so well when they attacked the bridges. They failed to knock them out and, by nightfall, XIX Corps' anti-aircraft gunners reckoned that they had shot down 150 Allied aeroplanes.

While the remains of the 2nd Panzer Division continued to cross the river, General von Rundstedt came up to see what was happening for himself. The 1st and 2nd Panzer Divisions were ordered to go south, cross the Ardennes Canal, then turn west with the aim of breaking through the French defences. By the evening, the 1st Panzer Division had crossed the canal and taken Vendresse and Singly against fierce opposition. The 10th Panzer Division had also broken through, capturing more than forty guns. The bridgehead was now secure and von Kleist halted the advance to allow the infantry to catch up. Guderian called him and asked for the order to be countermanded. The argument

Right: Men of the 1st Panzers with French prisoners at Floing

grew heated. Eventually von Kleist gave orders for the advance to continue for one more day to make room in the bridgehead for the infantry that were following.

Guderian's Panzer Corps were now tired, but their spirits were lifted when they had captured an order from the French army Commander in Chief General Maurice Gamelin that read: 'The torrent of German tanks must finally be stopped.'

Guderian read it to his men and he ordered them to push forward with all possible speed. The 1st and 2nd Panzer Divisions now broke through completely. At the town of Montcornet, they met the 6th Panzer Division under General Kempff, who had also crossed the Meuse. As the Panzer Group had laid down that there was to

be no demarcation between the corps, the three divisions agreed to press on together until they ran out of fuel. Lead elements were already 55 miles (88 km) from Sedan.

The following morning the order halting the advance came through again and Guderian was ordered back to see von Kleist, who upbraided him for disobeying orders and proceeding with the advance. When von Kleist stopped to draw breath, Guderian asked to be relieved of his command. Von Kleist ordered him to hand over his command to his most senior general. Guderian did so then, back at his headquarters, sent a message to von Rundstedt saying that he would fly to the Army Group headquarters to make his report. He got an immediate reply

ordering him to stay where he was. Then another message arrived from von Rundstedt's headquarters, which ordered him not to resign his command and explained that the order to halt the advance had originated, not with von Kleist, but with the High Command. The advance had been halted so that Guderian's headquarters would stay where they were – by then in Soize – and could be reached easily. However, he was free to continue with 'reconnaissance in force'.

Guderian went back on the offensive. He went forward with the Panzers but laid a land line between his new forward headquarters and his staff headquarters at Soize. That way the High Command would get the impression that he was still at Soize and he would be able to communicate without his orders being overheard by the High Command's radio intercept units.

By the time they had received the second order to halt on 17 May, the 1st Panzer Division and advanced elements of the 10th were 70 miles (112 km) from Sedan. And by 0900 on 18 May, the 2nd Panzers had reached St Quentin. The following morning the 1st Panzer Division crossed the Somme, capturing several French staff officers who had arrived at Péronne to find out what was going on. While the Panzers crossed the First World War battlefields of the Somme, tanks from General de Gaulle's newly formed 4th Armoured Division penetrated within a mile of Guderian's forward headquarters at Holon. Guderian also got news that a French reserve army, some eight infantry divisions strong, was mustering in the Paris area. But he did not think that they presented any threat, so long as his Panzers kept moving. That night, he moved his forward headquarters up again, this time to Marleville. Later that day,

he received orders allowing him freedom of movement once more and authorizing him to move on Amiens. This task was assigned to the 1st Panzers while the 10th guarded its extended left flank and the 2nd sped through Albert to Abbéville, securing another crossing on the Somme and then rounding up any Allied forces between Abbéville and the sea.

Rapid advance

Guderian himself headed for Amiens, arriving there at 0845 on 20 May, just as the 1st Panzers were launching their attack. By noon the city had fallen. At Albert the 2nd Panzer Division had captured a British battery. It was equipped only with training ammunition as no one had expected the Germans to turn up so quickly. The market square was soon full of prisoners of many nationalities and General Veiel, complaining that he was low on fuel, proposed stopping there. Guderian dismissed his gripes and ordered him on to Abbéville, where they arrived at 1900.

On the way to his new corps headquarters at Querrieu, north-east of Amiens, Guderian found himself under attack by German planes. His flak guns shot two of them down. Two Luftwaffe crew floated to the ground on parachutes only to be berated by a Panzer general. Once Guderian had said his piece, he fortified the two young airmen with captured champagne.

That night the 2nd Panzer Division reached the coast. The breakthrough had been so rapid that no orders had yet come through telling them which way to go next and Guderian was forced to halt. But the next day, orders came telling them to turn north and advance on the Channel ports. Guderian ordered the 1st Panzers to take

Calais, the 2nd to take Boulogne and the 10th were to advance on Dunkirk. However, the next day the 10th were removed from his command and put in the reserve. Guderian protested but his request to have the 10th back was refused.

The reason for this was that on 21 May, British tanks had attempted to make a breakthrough in the direction of Paris, cutting the German column in two and making contact with the remains of the French army to the south. At Arras, they came face to face with the SS *Totenkopf* (Death's Head) Division. Fresh troops, the SS men showed signs of panic. Even more panicky were the staff of von Kleist's Panzer Group, who immediately feared that the Panzers had overstretched themselves.

Coastal skirmishes

Nevertheless, the 1st and 2nd Divisions headed for the Channel ports, even though they were understrength as they had left units behind defending the Somme bridgeheads. The 2nd met stiff resistance from French, British, Belgian and Dutch units. And they were so far advanced that the Luftwaffe gave them little cover. The Allied air forces bombed them, but they too seemed to be on the limit of their range and Boulogne fell on 22 May.

The 10th Panzer Division was returned to Guderian's command. He sent it to replace the 1st Panzers at Calais, while the 1st went on to Dunkirk. He wanted to take Dunkirk urgently to cut off the Allied escape route. As the fighting around the Channel ports intensified, the SS Division *Leibstandarte Adolf Hitler* was put under Guderian's command to strengthen his drive on Dunkirk. Elements of the 2nd Division

Guderian aboard a German communications vehicle, May 1940

were also sent, while the artillery used at Boulogne was sent to Calais where the port was now encircled by the 10th Panzer Division.

It was then, on 24 May, that Hitler ordered the advance on Dunkirk to halt at the Canal d'Aire, just outside the port. Dunkirk, and the Allied troops bottled up there, were to be left to the Luftwaffe and, if Calais proved too difficult a nut to crack, it should be left to the Luftwaffe too. But the Luftwaffe was nowhere to be seen and Allied aeroplanes harassed the Panzers as they stood and waited. When Guderian arrived outside Dunkirk to check that the advance had indeed been halted, he found the *Leibstandarte* were still advancing. The divisional commander

Sepp Dietrich explained that they were at the mercy of anyone on the 235-ft Mont Watten on the other side of the canal, the only high point in the area. Guderian approved his decision and ordered the 2nd Panzer Division to move up in support.

Frustration

On 26 May, the 10th Panzer Division took Calais. But outside Dunkirk the Panzers could only sit and watch as a heroic fleet of small boats ferried the remains of the British army from the beaches. It was only late on 26 May that the order was given to advance again.

'By then it was too late to achieve a great victory,' said Guderian.

On the 29th Guderian's XIX Army Corps was withdrawn and replaced by the XIV Corps. Headed by the 9th Panzer Division, it took the city a few days later.

On 1 June, Maurice Few, a British officer, was captured near Godeswald by the 7th Panzer Division commanded by the already legendary Erwin Rommel, who had spearheaded another thrust to the north capturing Lille. Few said:

I found his troops to be correct but courteous and without the arrogance we were to experience later. The entire division seemed to be dressed in brand new British army battle dress trousers with a Wehrmacht jacket; many wore a gaily coloured silk scarf round their necks and had a tendency to long hair. I was told that everyone in the

Soldiers check their equipment as a Panzer 38 is serviced behind them

division was under 30 years old but no doubt this did not apply to Rommel [who was born in 1891] and perhaps some of his division staff. Somebody silently presented me with a 'hussif', presumably because my battle dress was in tatters. Someone else – obviously a Panzer humorist – held out his clenched fists, one above the other. The upper fist was then vigorously pumped up and down, while the lower first remained stationary to the chant: 'Chemblin, Chemblin'. (This was intended to take off Neville Chamberlain raising and lowering his famous umbrella.)

But the Panzers were not as well equipped as he had at first thought:

I noted an ingenious money saver. This was a 'mechanized' field cooker which simply comprised a horse-drawn field cooker run up on to the back of a lorry and its wheels lashed to ring bolts. The cook stood on the back of the lorry cooking just as he would have been doing on the line of march when his cooker had been drawn by two heavy draft horses. Maps throughout Rommel's division appeared to comprise Michelin tourist maps. They were bang up to date but, in so far as I can remember, without grid co-ordinates. Nonetheless they were vastly preferable to our ordnance survey sheets dated 1924. All the vehicles appeared to be fitted with Dunlop tyres and so did the aircraft.

Guderian said that the opportunity to capture the entire British Expeditionary Force at Dunkirk was wasted due to Hitler's nervousness.

'The reason he subsequently gave for holding back my corps – that the ground in Flanders with its many ditches and canals was not suited to tanks – was a poor one,' said Guderian.

Though he was robbed of the final prize, nothing could diminish the scale of the achievement of Guderian and his Panzers. In just 17 days, they had covered the 400 miles (640 km) from the German border to the Channel coast. On the way they had broken through the Belgian fortifications, forced a crossing of the Meuse, broken the French defences north of the Maginot Line, crossed the Somme, seized the important towns of St Quentin, Péronne, Amiens and Abbéville, and captured the Channel ports of Boulogne and Calais. The French had collapsed,

Wounded British soldiers are carried away for treatment aboard a German tank after the conquest of Calais, May 1940

the Belgians had been overrun, and the British sent scuttling home with their tails between their legs. Nobody could doubt that this astonishingly swift victory was due to the Panzers.

On a personal level, Guderian received news that his eldest son had been wounded. His second son, Kurt, had also been in action and had been awarded the Iron Cross, First and Second Class. Guderian's own reward was not long in coming. On 28 May, Hitler ordered that a Panzer Group be set up under his command. Panzer Group Guderian mustered at the beginning of June near Charleville in north-east France. He now had under his command the 1st, 2nd and 8th Panzer Divisions and the 20th and 29th (Motorized) Infantry Divisions. The 1st and 2nd Panzer Divisions had to drive over 150 miles (240 km) from the Channel coast and the destruction of bridges along the way put an extra 60 miles (96 km) on the journey. When they arrived the crews were tired and the tanks were in a poor state of repair.

> 'List upbraided Guderian, saying his men were not ready for action. Guderian said it wasn't his fault bridgeheads had not been taken'

The battle for France was not over yet. The German army still faced 70 divisions, including two British. However, most of the Allies' armour and motorized units had been destroyed. Now the Wehrmacht had to strike south. First Guderian needed to rest his men and get their tanks repaired.

Panzer Group Guderian was part of the Twelfth Army under General List, who deployed the Panzers behind the infantry. Guderian objected. He thought that the Panzers should be out in the lead again, otherwise their progress was hampered by the infantry's supply columns which would block the roads. But List wanted to save the Panzers for a decisive breakthrough and refused Guderian's request to put them at the front.

Held up

The attack was to begin on 9 June. The infantry were to establish eight bridgeheads over the Aisne, which the Panzers were to drive through with the motorized units following behind. The attack began at 0500. By 1200, Guderian received news that it had failed. Only one small bridgehead had been established, less than a mile and a half (2.4 km) deep. Guderian suggested that they move up all his tanks into the single bridgehead during the night, so that they were ready to break out the following morning.

List came to see Guderian, but on the way he spotted some of Guderian's men with their jackets off. Others were bathing in a stream. He upbraided Guderian, saying his men were not ready to go into action. Guderian countered by saying that it was not his fault that seven of the bridgeheads had not been taken and the eighth was too shallow for his tanks to occupy straight away. List took his point. The two men shook hands and then discussed the future of the attack.

During the afternoon, the infantry managed to establish two further shallow bridgeheads allowing the 1st and 2nd Panzers to move up. At 0630 on 10 June, the Panzers attacked. They advanced rapidly through the towns of Avançon, Tagnon, Neuflize and Retourne. By this time, the French had abandoned the open ground, knowing they could not challenge the Panzers there. Instead, they defended the woods and villages. The Panzers bypassed these, leaving the infantry to fight their way through well-defended woodlands and barricaded streets.

At Juniville in the early afternoon, the French counter-attacked with their remaining armour. A tank battle developed that lasted for two hours. The Panzers found that their 20mm and 37mm guns were ineffective against the French heavy Char B tanks. Even the shells of a captured 47mm anti-tank gun bounced off the Char's 60mm armour, which was twice as thick as the armour on the German tanks. The Char B had a 47mm gun in its turret and a 75mm fixed gun in the hull, but its one-man turret made it difficult to operate in battle. While commanding the tank, or even a phalanx of them, the tank commander had to load and fire the gun as well. The Panzers suffered heavy casualties. But the battle was won by the Germans when Guderian's riflemen captured the French colours.

Late in the afternoon, there was another engagement with French tanks, but the 1st Panzer Division managed to beat them off once again and took Juniville. Meanwhile the 2nd Panzer Division had crossed the Aisne to the west and was heading south. The group headquarters was brought up to Bois de Sévigny on the Aisne and Guderian caught three hours' sleep on a bundle of straw. He was so exhausted that he did not even take his cap off and a tent had to be erected around him.

French counter-attack

The following morning, he supervised the 1st Panzer Division's attack on La Neuville. After an artillery barrage, tanks and riflemen encircled the village and broke out towards Béthénville, a village Guderian had known during the First World War. The French counter-attacked with some fifty tanks. The French 3rd Armoured and 3rd Mechanized Divisions also attacked their flanks. This slowed the progress of the Panzers. The situation grew confused when the infantry caught up with the tanks and the two branches of the service competed for the lead. Guderian tried to get List to prevent the infantry from crossing the Panzers' line of attack, without success. The orders that came in now were confused and, sometimes, contradictory. So Guderian ignored them and pushed on south.

The 1st Panzer Division were ordered not to cross the Rhine–Marne Canal. But when Guderian arrived there, he found that they had already taken the bridge at Éptépy and established a bridgehead on the other side. So Guderian drove across the bridge. Instead of reprimanding the two officers responsible for crossing the canal for disobeying orders, he awarded them the Iron Cross, First Class on the spot and asked why they had not gone further. He then ordered them to advance directly on St Dizier. Once a breakthrough was made, Guderian believed, there was no place for hesitancy or delay. When the 1st Panzers took St Dizier, they expected a few hours' rest. But Guderian ordered them on to Langres. He said simply, 'The faster we could now continue our advance, the greater must be our victory.'

Communication breakdown

By the next morning, the 1st Panzer Division had taken the old fortress at Langres and three thousand prisoners.

Unclear as to what the High Command wanted him to do next, Guderian sent their liaison officer back to tell them that he intended to push on to the Swiss border.

However, their progress was hampered by the Luftwaffe who bombed the bridge at Gray. But Guderian was now out of contact with the Army Group and could not reprimand them.

As they pushed on they captured thirty tanks and took thousands of prisoners, including a number of Poles. On 17 June, as Guderian and his staff officers gathered to celebrate his birthday, his chief of staff Colonel Nehring handed him a special birthday present. It was a message saying that his 29th (Motorized) Infantry Division had reached the Swiss frontier. Guderian set off straight away to congratulate his troops. Meanwhile, he sent a message to the High Command that his men had reached the Swiss border at Pontarlier.

'Your signal based on error,' Hitler signalled back. 'Assume you mean Pontailler-sur-Saône.'

'No error,' was Guderian's reply. 'Am myself at Pontarlier on Swiss border' – which was 70 miles (110 km) further on.

Guderian now turned his column north-east

German top brass oversee the German push towards Verdun – police chief Kurt Daluege holds a map or newspaper behind his back

to attack the French defences along the border with Germany from the rear. This would trap the French forces in Alsace-Lorraine and force them back against the Seventh Army under General Dollmann who was advancing over the German border. Guderian's well-trained troops executed the 90-degree turn without difficulty. It was only then that Guderian received orders telling him to turn to the north-east. He signalled back that the order had already been carried out.

That evening Guderian received another birthday present. His younger son, Kurt, turned up. He had just been transferred from the 3rd Armoured Reconnaissance Battalion into Hitler's bodyguard, the Führer Escort Battalion.

Again the speed of the Panzers' advance took both the enemy and the Army Group by surprise. Thousands of prisoners had surrendered, along with their artillery and transport. They

reached Belfort, the objective the Army Group had set them, that night. By morning the town had been taken and the troops in the barracks there had surrendered. Only the fort held out. Guderian organized a lightning assault. After a short barrage by the artillery of the 1st Panzer Division, an 88mm anti-aircraft gun and a rifle battalion in armoured troop-carrying vehicles were rushed up to the foot of the fort. They clambered over the entrenchments and scaled the walls while the anti-aircraft gun ensured that the defenders kept their heads down. The speed of the attack took the French by surprise and they were forced to surrender.

Although Belfort was their objective, while the fort was being taken, lead elements of the 1st Panzer Division went on to Giromagny to the north where they took 10,000 prisoners and captured seven planes and forty mortars.

A police post in Alsace-Lorraine in 1940 as the Germans begin to tighten their grip on neighbouring countries

Meanwhile the French government had fallen and, on 16 June, the First World War general Marshal Pétain began to negotiate an armistice. Even so Guderian saw no reason to slacken the pace. He pushed on to make contact with General Dollmann and encircle the French. By the time the 2nd Panzer Division reached the upper Moselle at Rupt and the 6th Panzer Divisions took the fort at Épinal, 40,000 more prisoners had been taken.

On 19 June, contact was made with the Seventh Army. The infantry of I Army Corps then arrived in the area, but Guderian halted their advance as the roads were already choked with his Panzers. The infantry complained to Army Group headquarters. It did no good as the Panzers had already taken the remaining forts of the Maginot Line. They then pushed on into the Vosges region of Lorraine, taking a further 150,000 prisoners. Since crossing the Aisne, Panzer Group Guderian had captured a quarter of a million men.

Ceasefire

The French government agreed to an armistice on 22 June. With the Panzers leading the attack, the German army had overrun France in just six weeks, something it had failed to do in four years without armour in the First World War. The following day Guderian went to visit General Dollman whose headquarters were in Colmar. This was where Guderian had spent his childhood. He also visited his elder son in hospital in Lyon. Heinz Günter had been wounded for a second time, but had received a promotion for his pains.

Guderian himself played host to Dr Fritz Todt, the minister for armaments and war production, who sought his advice on the development of tank production in the light of his experience in action. As a result Hitler ordered that the Panzer III's 37mm gun be replaced with a 50mm gun, the L60. In practice the L42, also 50mm, was used because it had a much shorter barrel. Hitler was angry when he found out, even though a shorter barrel was far better for the tanks' manoeuvrability.

Panzer Group Guderian was dissolved on 30 June 1940. In his farewell address to his men, Guderian said, 'The victorious advance from the Aisne to the Swiss border and the Vosges will go down in

Hastily erected traffic signs in Gothic script reveal a new direction in Colmar, Alsace

As part of the preparations for Operation *Sealion*, a German tank is refitted to make it amphibious on the French coast

history as an heroic example of a breakthrough by mobile troops.'

Some of Guderian's Panzer Group went back to Germany. Other elements, along with the staff, went to Paris. Guderian went with them and took the opportunity to visit the Napoleonic Museum at Malmaison. Afterwards Guderian returned to Berlin where he was promoted to colonel-general. Preparations for Operation *Sealion* – the invasion of Great Britain – were now under way. Panzer IIIs and IVs were modified to operate underwater for the invasion. They were tested at Putlos, in Holstein but were never deployed against the British. Instead they would be sent into the Soviet Union the following year.

The Panzers had played such a vital role in the battle for France that Hitler ordered production to be raised from 800 to 1,000 tanks a month. But the Army Ordnance Office pointed out that 10,000 extra skilled workers and specialists would be needed.

The cost, they reckoned, would be two billion

marks and Hitler was forced to abandon his plan.

Hitler also ordered a doubling of the number of Panzer divisions. The result was simply a halving of the tank strength of each of them. He also increased the number of mechanized units, but the German automobile industry could not cope with the demand for new vehicles. Captured vehicles had to be used instead. These were generally inferior in quality to those produced by the German industry and quite unsuited to the conditions in the Soviet Union and the North African desert where they would be deployed.

Guderian was occupied in training the new Panzer and mechanized units, and, during this period, he had no contact with the Army High Command or the general staff.

'My opinions were not sought,' he wrote, 'either concerning the reorganization of the armoured force' – an area in which he was the expert – 'or as to the future prosecution of the war.' He had already made it clear in *Achtung – Panzer!* that he thought that war with Russia was a mistake.

5. INTO THE DESERT

'**O**f all theatres of operations, North Africa was probably the one where the war took on its most modern shape,' wrote the brilliant Panzer commander Erwin Rommel. 'Here fully motorized formations faced each other over flat desert, free of obstructions, offering hitherto unforeseen possibilities. Here the principles of motorized and tank warfare, as they had been taught before 1939, could be applied fully and, more importantly, developed.'

Rommel's ability to handle Panzer formations in the field, it is said, even surpassed that of Guderian and earned him the grudging respect of the British who called him the 'Desert Fox'. Born in Heidenheim an der Brentz on 15 November 1891, he joined the 6th Württemberg Regiment in 1910. Like many of the great Panzer commanders he served with the infantry in the First World War. He first saw combat on the Western Front at Verdun in 1914, earning the Iron Cross, Second Class. His Iron Cross, First Class came after he staged a daring raid on the French trenches at Argonne the following year. In 1916,

he was posted to the newly formed Württemberg Mountain Regiment and fought with the Alpine Corps in the Romanian campaign. During the 1917 Caporetto campaign where *Stosstruppen* were first employed, his battalion fought their way from Isonzo to Piave, deep behind Italian lines, capturing 81 guns, 9,000 men and 150 Italian officers. Away from the trenches, it taught Rommel a different kind of warfare.

'I was under the impression that I must not stand still or we were lost,' he wrote in his book *Infantry Attacks*, published in 1938, based on the lectures he gave as an instructor at the Infantry School in Dresden.

He spent four years there studying tactics. Strategy and the political and diplomatic aspects of military operations did not interest him and the limit of 4,000 officers imposed on the army by the Versailles Treaty prevented him being promoted beyond company commander. Although he had no particular liking for the

Top: Himmler and Heydrich are part of a summit meeting in Rome

Nazis, the Third Reich presented opportunities for an ambitious military man. When he met Hitler in 1934, he was impressed. In his turn, Rommel made a favourable impression on Hitler's propaganda minister Josef Goebbels, who sought to promote him as a popular hero. Promoted to major, he was given the command of the 17th Infantry Regiment. Then in October 1935, Hitler made him a military instructor at the newly reopened War Academy. He also served as a military instructor to the Hitler Youth. And when Hitler marched into the Sudetenland in 1938, Rommel headed his personal escort, the *Führerbegleit* Battalion.

When Rommel showed particular skill in organizing Hitler's motorcade, Hitler appointed him commander of the 7th Panzer Division, one of the light divisions that was undergoing an upgrade in armour after the Polish campaign in February 1940. He had been a Panzer commander for just three months when the battle for France began. But he discharged himself well, playing a crucial role in crossing the Meuse at Dinant. In the race across northern France to the Channel, he outpaced the other divisions to such an extent that the 7th earned the nickname the 'Ghost Division'. Rommel was also commended for his personal bravery as he came under fire many times during that campaign.

War spreads

The war in North Africa started when the Italian dictator Benito Mussolini ordered Marshal Rodolfo Graziani, his commander in Libya,

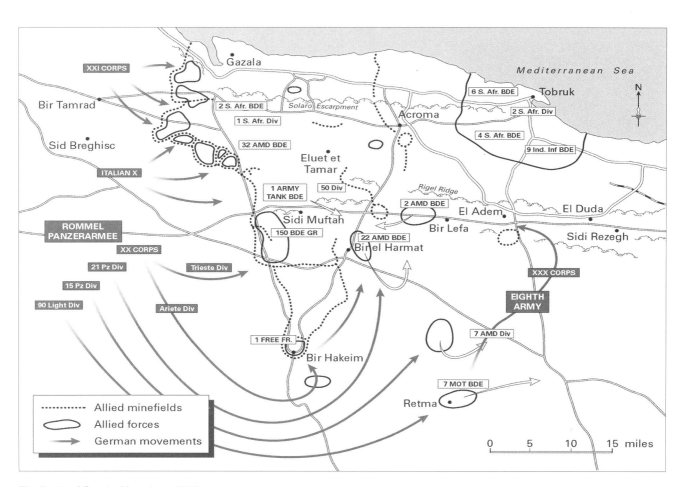

The Battle of Gazala, May–June 1942

which had been in Italian hands since 1911, to take Egypt, which had been British since 1882. On 13 September 1940, the Italian Tenth Army took the small border port of Sollum. They then advanced a further 50 miles (80 km) into Egypt and occupied the British base at Sidi Barrani on 16 September. Six weeks later the British Western Desert Force under Lieutenant General Richard O'Connor executed a short 'end run' around the Italian southern flank. This would be a tactic used by both sides in the desert war. Both armies' northern flank was secure as it was bounded by the sea and the opposing armies clung on to the coast road. But the southern flank was open

desert. O'Connor then turned and hit the Italians in the rear with fifty heavy Matilda infantry tanks reinforcing the 4th Indian Infantry Division. This avoided a frontal assault on the fortifications and caught the Italians by surprise. With the Italians in total confusion, the 7th Armoured Division rode in, the hulls of their tanks hidden in clouds of dust, only the menacing gun turrets showing, with commanders' heads emerging and two pennants fluttering high above on the radio aerials. The British hit hard into the flank and rear, cutting off the forward units. Some 40,000 prisoners were taken.

By 10 December, those Italians who could get

Displaying a captured Italian flag, a British Matilda tank on its way into Tobruk, 24 January 1941

Throwing up dust, Italian tanks advance on Marmarica, Tunisia

away had fled back across the Libyan border into the province of Cyrenaica, where the remnant of the Italian forces from Sidi Barrani shut itself up in the fortress of Bardia. O'Connor's tanks quickly encircled it. On 3 January 1941, the British assault on Bardia began, and three days later the whole garrison of Bardia – 45,000 men in all – surrendered.

Reinforced by the Australians, the Western Desert Force continued the advance. The next fortress to the west, Tobruk was assaulted on 23 January and captured the next day: 30,000 prisoners were taken in the process. After taking Mechili and Msus, it remained for the British to take the port of Benghazi to complete their conquest of Cyrenaica. On 3 February 1941, however, O'Connor learned that the Italians were about to abandon Benghazi and retreat westward down the coast road to Agheila. Thereupon he boldly ordered the cruiser tanks of the 7th Armoured Division to cross the desert hinterland and cut across the great bulge of Cyrenaica, intercept the slow-moving Italian retreat by cutting the coast road well to the east of Agheila, and hold them up for the 4th Indian Infantry Division and its Matildas. On 5 February, after an advance of 170 miles (270 km) in 33 hours, the British tanks blocked the Italians' line of retreat south of Beda Fomm. On the morning of 6 February, the main Italian columns appeared and the battle of Beda Fomm began. Though the

A column of Italian prisoners, captured during the assault on Bardia, Libya in January 1941, shuffles off towards a British POW camp

Italians had nearly four times as many cruiser tanks as the British, by the following morning sixty Italian tanks had been crippled, forty more abandoned, and the rest of Graziani's army was surrendering in droves. The British, numbering just 3,000 and having lost only three of their 29 tanks, took 20,000 prisoners, 120 tanks, and 216 guns. By the time the Italians surrendered at Beda Fomm on 7 February, the British had driven them back 500 miles (800 km), taking in all over 130,000 prisoners, along with 400 tanks and 1,290 guns. Meeting no further resistance, the Western Desert Force could have gone on to take Tripoli, but their supply lines were already overstretched and Churchill wanted to divert men and resources to Greece.

Then Hitler came to Mussolini's aid. He sent a Panzer force – never meant to be more than two divisions – 'to render services to our allies in the defence of Tripolitania – particularly against the British armoured division'.

After distinguishing himself in the French campaign, Rommel was sent to Libya. On 12 February, he arrived in Tripoli. The following day there was a parade of Panzers in the main street. Rommel gave a speech which was translated sentence by sentence into Italian. The crowd only applauded when Rommel made reference to the 'achievements' of the Italian troops. However, the Italians were impressed by the Panzer parade, though they were alarmed at the damage the tracks of the heavy Mark IVs did to the street. British spies in Tripoli were also impressed.

'Broadcasts made it clear that GHQ Middle East was astonished by the strength of the German expeditionary force in Tripolitania,' said Lieutenant Heinz Schmidt, Rommel's South African-born aide-de-camp.

Within two hours of the end of Rommel's speech the Panzers were heading out of Tripoli, bound for the front. Rommel immediately abandoned any defensive posture and prepared to attack. This alarmed Hitler and the High Command. They thought that a major offensive in North Africa was a waste of men and materiel and they feared that Rommel might wreck his Panzers which were needed in the build-up to the attack on the Soviet Union.

General Halder wrote in this diary, 'Reports from officers coming from this theatre… show that Rommel is in no way equal to the task. He rushes about the whole day between the widely scattered units, stages reconnaissance raids and fritters away his forces. No one has any idea of their disposition and battle strength. The only certainty is that the troops are widely

---

AXIS TROOP COMMITMENT TO NORTH AFRICA, 1941

JUNE 27, 1941
Deutsches Afrikakorps (Rommel)
5th Light Division (Streich)
15th Panzer Division (von Esebeck)

AUGUST 15, 1941
PANZERGRUPPE AFRIKA (Rommel)

Afrikakorps (Cruwell)
15th Panzer Division (Neumann-Silkow)
21st Panzer Division (von Ravenstein)
"Afrika" Division (Summermann)
55th Savona Infantry Division (Giorgis)

Italian XXI Army Corps (Navarrini)
17th Pavia Infantry Division (Franceschini)
27th Brescia Infantry Division (Zambon)
25th Bologna Infantry Division (Gloria)
102nd Trento Mot. Infantry Div. (de Stefanis)

Italian XX Corps (Gambarra)
132nd Ariete Armored Division (Balotta)
101st Trieste Mot. Infantry Division (Piazzoni)

dispersed and their battle strength reduced.'

Halder even sent Panzer general Friedrich Paulus to Libya with orders to 'head off this soldier gone stark raving mad'. Throughout the North African campaign Halder considered Rommel a man who 'cannot cope with the situation'. The anti-Panzer faction in the High Command began making advances again. But Rommel was ambitious. The British were weak and he believed that he could single-handedly kick them out of Egypt. There was all to play for.

'Ahead of us lay territories containing an enormous wealth of raw materials,' he said. 'Africa, for example, and the Middle East – which could have freed us of all our worries.'

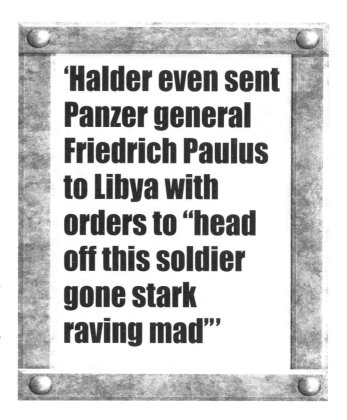

'Halder even sent Panzer general Friedrich Paulus to Libya with orders to "head off this soldier gone stark raving mad"'

False projections

In 1940, General von Thoma wrote a report saying that Egypt could be taken with just four armoured divisions. Rommel was given two: the 15th Panzer Division and the 21st Panzer Division, the old 5th Light Division which had become a Panzer division in October 1941. He also had one light division and one division of infantry. Together these formed the famous 'Afrika Korps'. Rommel was also in command of the Italian motorized forces in North Africa and was himself theoretically under the command of Marshal Graziani and Mussolini. In fact, he reported directly to Hitler.

Paulus wrote in his report to Halder that, not only did the Afrika Korps lack logistical support, it did not have the number of men or the materiel to mount a successful offensive. Rommel was starved of resources because his plans for an offensive did not have the backing of his superiors.

'Of course, if the opportunity for offensive action presented itself we would take it,' Halder wrote, 'but on the whole we regarded the matter as a fight for time.'

The situation did not improve when Rommel surprised everyone by winning battle after battle.

Liddell Hart wrote:

Even when he had shown how far he could go with such a small Panzer force, Hitler and Halder remained unwilling to provide the relatively small reinforcement which would in all probability have decided the issue. By that refusal they forfeited the chance of conquering Egypt and ousting the British from the Mediterranean area at a time when the British were still weak – while they were led to make a much greater commitment, and sacrifice, in the long run.

Rommel had another problem. The Royal Navy

still controlled the Mediterranean, so his supply convoys that were sent to him were in constant danger of being seized or sunk, and the loss of a large number of paratroopers during the invasion of Crete had caused Hitler to cancel his planned invasion of Malta. This left the RAF with a large airbase in the middle of the Mediterranean.

Halder complained that Rommel simply ignored the fact that it was not possible to supply his troops adequately when they were on the attack, but Rommel said, 'With a certain amount of goodwill, supplies for these formations could have been organized in sufficient quantities. Later on, when it was, of course, too late, it proved perfectly possible suddenly to double the amount of supplies.'

The excuse was that men and materiel were needed in Russia. But the doubling of supplies to North Africa in 1942 came at a time when Germany had never been so fully committed to the fighting in the Soviet Union. Until then, Rommel complained of the 'exhaustion of the Panzer Army in all the essentials of motorized warfare'. But Rommel did have one great advantage: Hitler was too far away to interfere.

Undeterred, Rommel set to work with what little he had. As it would take until mid-May for his Panzers to get up to their full strength, Rommel got workshops in Tripoli to build a large number of dummy tanks mounted on Volkswagens which, Rommel insisted, were 'deceptively like the original'.

He organized his Panzers so that they worked in close co-operation with mobile infantry units and artillery, especially anti-tank guns. An 88mm

FLAK (*Flieger-abwehrkanone* – anti-aircraft gun), was used. The British considered that this was rather 'unsporting', though it proved devastatingly effective.

When Rommel began his advance in February 1941, he had fifty tanks; the British double that number. By the end of the year, the British superiority had risen to seven to one and continued rising. But Rommel's successes came not from the strength of his forces, but from his masterful command of Panzer tactics. On the attack, he deployed highly mobile reconnaissance units, followed by anti-tank guns protected by infantry. Close behind this forward screen came the main body: the Panzers and the motorized infantry.

He developed defensive manoeuvres that would lure the British forward to attack the

Originally an AA gun, the 88mm FLAK was an effective tank-killer

German anti-tank screen. The British would charge with their tanks, unsupported. They would break through the outer German defences on to batteries of 88mm FLAK guns and other artillery. These would be positioned so that they hit a vulnerable flank – the 88s in particular wreaking havoc on the British armour, leaving the battlefield littered with burning British tanks. Meanwhile the Panzers would attack to the flank and rear of the enemy position, while mobile troops disrupted the British lines of communication and retreat. Although an infantryman by training, Rommel used his Panzers like cavalry, making quick changes of direction, feints and sudden withdrawals which earned him his nickname, the 'Desert Fox'.

Hotting up

Rommel had other advantages. Although his Panzers were fresh to desert conditions, the tanks were new. The British tanks were exhausted mechanically after the long campaign they had just waged.

Sand and dust effectively halved the machinery's mechanical life and the British tanks were much in need of maintenance. Many of them had been taken back to Egypt for repair.

Others had been sent to the defence of Greece, which was being invaded first by Italy, then later by Germany. Rommel also found that the climate of North Africa rather suited him. It was not so good for the tanks though. In June the temperature soared to 107°F (42°C) and the temperature of tanks left standing in the sun rose to 160°F (71°C) – too hot to touch.

Lieutenant Kurt Wolff, who was with Panzer Regiment 5 which went into action with the 21st Panzer Division in North Africa, described the situation:

A Panzer regiment is a gigantic organisation. Ammunition trucks and fuel tanks move forward and often get blown up in the course of battle. Field kitchens and ration trucks search for the tracks of the Panzers of their units. However, the important movements in the dusk are the repair groups. Men who repair the engines, clean and adjust the carburettors. Springs, track rollers and track links have to be seen to and fixed. Guns and machine guns have to be checked. You can hear the swearing of hard-working men, the clanging of hammers in the wet and cold night. But thousands of other things come together before a battle is won. In the yellow moonlight long convoys of trucks move along the coast road, now and again attacked by English bombers. Water, fuel, ammo, bread, food and people, everything moves though the dark night which is no different from the glowing heat of the day. As soon as the sun rises through the morning mist, the regiment starts to roll forward. We disperse into the desert, but forward we go, 40–50km per hour we read on our tacho. But the nicest is the attack… the German Panzer, our beautiful wide, humming Panzer. We are secretly proud that everyone needs us when the danger is great. Panzer! Panzer to the fore!

On 31 March, Rommel attacked at Agheila, even though his Panzers were not yet up to strength. He had been told he could not expect reinforcements, but he did not want to give the British time to prepare defences. Believing Rommel's dummy tanks to be real, the British withdrew. The Panzers pursued them.

On 2 April, the 5th Panzer Regiment ran up against British tanks. Soon seven of them were burning on the battlefield. As the British put up little resistance, Rommel decided to seize the whole of Cyrenaica in one stroke.

'Probably never before in modern warfare had such a completely unprepared offensive as this raid through Cyrenaica been attempted,' said Rommel. He was informed that any such move was in direct contradiction to orders from Rome. He went ahead anyway and Rommel was preparing to seize Benghazi when a signal came from the German High Command giving him complete freedom of action.

At Benghazi, the British had already burnt their stores and fled. Rommel wrote home to his wife Lucie-Maria that he could not sleep for happiness. And he threw his Panzers forward once again. 'Speed was now everything,' he wrote. 'We wanted at all costs to bring some part of the British force to battle before they all managed to withdraw.'

The advance was so rapid that Rommel had to take to the air with the Luftwaffe to keep up with the action. This took the Italians by surprise and they opened fire. 'It was a miracle we were not shot down,' wrote Rommel, 'and it did not speak well of Italian marksmanship.'

On 5 April, he took command of the forward troops with his *Gefechtsstaffel* – a small headquarters team of signals and combat troops, with a wireless truck and troop-carrying vehicles that Rommel took with him into action. On several occasions Rommel's headquarters group got the opportunity to attack the rear of the retreating British column. And on 8 April, the advancing Panzers captured General Sir Richard O'Connor, recently knighted for his success against the Italians, and the whole of his staff. Rommel noted that the British generals had caterpillar trucks, equipped with radios and office space, which were dubbed 'mammoths' by the Germans. He took one and made it his own command truck. And, in the sand, he found a pair of large British sun-and-sand goggles and took a fancy to them.

'Booty is permissible, I believe,' he said, 'even for a general.'

Those goggles over the gold-braided rim of the peak of his cap became the trademark of the 'Desert Fox'. Thus equipped, the Panzers pressed on. And by 10 April, the whole of Cyrenaica was in German hands. Paulus was furious. He blamed Rommel's unplanned advance across Libya for the British withdrawal from Greece, but Rommel said that he doubted that the Germans could have trapped the British in Greece. The British had always been good at evacuating their troops by sea when necessary.

The Balkans

As it was the Panzers had taken 20 days to overrun the whole of the Balkans. In order to secure Germany's southern flank, Hitler had put pressure on Yugoslavia's prince regent, Paul, to join the German–Italian Axis. Meanwhile the British had moved troops from the Middle East to defend Greece against an attack by Mussolini. This encouraged anti-German elements in Yugoslavia to overthrow Paul. Hitler responded by ordering the High Command to attack both

Yugoslavia and Greece. They drew up a plan of attack in just ten days. It involved Field Marshal List's Twelfth Army and a special Panzer group under cavalry General von Kleist. These were already massed in Hungary and Romania, both of which had pro-Nazi governments. They were moved into south-west Romania and Bulgaria, another pro-Nazi state, opposite the Yugoslav and Greek borders. General Maximilian von Weichs' Second Army also began to assemble in Austria and Hungary, opposite northern Yugoslavia.

There were few roads in the Balkans and practically no railways, and the German High Command concluded that the peninsula could only be taken swiftly by mechanized troops. A third of Germany's tanks were deployed in the attacking formations. The Yugoslavs and Greeks believed that they were safe in the natural fortress of this mountainous region and that the *Blitzkrieg* methods used in Poland, France and the Low Countries would not work there. They were in for a surprise.

On 6 April 1941, the Luftwaffe bombed Belgrade, paralyzing the Yugoslav High Command. Panzers poured over the borders from the north-east and south-east. Yugoslavia had three cavalry and 17 infantry divisions holding the mountain passes, but they had no anti-tank weapons. So while German mountain troops attacked the Yugoslav positions, the tanks drove straight through the valleys. The 2nd and 9th Panzer Divisions, on the left flank of List's Twelfth Army attacking from Bulgaria, pushed through Skopje, turning south-west to link up

During the Yugoslavian campaign, a German soldier fires from behind a looted French R-35 which now carries German markings

with the Italians fighting in Albania. The 2nd Panzer Division then turned south-east and pushed on into Greece.

The 5th Panzer Division and the SS-Panzer Division *Das Reich* on the Twelfth Army's right flank turned north and ran up the valley of the River Morava towards Belgrade, ignoring the Yugoslav forces on their flanks. Meanwhile from the north, the 14th Panzer Division with the 16th Motorized Infantry Division also descended on Belgrade, while the 8th Panzer Division drove on towards Zagreb.

The lack of adequate roads presented no obstacle to the tanks which could operate over open country. But it did cause problems for the supply columns following behind them, especially when it began to snow in the mountains. Nevertheless, Zagreb fell on 10 April. Two days later Belgrade fell when the 14th Panzers from the north met up with the 5th Panzers from the south. Sarajevo fell on 15 April and the Yugoslav forces surrendered unconditionally on the 17th. German losses were just 558, while they took 345,000 prisoners of war.

With Yugoslavia pacified, it could be occupied by the infantry, while the Panzers were thrown against Greece. German mountain divisions had already penetrated the Greek army's mountain defences and the German spearheads reached Salonika on 9 April. This cut off the Greek Second Army in eastern Macedonia which surrendered, allowing Kleist's Panzers to move westwards against the British who were preparing defensive positions between Mount Olympus and Salonika. The 5th Panzer Division, driving south from Skopje, hit a Greek division holding the Monastir Gap on the British left

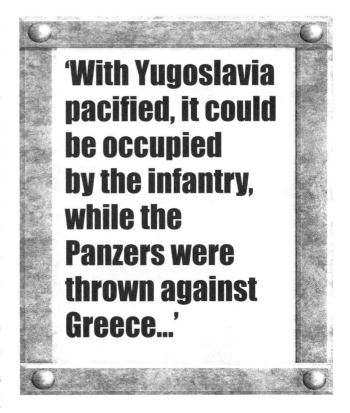

'With Yugoslavia pacified, it could be occupied by the infantry, while the Panzers were thrown against Greece...'

flank. The Greeks crumbled, leaving the road to Mount Olympus open.

The going gets tough

The 2nd Panzer Division reached Mount Olympus on 13 April, but was ordered to bypass the stronghold. The terrain there was barely passable, even for pack animals. However, some of the 2nd Division's Panzergrenadiers managed to slip around the British positions at night. Fearing they would be encircled, the British fell back to Thermopylae, where the Spartans had once held off the Persian army.

But the Greeks capitulated on 23 April and the British withdrew to the Peloponnese, where they were evacuated by the Royal Navy with the Panzers hard on their heels.

Once again the Panzers had triumphed. Their bold moves had systematically carved up the opposition, so that it could be annihilated piecemeal. The tanks had shown that they could

Panzer IVs pour across open ground in Greece. The British found themselves encircled in the Peloponnese and had to be evacuated

negotiate terrain previously thought 'untankable', even in adverse weather conditions. However, this did cause wear and tear on the vehicles, with every tank going off the road for a three-week overhaul.

Rommel thought that, if the aim was to drive the British out of the Mediterranean, the men and materiel expended in Greece would have been more effectively deployed supporting his motorized forces in North Africa. As it was, Rommel attributed his success in Cyrenaica to the fact that the British had been deceived as to his real strength.

'Their moves would have been very astute, if they had in fact really been attacked by a force as strong as they had supposed,' he said.

Rommel was particularly impressed by the

British commander in Egypt General Sir Archibald Wavell's decision to hold Tobruk while the rest of the British retreated into Egypt to regroup.

'Assuming that our first attacks on the fortress did not succeed,' he said, 'I know that we should then find ourselves in an extremely unpleasant situation, both tactically and strategically.'

As Tobruk had fallen easily to the British on 21 January, its fortifications were largely intact. It had classic First World War zig-zag defensive line strongpoints laid out in alternating rows. The 3-foot-thick (90 cm) concrete walls offered protection against 15cm guns, the heaviest the Afrika Korps had. It also had an anti-tank ditch, covered with planks and camouflaged with sand. The perimeter defences ran 9 miles (14 km) inland and formed an arc 28 miles (45 km) long round the

The Afrika Korps in 1942: by 11 April the encirclement of Tobruk was complete and all British supplies had to be delivered by sea

harbour. It was defended by the 9th Australian Division under Major-General Leslie Morshead, reinforced by a brigade of the 7th and the Sikhs of the 18th Cavalry Regiment.

The artillery support was supplied by the Australian Royal Artillery and Royal Horse Artillery. Although their 25-pounder field guns were not designed as anti-tank weapons, they were very effective against Rommel's Panzers, bearing in mind that the standard anti-tank gun was the 2-pounder. Tobruk was also defended by anti-aircraft batteries with 75 guns between them and in the early days of the siege four Hurricanes, but these had soon been shot down or withdrawn.

On 10 April, Rommel reached Tobruk. He knew it was important to start the attack as soon as possible, while British morale was low and before they had a chance to organize their defences. He sent a motorized detachment to storm the town, but it was repulsed by heavy gunfire which killed its commander General von Prittwitz. Rommel had been prevented from leading the attack himself by a sudden sandstorm, but the next day he reached the front, risking shellfire and the possibility of being picked up by a British scouting party. The roof of his Mammoth, he said, made an excellent observation tower. For Rommel, like Guderian, it was necessary to command from the front.

'It is often not a question of which of the opposing commanders is the most qualified mentally, or which has the greater experience,' he said, 'but which of them has the better grasp of the battlefield.' And in mechanized warfare 'reports received second-hand rarely give the information he needs for his decisions'.

By 11 April, the encirclement of Tobruk was complete. Meanwhile elements of the Afrika Korps had bypassed Tobruk and had reached the Egyptian border. From then on, the 22,000 men at Tobruk would have to be supplied by sea. This was a dangerous business as the Luftwaffe had complete air superiority, flying hundreds of sorties against Tobruk. However, the anti-aircraft gunners managed to keep the harbour open. Rommel now fortified the Egyptian border to prevent a British counter-attack. And with much of North Africa in German hands, the Luftwaffe could bomb the Malta convoys and disrupt Allied shipping in the Mediterranean.

Waiting for back-up

The following day, Rommel ordered a fresh attack from the south. This time Rommel in his Mammoth drove in behind the tanks. The 5th Panzer Regiment came under heavy artillery fire and were eventually halted by the anti-tank ditch. It was only then that Rommel got a good view of the defences, which were much more extensive than he had imagined, and he decided to delay an all-out attack until more artillery had been brought up.

On the night of 13 April, Rommel ordered a reconnaissance raid by an infantry battalion of the 5th Light Division to blow the anti-tank ditch. Early on the morning of the 14th, the main attack started with an artillery barrage. Just before dawn on 14 April Rommel threw his tanks into the attack on Tobruk for the first time. Soon the Panzers were reporting good progress.

Thirty-eight tanks had broken through the two lines of the zig-zagged perimeter defences and headed for the town itself. Rommel drove up to within 100 yards (91 m) of the wire to see for himself but was forced to withdraw when the British started shelling his position and the aerial of his signals truck was cut by a splinter.

When he returned to corps headquarters at 0900 he heard that the tanks had come under murderous fire. Three miles (5 km) in they had hit the British second line of defence, which was called the Blue Line. There they met fire from British 25-pounders at close quarters. The Australian infantry had stayed in position when the tanks broke through and held up the Panzers' artillery, infantry and machine-gun support.

Faced with the lethal fire of the 25-pounders, the Panzers were forced to retreat. As they headed back to the German lines, Australian anti-tank guns and British tanks pounded their flanks. They left 17 blazing tanks behind on the battlefield. Some 110 men were killed and 254 captured. The survivors had withdrawn, leaving the infantry undefended. Rommel ordered the tanks back to get the infantry out, but again they were halted by heavy artillery fire.

The Italian Ariete Division which Rommel ordered into battle broke up in confusion under the British shelling.

That night the Panzers established contact with the infantry, only to discover that a large part of the battalion had been wiped out, including its commander Lieutenant Colonel Ponath, who had received the Knight's Cross for his exploits during the advance through Cyrenaica. Only the following year, when the Panzer Army Afrika eventually broke into

Tobruk, did Rommel discover that, that night, his tanks had taken all-important Hill 209 which overlooked the defences from the south-west corner of the perimeter. If the flanks had held, Rommel believed that the fortress would have fallen. As it was, they were destroyed and, after 18 months of spectacular victories, the Panzers tasted defeat for the first time.

When Rommel eventually got the plans of

> **'Rommel became convinced that Tobruk could not be taken using his usual tactics. What was needed was all-out attack'**

Tobruk from the Italian High Command, he became convinced that Tobruk could not be taken using his usual tactics. What was needed was an all-out attack, but he did not have the men and materiel for such an offensive. His men were tired and their tanks had suffered in the desert conditions. He called for reinforcements, but the Royal Navy caught up with a convoy carrying supplies for the 15th Panzers. Tanks particularly were in short supply, as by then they were also being deployed in the Balkans and readied for the attack on Russia. Clearly Rommel was going

to have to make do with what he had got. He spent two weeks sitting on his hands while he marshalled his forces. His Panzers, he thought, would give him a decisive advantage. By the end of April, he had some 400 German and Italian tanks outside Tobruk, while inside the British had 31.

On the evening of 30 April, Rommel launched an attack on the all-important Hill 209 which overlooked the defences from the south-west corner of the perimeter. Twenty-two Stukas began dive-bombing the Australian positions and an artillery barrage opened up. This neutralized the front-line defences and cut the lines of communication. Under cover of the air and artillery attack, his men blew gaps in the wire and cleared paths through the minefield. By 2115 a German machine gun battalion was a mile (1.6 km) inside the perimeter and opened fire. The Australians tried to counter-attack, but with their communications knocked out, they could not find beleaguered perimeter posts in the darkness. In the light of the following morning, they could see that the Germans had knocked a hole a mile and a half (2.4 km) wide through the outer defences, taking more than 100 prisoners and capturing seven perimeter posts. But the determined Australian resistance had taken the steam out of the German attack. Rommel was furious that his troops had stopped to take out strongpoints, rather than pushing on with the main attack. So the Panzers were called on again. Soon after 0800, forty German tanks rolled into action, but were halted by a minefield. Heavy shelling forced them to flee, though they were saved from severe damage by a dust storm that covered their withdrawal.

Rommel then tried to draw off the Allied armour with around 20 tanks, but the British were now wise to his diversionary tactics. Morshead was reluctant to commit his precious tanks and preferred to let the artillery and mines take their toll on the Panzers. Rommel responded by sending the Luftwaffe against the British artillery. But repeated air attacks failed to knock it out and the German attack stalled. In this one assault the Germans lost more than 1,200 men.

'This shows how sharply the rate of casualties rises when one reverts from mobile to position warfare,' Rommel wrote.

One thing that particularly annoyed him was that the Luftwaffe was not under the command of the Afrika Korps. He thought it would be more effective if its fighter and ground-strafing groups were used in tactical support of his troops.

Further setbacks

The Panzers and their infantry support then turned their attention to the strongpoints at the mouth of the German bridgehead. One fell at noon, but the heavy shelling prevented the Panzers co-ordinating with their supporting infantry and they failed in their attempts to take the other.

However, 25 light tanks got beyond the perimeter posts and ran around the southern edge of the minefield behind them under heavy shellfire. Eventually they were halted by 14 cruiser tanks. Rommel reinforced them with another nine tanks and a loose tank battle ensued. The Panzers clearly outnumbered the British tanks, but after they had lost three they withdrew.

But Rommel was not going to give up that easily. He had the Panzers refuelled and they attacked again that afternoon. Once again they faced accurate British shelling. The Australians in the perimeter posts were armed only with rifles and Bren guns: nevertheless they put up fierce resistance. Two Panzers attempted to pound one post into submission from 75 yards (69 m), but their infantry support was beaten back repeatedly. The Panzer attack took its toll on the defenders though. By dusk half of them were wounded. And as darkness fell, the Panzers attacked again, this time with flame-throwers, and took the post at 1930 hours. Another perimeter post was overrun the following morning.

Any forward drive on the port was blocked, so the Panzers pushed along inside the perimeter until they could swing around the edge of the southern minefield. But that evening the British counter-attacked. The fading light and dust kicked up by German shells made visibility poor and the Australians moved forward over a mile (1.6 km) before they came under fire from the machine guns and anti-tank emplacements on Hill 209. By then they were out of range of their own artillery support and had no machine guns, so they pulled back. Even though they had not succeeded in retaking Hill 209, they had thrown the Germans back on the defensive and prevented the Panzers pushing on around their critical defensive minefield.

A sandstorm blew up, halting any further German advance. This gave the defenders time to bring up fresh infantry, strengthen their positions and lay new minefields. Despite the poor visibility, the British artillery was zeroed in on the German positions and continued to

British Matildas, heavy infantry tanks, line up on parade

pound them. When the storm cleared, Rommel found he was in no position to resume the offensive. In the fighting 12 Panzers had been destroyed completely and a further 34 were out of action, leaving well over half Rommel's tank force *hors de combat*. Meanwhile the British had lost just five tanks. The Germans had succeeded in breaching the fort's outer defences and occupied a large salient, but the Panzers had not managed to capitalize on it. This was not the pushover they had experienced in Poland and France. The Panzers had suffered their second defeat and morale was flagging.

Now the British went on the offensive. Morshead sent two battalions to attack the mouth of the salient. If they could retake the perimeter posts, they would cut off the enemy spearhead. A third battalion would make raids deep into enemy-held territory to throw the Germans off balance. With the Germans still holding Hill 209, they knew an attack was imminent as they could see the Australians assembling. Nevertheless, under the cover of darkness, the Australians attacked behind a rolling artillery barrage. Heavy German

artillery fire and mortars halted the Australian advance on the northern flank. But to the south, the Australians retook one perimeter post. They attacked another, failing to retake it, but other advances forced the Germans back over half a mile (800 m). British casualties were 797, including 59 killed. The Germans lost 1,700 men and Rommel was ordered not to attack again. The British felt that, at last, they were making some headway against the Panzers.

'The actions before Tobruk in April and May are the first in which armoured formations of the German Army have been defied and defeated,' wrote Morshead.

This was psychologically important for the Allied cause. It showed, for the first time, that the Panzers were not invincible. They could be stopped by artillery fire, minefields and infantry who stood their ground.

Ignoring the fact that Rommel had been stopped in his tracks, German propaganda began sneering at the defenders, saying the British were caught like rats in a trap. The 'Rats of Tobruk' embraced the sobriquet, relishing the

A British Crusader tank, which was fast but lightly armoured

idea that mere rodents could halt the Panzers and thwart the Desert Fox.

Even the stalemate played directly into British hands. It took three battalions of Rommel's best troops and four Italian divisions to hold the salient around Hill 209. Aggressive night patrolling meant that the British dominated no man's land, and raids deep behind German lines further weakened German morale. And a handful of British tanks kept up harassing attacks on the German forces on the Egyptian frontier to prevent Rommel regrouping his army there and turning it back on Tobruk.

With the fall of Greece on 11 May 1941, fifty tanks were diverted to Egypt and Wavell used these to mount an operation to relieve Tobruk. On 15 May, the British took the Halfaya Pass: the Halfaya Pass and Sollum Pass were the only ways to cross a 600-foot (183-m) escarpment which barred the entrance to Egypt. Rommel sent a Panzer battalion reinforced by two anti-aircraft guns. He drove up to the front himself to oversee the attack on the morning of 27 May. The Germans retook the pass. It was then fortified with 88mm anti-aircraft guns positioned so that their barrels were horizontal and could not be seen above the ground. Liddell Hart said that the Germans not only mastered the art of armoured warfare, but also the defensive counter to it.

'Rommel was the first Panzer leader to demonstrate the modern version of the "sword and shield" combination, and prove the value of the "defensive-offensive" method in mobile mechanized warfare,' he wrote. 'The effectiveness of his offensive strokes was greatly aided by the skilful way he laid defensive traps for his opponents' attacks – blunting the edge of his "sword" on his "shield".'

'The British dominated no man's land, and raids deep behind German lines further weakened German morale'

Fierce fighting continued at Tobruk with the Australians, who Rommel considered the elite troops of the British Empire, making some gains. Tobruk barred the coast road and trucks carrying supplies to the Sollum–Halfaya–Bardia front line had to be carried across the open desert on tracks that became so badly worn that they were almost impassable. Nevertheless the rest of the 15th Panzer Division had now arrived and moved up to the Egyptian border.

On 15 June, Wavell made a second attempt to relieve Tobruk. Some 200 British tanks of the 7th Armoured Division, reinforced by the 4th Indian Division and the 22nd Guards Brigade, was beaten back by the eighty tanks of the 15th Panzer Division, reinforced by the 21st, giving the Germans a total of 150 tanks of which 95 were Panzer IIIs and IVs. The British, though, still had Matilda infantry tanks that were slow, lightly armed, but heavily armoured. They also had the Mark VI cruiser tank, the Crusader,

'But Rommel not only had plans of his own, he also had Cunningham's – captured from a careless British officer'

which was fast, with a top speed of 40 mph (64 kph): Rommel, however, considered it too lightly armed to give his Panzers too much trouble.

After three days of tank battles, the British were running low on fuel and ammunition and were forced to withdraw. Two-thirds of the British tanks were out of action by the end of the engagement: Rommel estimated 220 British tanks were lost, but the number destroyed or captured was actually 87.

Rommel also claimed that only 25 of his tanks were lost; the British estimated 100. Even so, the Panzers celebrated that they had found their winning streak again. Rommel lavished praise on Wavell's strategic planning, attributing his defeat to the slow speed of his heavy infantry tanks that could not react quickly enough to the moves of the faster Panzers. Nevertheless a disappointed Churchill replaced Wavell with General Sir Claude Auchinleck.

While Rommel planned a new attack – against

the advice of the German High Command – Auchinleck began organizing a third attempt to relieve Tobruk, called Operation *Crusader*. To carry it out, he formed a new army, the Eighth, under General Sir Alan Cunningham. Cunningham's plan was to send his XXX Corps across the border into Libya well to the south. He felt that Rommel and his Panzers, now 260 strong with 150 Panzer IIIs and 55 Panzer IVs, were still itching for a tank battle and would seize the opportunity to engage them at a place called Gabr Saleh. While the Panzers were being crushed in the desert, Cunningham would send XIII Corps up the coast road towards Tobruk. Despite the Panzers' fearsome reputation, the British and South African forces under Cunningham's command were more numerous and, he believed, better equipped. They had 724 tanks with 200 in reserve that were being sent up at a rate of forty a day.

But Rommel not only had plans of his own, he also had Cunningham's – captured from a careless British officer who had taken them to the front. Rommel was still determined to take Tobruk, so instead of moving south to engage XXX Corps at Gabr Saleh he kept his Panzers around Gambut on the coast road. Given his inferior strength, Rommel intended to attack the British formations one at a time. The British had no choice but to press on northwards, obliging Rommel by sending their armoured brigades in as separate units which could be picked off individually. On 19 November, they tried to take Bir el Gubi to the south of Tobruk and fifty of their new Crusader tanks were destroyed. The 21st Panzer Division caught another column at Sidi Rezegh and destroyed much of its armour.

Strategic discussions involving General Sir Archibald Wavell and General Sir Claude Auchinleck, 8 September 1941

The 15th drove into the flank and rear of the attacking force, overrunning the headquarters of the British 4th Armoured Brigade, capturing its commander and disrupting the brigade.

Thrust and counter-thrust

While XXX Corps were taking a drubbing in the south, XIII Corps had made progress along the coast road. General Cruwell, now left to his own devices, left his headquarters at Gasr el Arid at 0530 at the head of his troops. Half an hour later his whole headquarters staff was taken prisoner by the New Zealand Division who had advanced unobserved, though General Cruwell himself escaped to lead his 15th Panzers against the enemy's rear the next day. He came across extensive formations of British vehicles parked in the desert and a huge tank battle erupted. The aim was to push the British back against the 21st Panzers.

For the Germans, the attack started well, but they soon came up against a South African artillery and anti-tank screen. Tank after tank split open and it was impossible to make progress. The Germans' artillery was also taken out. However, by late afternoon, the Panzers had punched a few holes through the front. And as the Panzers pushed forward again, tank duels broke out over a huge area.

'In fluctuating fighting, tank against tank, tank against gun or anti-tank nest, sometimes in front, sometimes in flanking assault, using every trick of mobile warfare and tank tactics, the enemy was finally forced back into a confined area,'

In a desert area scarred by tank tracks, a British Crusader closes in on a burning Panzer IV during Operation *Crusader*

wrote Lieutenant General Fritz Bayerlein, who was with General Cruwell.

During the battle General Cruwell's Mammoth found itself ringed by British tanks. Thanks to conditions on the battlefield, the German crosses on the sides were not easy to see and, as the Mammoth had originally been captured from the British, the tank commanders assumed it was one of theirs.

One clambered out of his turret, walked over to the Mammoth, and tapped on the armour plate. General Cruwell opened the hatch and found himself face to face with the British soldier, to the astonishment of both. At that moment a German 20mm anti-aircraft gun opened fire on the tanks and the British fled. Once again General Cruwell had escaped capture.

The battle did not end at dusk. Hundreds of burning tanks and guns lit the battlefield. But when, long after midnight, the commanders counted up their losses, the British found that they had lost two-thirds of their tanks and the remaining 150 were badly dispersed. The Panzers could have wiped out the whole of XXX Corps if they had followed up the next day. Instead, Rommel took a gamble. He took 100 Panzers and made a flanking move across the desert to the Egyptian border in the hope of cutting off the Eighth Army and attacking it from the rear. Rommel explained:

The greater part of the force aimed at Tobruk has been destroyed. Now we will turn east and go for the New Zealanders and Indians before they have been able to join up with the remains of the main force for a combined attack on Tobruk. At the same time we will cut off their supplies. Speed is vital. We must make the most of the shock effect of the enemy's defeat and push forward.

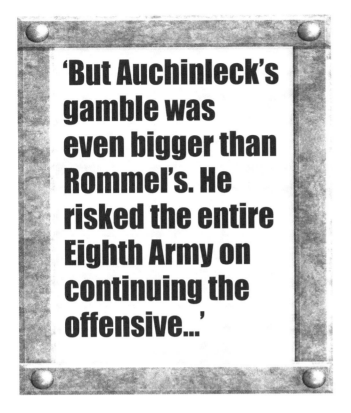

'But Auchinleck's gamble was even bigger than Rommel's. He risked the entire Eighth Army on continuing the offensive...'

Rommel's intention was to exploit the disorganization and confusion which he knew must exist in the British camp by making an unexpectedly audacious raid into the area at the south of the Sollum front.

According to General Fritz Bayerlein:

> *He hoped to complete the enemy's confusion and perhaps even induce him to pull back into Egypt again. Our entire mobile force was to take part in the operation... This decision of Rommel's – probably the boldest he ever made – has been severely criticized by certain German authorities, who were forever incapable of understanding the African theatre, but has been praised and admired by the enemy.*

Cunningham's plan was now in tatters and he wanted to withdraw. But Auchinleck believed Rommel's daring flanking move to be misguided.

He replaced Cunningham with his own deputy chief of staff, Major-General Neil Methuen Ritchie, effectively taking command himself.

Rommel claimed his 'dash to the wire' as a huge success. But the 21st Panzer Division were fought off by the New Zealanders and the 4th Indian Division who held the rear. Rommel found himself on foot at night in the desert when his Mammoth broke down. By sheer luck General Cruwell came by and he cadged a lift.

The British were far stronger at the rear than he had expected, thanks to Auchinleck's cancellation of Cunningham's planned withdrawal, and Rommel failed to cut the Eighth Army's supply lines. What is more, his radio vehicle had got stuck in the sand and he had driven on without it, so his Panzer group headquarters were left without orders for four days.

This was the great defect of Guderian's 'command from the front' if the commander is someone as audacious as Rommel.

But Auchinleck's gamble was even greater than Rommel's. He risked the entire Eighth Army on continuing the offensive. And it paid off. Rommel had all but won the battle when he struck out for the Egyptian border. By the time he finished his raid, the advantage lay with the British.

On 25 November, the New Zealanders contacted Major-General Scobie, whose British 17th Division now held Tobruk, telling him that they would attack at Sidi Rezegh the next day. The garrison was to try and break out at the same place. After fierce fighting, Eighth Army broke through and the siege of Tobruk was lifted. But only briefly. With Rommel out of contact, the 21st Panzer Division, which had been sitting on the Egyptian border, received orders to turn back on Tobruk. In the confused battle that followed, the New Zealand Division was cut in two and the commander of the 21st Panzer Division, General von Ravenstein, was captured. But the Panzers succeeded in closing the siege of Tobruk once again.

Auchinleck quickly regrouped XXX Corps and

> 'Rommel was now running short of Panzers and knew he was not going to be resupplied until the end of December'

sent it back to Tobruk. Rommel was now running short of Panzers and knew he was not going to be resupplied until the end of December, so he pulled back his forces to the east of Tobruk. They came up against a fresh British Guards Brigade and refitted brigades of the 7th Armoured Division. Meanwhile the defenders of Tobruk tried to break out. On 6 December, the Panzers made one final attack. They came up against the 1st Armoured Division, which had just arrived from England, and Rommel, finding that he was now considerably outnumbered, ordered his Panzers to make a general retreat. Rommel was too busy to write his daily letter to his wife that day, but his batman Lance-Corporal Herbert

Guenther wrote instead, saying that the general and the two chickens they now had with them as mascots were well.

An Italian division was left behind at Tobruk with orders to hold out for as long as possible to slow the British pursuit. It surrendered on 17 January, down to its last food and ammunition.

After the relief of Tobruk, Rommel intended to establish a defensive line at Gazala, but it risked being outflanked.

'After four weeks of uninterrupted and costly fighting,' Rommel reported to the German High Command, 'the fighting power of the troops – despite superb individual achievements – is showing signs of flagging, all the more so as the supply of arms and ammunition completely dried up.'

Instead of stopping at Gazala, over the objections of Italian High Command the Panzers drove back all the way to Agheila, where they had first halted the British in February 1941. But on the way, the British had not managed to detach any of the fleeing units by flanking manoeuvres as they were hampered by their lengthening supply lines. Then in December 1941, the logistical situation changed dramatically. When the Japanese hit Pearl Harbor on 7 December, they also hit British colonies in the Far East and supplies were diverted to Asia. Suddenly it was the British who were facing shortages. Meanwhile, Rommel had received some two new Panzer companies and some fresh artillery during his retreat from Tobruk, though two other Panzer companies and a battery lay at the bottom of the Mediterranean. Then in January 1942 a convoy got through to Tripoli, carrying more reinforcements. Soon the Afrika Korps could roll out some 111 tanks with 28 more in reserve, and the Italians still had 89.

The Germans fight back

Bolstered by the Japanese victories in the Far East, Rommel quickly turned his Panzers around, again without Italian approval, and attacked, knocking out nearly half the British armour. Suddenly the British were on the run.

More British armour was lost on the retreat and, as the Desert Fox dashed eastward, he acquired captured British supplies. The Luftwaffe stepped up its attacks on Malta and the British supply ships now had to make their way all the way around the Cape. However, the British were well supplied with fuel as they owned refineries in the Middle East. And leaving aside the logistical position, the Panzers' tactics were superior to those of the British who still lagged behind in the theory and practice of tank warfare.

Heinz Schmidt of the 21st Panzer Division wrote:

We had our first skirmish with the British on the second day of the march [22 January]. We sighted about thirty tanks stationary at the foot of a rise in hilly ground. When we received the order to attack, we were certain we had not been observed. We brought out 50mm anti-tank guns into position in a hollow. The enemy was totally surprised when we opened fire, and a dozen Panzers raced down against the tanks. He decided his position was untenable with the loss of a few tanks. We had now developed a new method of attack. With our twelve anti-tank guns we leapfrogged from one vantage point to another, while our Panzers, stationary and hull-down, if possible,

provided protective fire. Then we would establish ourselves to give them protective fire while they swept on again. The tactics worked well and, despite the liveliness of the fire, the enemy's tanks were not able to hold up our advance. He steadily sustained losses and had to give ground constantly. We could not help feeling that we were not then up against the tough and experienced opponents who had harried us so hard only a few weeks before.

By 6 February, the British were just 30 miles (48 km) west of Tobruk. There the British stopped to fight. They laid an unbroken minefield that ran from Gazala on the Mediterranean coast 30 (48 km) miles inland to Bir Hacheim in the desert, connecting it to Bir Harmat 15 miles (24 km) to the north-east by another minefield: over a million mines had been laid. The two were joined by a belt of mines 5 miles (8 km) south of the Aslag Ridge, forming what was known as the 'Cauldron'. 'The whole line had been planned with great skill,' said Rommel. 'It was the first time that an attempt had been made to build a line of this kind so far into the desert... All defence positions and strongpoints conformed to the most modern requirements of warfare.'

However, he did spot that the British defences were a 'second-best solution' as they had been planned primarily with a view to an offensive, due to pressure from the War Cabinet.

Behind this defensive line, the British regrouped and started building up their strength for a new offensive. They soon had some 900 tanks. But Rommel, with 320 German tanks and 240 Italian, attacked first, believing his

Grant tanks in the western desert – these US-built tanks could only be matched by long-barrelled Panzer IVs and Rommel only had four of these

88mm guns gave him the advantage. The British tanks with their 40mm gun were no match for Panzer IIIs, let alone Panzer IVs. But the Panzer III, even with a 50mm gun, was outclassed by the new US-built Grant tanks with a 75mm gun that the British were now beginning to receive. The only serious opposition to the Grants were the long-barrelled Panzer IVs, but Rommel had only four of them. His short-barrelled Panzer IVs were faster and more manoeuvrable than the Grants, but the Grants could shoot them up at a distance where the Panzers' shells were unable to penetrate the Grants' heavy armour.

And the Germans had just forty short-barrelled Panzer IVs against 160 British Grants. The 240 Italian tanks hardly entered into the equation and had long been talked of by their crews as 'self-propelled coffins'. The British also had an advantage in artillery of about eight to five. So it was with inferior forces that the Panzers once again took on the enemy.

The Italians, with one Panzer regiment leading each Italian formation, kept up the pressure on the front of the line as the main body of the Panzers swept around the southern flank of the Gazala Line in the moonlight on the night of 26

May 1942. The 15th and 21st Panzer Divisions destroyed the 3rd and 7th Indian Motor Brigades in a great armoured battle south-east of Bir Hacheim, then turned north, driving up behind the Gazala Line towards the coast to attack the defenders from the rear. Meanwhile the German 90th Light Division headed for Tobruk itself. It took with it aeroplane engines mounted on trucks. These were use to kick up great plumes of dust, which would lead the enemy to believe that a large formation of Panzers was on its way.

But this attack was not the coup Rommel had envisaged. The British 4th Armoured Brigade hit back with its Grants and their 75mm guns and anti-tank guns on both sides blazing away. 'Tank after tank, German and British, was shattered in the fire of the tank-guns,' wrote Rommel. 'Finally we succeeded in throwing the British back, although at the cost of heavy casualties.'

Merciless fire

The 15th Panzer Division lost 100 tanks on the first day and, at around midday, a counter-attack by the 2nd Armoured Brigade at Bir Harmat forced the Panzers on to the defensive. Under merciless artillery fire, some columns broke and fled to the south-west. The 21st Panzers' advance was brought to a stop ten miles (16 km) north-west of 'Knightsbridge', the British 1st Armoured Division's stronghold. And the 90th Light Division was halted just outside Tobruk's defensive perimeter at el Adem.

At the end of the first day, it was clear that Rommel's plan had not succeeded. The push to the coast had failed and he had been unable to cut the British 50th and South African 1st Divisions from the rest of the Eighth Army. This was entirely due to the new Grant tanks, Rommel said. However, his Panzers had managed to inflict serious damage on them, as Ritchie had committed his tanks piecemeal.

On 28 May, Lieutenant GPB Roberts' 3rd Battalion of the Royal Tank Regiment, part of the 7th Armoured Division's 4th Armoured Brigade, went into action in a counter-attack south-west of el Adem.

Lieutenant Roberts gave this account:

We continued to move forward slowly, closing up on the light squadron and looking for a suitable hull-down position. Then there they were. More than 100: twenty in the first line with six or, maybe, eight more lines behind them in the distance. A whole bloody Panzer division was quite obviously in front of us. Damn it, I thought, this is not the plan at all. Where the hell are the rest of the brigade?

Seeing no alternative, Roberts deployed his men to attack the Panzers' flank. The Grants were told to hold their fire until the enemy was with 1,200 yards (1,100 m) or had halted. Meanwhile the British gunners had overheard the tanks' radio traffic and joined in behind.

'The leading enemy tanks had halted about 1,300 yards (1,190 m) away,' said Roberts. 'All our tanks were firing, there was no scarcity of targets, certainly two of our tanks were knocked out, but the enemy had also had losses. I could see one tank burning, and another slewed round with its crew "baling out".'

Although they were knocking out tanks, the Panzers simply used their rear lines to replace the casualties and Roberts got his adjutant to signal to the brigade that they were going to have to pull out before they were cut off. Next he told his driver to advance slightly to come in line with the other tanks, then told the 75mm gunner to engage the Panzer straight ahead. At the same time Roberts spotted a German tank to the left – 'just the job for the 37mm'.

'37 gunner traverse left,' he ordered, 'traverse left – on; enemy tank broadside – 500 yards (450 m) – fire. 37 gunner – good – have a couple more

> ## 'There was no communication between the various parts of the Panzer army and the British hunted down their supply columns'

shots and then get ready with the co-ax [co-axial machine gun]'.

Another Panzer was dispatched.

The Panzers were now dangerously dispersed and short of ammunition and fuel. There was no communication between the various parts of the Panzer Army and the British hunted down their supply columns. General Cruwell was captured and the commander of the 15th Panzer Division, General von Vaerst, was wounded. Rommel's command post came under attack and

the windscreen of his Mammoth was shattered before he got out of range.

Rommel then went on the defensive. He pulled his Panzers back to the Cauldron. Once inside they were protected on three sides by the British minefields. The Italian X Corps cut two lanes through the front of the Gazala Line to resupply the Panzers along lines that were no longer vulnerable to disruption by the strong British forces to the south.

But the northern supply route was in range of the British 150th Brigade, supported by the 1st Army Tank Brigade, at Got el Ualeb. New 57mm 6-pounder anti-tank guns and infantry tanks were brought up. The British force at Got el Ualeb soon found themselves surrounded. Hugely outnumbered, they were forced to surrender. The Germans took over 3,000 prisoners, 124 guns and 101 tanks.

At around this time, an order issued by the 4th British Armoured Brigade saying that German and Italian prisoners should be given nothing to eat or drink before they were interrogated fell into German hands. Rommel conveyed his objections at the highest level, fearing that the war between Germany and Britain, which he considered tragic, would descend into bitterness, and the British order was eventually withdrawn. During a lull in the fighting, the Afrika Korps set about making repairs. On 2 June, they had only 130 serviceable tanks left out of the 320 they had had at the start of the battle. That number slowly rose again. Rommel's command post came under attack once more and his Chief of Staff, General Gause, was wounded. He was replaced by Colonel Bayerlein.

At the north end of the Gazala Line, the Italian

advance was held off by the South Africans who were well dug in. On 4 June General Ritchie then launched Operation *Aberdeen* to crush the Panzers in the Cauldron. It had been planned for 2 June, before the Italians had cut through and established supply lines and before 150th Brigade had been crushed. But now Rommel was in a much stronger defensive position and the attack faltered as the 15th Panzer Division made a daring thrust to the rear of the British.

'Soon the guns of our tanks were firing from three sides on the British, who fought back in their usual way with extreme stubbornness but far too little mobility,' wrote Rommel. 'By the evening, more than fifty British tanks lay shot up on the battlefield.'

The next day, the 21st Panzer Division engaged the British in a fierce tank battle. Over the next two days, they took 4,000 prisoners and wiped out the newly arrived 10th Indian Brigade.

Ritchie tried again on 7 June. Realizing that the Panzers were now in a strong position, Ritchie ordered the South Africans to attack the Italians, hoping to turn the northern flank. But by then the Italians were also well dug-in and had laid minefields. Even when lines through them had been clear, they limited the size of the attack and it was never big enough to overrun the defenders.

With supply lines open to the west, the Cauldron formed a huge salient in the Gazala Line and the Free French holding Bir Hacheim to the south were isolated. On the night of 1 June, the 90th Light Division had attacked Bir Hacheim from the north, while the Italian Trieste Division attacked from the west, supported by heavy bombardment by the Luftwaffe. The Free French mounted a stout resistance for 11 days, but once the 15th Panzer Division was freed from fighting the British to the north their position was hopeless and they surrendered.

Desperate times

The Panzers regrouped at Bir Hacheim. Then on 12 June they made a lightning advance on el Adem, destroying four armoured brigades on the way. The British lost fifty infantry and 185 cruiser tanks. The next day Rommel's Panzers smashed the remaining British armour at Acroma behind the northern sector of the Gazala Line. And by 14 June, the British only had twenty infantry and fifty cruiser tanks left.

Auchinleck wanted to abandon Tobruk, but Churchill ordered him to hold it. Auchinleck therefore sent orders to Ritchie telling him to hold an outer defensive line, assuming Ritchie had the two divisions that had held the northern half of the Gazala Line at his disposal. However, Ritchie had already ordered the 1st South African Division and the British 15th Division back to Egypt. Their direct line of retreat had already been cut by Rommel's Panzers who were making a dash for the sea, so they broke out westward through the Gazala Line then swept around to the south through the desert and back to Egypt. Without these two divisions, Ritchie did not have the manpower to hold the line and 'Knightsbridge' had to be evacuated. After this unexpected defeat, Ritchie came under severe criticism. Later Rommel came upon an article by Liddell Hart which attributed the shortcomings of the British commanders during the North African campaigns to the fact that they had been trained as infantrymen. Rommel, an infantryman himself, was forced to agree.

'I think that my adversary, General Ritchie, like so many generals of the old school, had not entirely grasped the consequences which followed from the fully motorized conduct of operations and the nature of the desert battlefield,' he said.

On 18 June, the Afrika Korps cut the coast road to the east of Tobruk and the port found itself under siege again. Once again the main force bypassed the fortress and sped on eastwards towards the RAF airbase at Gambut, forcing a withdrawal and consequently denying the besieged garrison air support.

Jubilation for Rommel

Rommel dusted off his plan to punch a hole through the south-east section of the defensive perimeter, as he had intended to do in November 1941 before being beaten to the punch by Operation *Crusader*. This time it went like clockwork. Shortly before 0520 on 20 June, the Luftwaffe began pounding the outer defensive line, tying up the Mahratta Light Infantry who were holding that area. By 0830 the 15th Panzer Division had crossed the anti-tank ditch. Rommel himself crossed it with Bayerlein half an hour later. Together, the 15th and 21st Panzer Divisions drove for 'King's Cross', a key intersection inside the perimeter. At 0930, the 22nd Army Tank Brigade attacked the column, but it was repulsed and by 1330 King's Cross was in German hands. The 21st Panzer Division then headed for the harbour, while the 15th Panzer Division drove along the Pilastrino Ridge which ran to the west. The British forces were cut in two and, by dusk, only isolated pockets of resistance remained.

Major General Klopper of 2nd South African Division, then commander of the garrison at Tobruk, had to move his headquarters. He had no tanks left and few guns: the Panzers were now unstoppable. Early the following morning, any troops that still had transport were evacuated, but most British vehicles were now in German hands. Klopper ordered the destruction of the port facilities, and the remaining stock of petrol. Soon after 0630, he surrendered. Some 32,200 prisoners were taken, plus a large quantity of stores. The Panzers had triumphed again. Rommel was jubilant.

'For every one of my "Africans", that 21st of June was the highest point of the African war,' he wrote.

He issued an order of the day to his Panzer Army congratulating them and exhorting them to make one more great effort.

'Now for the complete destruction of the enemy,' it read. 'We will not rest until we have shattered the last remnants of the British Eighth Army.'

The following day Rommel was promoted to the rank of field marshal. In the busy days that followed, he forgot to change his shoulder badges to those of his new rank – two crossed batons. Later, at el Alamein, Field Marshal Kesselring noticed this and gave him two of his own. In Berlin in September, after the tide had turned decisively against him at el Alamein, Rommel was given his field marshal's baton by Hitler.

'I would rather he had given me one more division,' he told his wife.

Although his troops were exhausted, Rommel had captured enough ammunition, fuel, food and other materiel at Tobruk for the Panzers to

Beneath a pall of smoke, Erwin Rommel (left) and Fritz Bayerlein in an open-topped Kfz.15 Horch, with a Panzer III to their left, June 1942

push on into Egypt before the British had time to regroup. Rommel believed that if he could destroy the tattered remnants of the Eighth Army, the British could do nothing to prevent him reaching Alexandria and the Suez Canal. Ritchie thought he could stop the Panzers with a new line of fortification running south along the Egyptian border from Sollum to Sidi Omar. But like the Gazala Line, it had an open flank to the south. On 24 June, 44 Panzers swept around it. They were advancing at over 100 miles (160 km) a day. The Eighth Army was quick enough on its feet not to be caught by this flanking movement. It had already fallen back to Mersa Matruh, 120 miles (193 km) east of the frontier, where Ritchie was preparing another defensive line. Already the Luftwaffe were in range of Alexandria and the Panzers were on the brink of taking Egypt. Once they had done that, there would be nothing to stop them steaming on to take the oilfields of the Persian Gulf. Germany

had already attacked the Soviet Union and, from the Gulf, Rommel's Panzers could smash into the beleaguered Russians' southern flank. Rommel was so confident that the war in North Africa was almost over that he was planning a holiday in Italy with his wife.

Auchinleck realized that a defensive line at Mersa Matruh would be no better than the lines at Gazala and Sollum. So he sacked Ritchie, took command of the Eighth Army himself and issued new orders. There would be no new line at Mersa Matruh. Instead, he would take Rommel on at his own game. He would keep his formations fluid, brigade-sized battle-groups made up of artillery, armour and infantry. These mobile columns would strike at the enemy from all sides.

On the run again

On 27 June, the Germans caught up with the Allies again, but British mobile battle-groups

British soldiers captured by the Germans during the siege of Tobruk are marched off into custody with their hands on their heads

were no match for the Panzers. British units were bypassed and had to fight to get back to their own lines. They fell back on el Alamein, which was just 60 miles (96 km) from Alexandria. Auchinleck blocked the Panzers' advance with a new defensive line. The difference this time was that this line did not have an open flank in the desert. To the south was the Qattara Depression, 7,000 square miles (18,000 km^2) of marshes and salt lakes that lay 435 feet (132 m) below sea level. Impassable to tanks and heavy military vehicles, the Germans could not just skirt round it. This time they would have to take the British on head to head.

The Panzer spearhead had reached el Alamein on 30 June. It was defended by Australians who had been the original 'desert rats' of Tobruk, along with New Zealand, Indian, South African and British troops who had been pushed back across the desert by the Afrika Korps. But they would be pushed no further. Here, at last, at el Alamein, they would be supported by the RAF. But first there would be more fighting before the line would become consolidated.

'Oh Lord, when I remember 2 July, my eyes burn,' wrote the Panzer veteran Kurt Wolff. 'More than a hundred tanks stood in our area as far as we could see, shot to pieces, on fire.'

The day had not started well though. The repair shop was 60 km to the rear and immobilized Panzers had been moved on to the coast road to block any counter-attack. That night the New Zealanders had broken through into their right-hand position, so the Germans had pulled in their defensive ring. Two men guarded each tank: one inside with the Panzer's machine gun; one outside with a machine-pistol. They were jumpy because the moon had set early and you could see no more than 20 metres.

Wolff acted as a runner and was stationed next to his commanding officer who had a telephone connected to division. They expected the New Zealanders to attack and for British planes to drop 'Christmas tree' flares to light up the landscape for their troops. Further back, bombs fell on the German transports, but the artillery was silent. Wolff found this wearing as the British had not let them sleep the night before either. Meanwhile, in the darkness, the repair crews went about their work.

At 0200, a guard returned with a prisoner who had lost his way. He also brought with him a wounded German NCO who was unconscious, but moaned constantly. Then at 0300 came the news that a British rifle brigade had broken through and overrun the German infantry positions. The Panzers were ordered in.

'The company is immediately battle ready,' wrote Wolff. 'The engines were running warm, orders came through by radio, the unit comes to order and is on the move.'

It was still twilight with the morning star slowly fading over in the east. The morning fog that had formed was blown away by the wind and the desert was silent, apart from the roar of the Panzers.

The 5th Panzer Regiment was ordered to take the heights to the right. The British were reported to be just 1,200 metres way. Soon targets were acquired and the fighting started.

'The New Zealanders seemed just to wake up and run about, as if the Germans should not have reached their position,' continued Wolff. 'When at long last they got their guns in position, some of their transports were already on fire.'

In a quick fight, the Panzers got within 800 metres of the British, though they took care always to cover each other as, in the past, they had often run past a concealed British anti-tank gun. Then German tanks and anti-tank guns broke through on the left, adding to the enemy confusion.

Wolff wrote:

I don't know how it came about, as I destroyed an English tracked vehicle and observed the hit with my binoculars, a shell from an American tank exploded next. I managed to pull my head in. Then I felt pain in my right arm and saw blood drip onto the shoulder of my gunner. He had the first-aid box ready, rolled up my sleeve and bandaged me up. I was lucky, a small splinter of shrapnel had lodged a centimetre above my elbow joint. Where before there had only been a few artillery pieces, some anti-tank guns and some tracked vehicles, suddenly from holes in the ground, first ten, then fifty, and finally about six hundred Tommies emerged, waving at us. Some half-heartedly saluted. Some threw their arms away as they came towards us in a line. The whole New Zealand outfit had surrendered.

His commanding officer called on the radio to ask whether he was hurt. As they had already fallen behind, Wolff ordered his driver to stop for a moment, so that he could show off his bandage.

The attack had progressed at great speed. One company moved forward to attack the British tanks, while the rest overran the British positions.

Wolff's commanding officer was pleased. After days of British artillery attacks, now they had at their mercy four burning tanks, around ten self-propelled guns, eight cannon, some tracked vehicles, machine guns and bazookas. And in the trenches they could see rifles with fixed bayonets lying about.

'"Those dogs", we thought,' said Wolff. 'But the rifle battalion following us would have sorted them out.'

The commanding officer ordered a halt while they reformed their units. Then they went after 14 tanks that were reported ahead of them. They shelled the retreating New Zealanders. Then they received a message saying that a British tank brigade had broken through their lines and was attacking the ack-ack guns. They then realized that the New Zealanders had been in position to attack them from the south, while the tanks encircled them. If this move had been successful, a large part of the 21st Panzer Division would have been destroyed. As it was, they found themselves beleaguered.

'No General is with us, no anti-tank gun, no flak, no artillery, only the shrunken Panzer unit that came from Derna and fought forward as far as el Alamein, more than 1,000km,' wrote Wolff.

On the way they had destroyed more than 250 British tanks, along with numerous anti-tank guns, artillery pieces and tracked vehicles. But despite their losses, the British grew stronger. 'Now the enemy is in front to the left and at our backs, stronger than ever before, in a better position. They knew their superiority – but whatever happens, we have to make the next move.'

First they succeeded in turning around, not an easy manoeuvre, especially with British tanks to their rear. Section by section they had to move left and right to reform facing westwards, while urgent messages from division urged them to hurry. Then as the heavy Panzers regrouped

'They shelled the retreating New Zealanders. Then they heard that a British tank brigade had broken through their lines'

behind a ridge, a British tank brigade appeared in the depression on the other side.

'No order was necessary,' said Wolff. 'We were well positioned. Our minds were clear and, without rushing, the battle commenced… As our tank gunner is loading for the second time, the first shell already brings smoke and fire from the enemy tanks. The commander and I, standing next to him, breathe a sigh of relief.'

While the Panzers stood out of sight behind the ridge, the British armour had driven into the German field of fire.

'The leader of the 4th Company shot up seven tanks, another tank commander five, almost everyone could later account for two or three destroyed. We, apart from my laughable wound which only later came to mind, lost two dead and two wounded. This was meaningless compared with the sixty enemy tanks we counted later.'

Most of them had been burnt out. The rest of the British armour fled from an enemy they could not see and had not expected. In their rapid retreat, the British tanks ran into a minefield, missing the narrow path they had cut through it earlier, causing more casualties.

More of the British armour was destroyed by German howitzers and anti-tank guns and reports from division said that all but 12 of them had been finished off by anti-aircraft guns.

'The sweat ran down our dirty faces, it was well earned after a good job,' said Wolff. 'Watchful, tired, unwashed and oily, we stand watch for Germany in the African night.'

They would get no peace. The British artillery responded that night, destroying some 131 AFVs.

'The next day was very hot again, very heavy. How do we bear it?' wrote Wolff. 'Hundreds and thousands of flies crawl over our faces. Our mosquito nets got lost a long time ago. We shall have patience. The steel on our Panzer is red hot. The water is almost undrinkable. A sandstorm at midday remains our only hope.'

Having come so far, so fast, the Panzers were now exhausted. They were at the end of a very long supply line. Their nearest port safe from air attack was 680 miles (1,100 km) away at Benghazi and they were being starved of supplies by Rome. When the Panzers' first assaults failed to break through the Alamein Line, they began to lay extensive minefields of their own to give Rommel time to build up his forces.

Reinforcements arrive

By 13 July, the Afrika Korps had been reinforced with 260 tanks and Rommel launched what became known as the First Battle of Alamein. Denied room to manoeuvre, the Panzers had to make a frontal assault and were stopped

once more. That night, Eighth Army seized the opportunity to counter-attack. Two Italian divisions were overrun by New Zealand and Indian troops, who also held off a counter-strike by Rommel's 21st Panzers. In the following war of attrition, Rommel quickly exhausted the supplies that he had taken at Tobruk and the supply situation now turned once again in the British favour.

With American industry now on a war footing, the US sent 300 Sherman tanks and 100 self-propelled guns. The British also had much of the resources of the British Empire at their backs – their possessions in the Middle East and India – and Port Said was only 200 miles (320 km) away. Meanwhile, Rommel's supply convoys were being harassed by the RAF and the principal wharf at Tobruk was knocked out by a British bombing raid. The coastal railway had also been rendered unusable. Rommel reckoned that by the end of August his 371 Panzers would face 900 British tanks.

The British had been supplied throughout with fresh troops, while the 17,000 men of the Panzer Army had been in Africa from the beginning of the campaign.

All of them had suffered from the effects of the climate. Rommel said, 'In most cases, only their enthusiasm and remarkable esprit de corps kept them with the Panzer Army.' Reluctant as he was to lose these veterans, he knew they were worn out and had to ask for fresh troops. But even when reinforcements came, Bayerlein estimated that the Germans had only 34,000 men – some 17,000 below strength.

Auchinleck had stopped the Panzers once again, but Churchill was impatient for a victory to avenge Tobruk. He sacked Auchinleck, replacing him with Sir Harold Alexander as Commander in Chief in the Middle East. Command of the Eighth Army was given to General Bernard Montgomery, who had commanded the 3rd Division in France.

Montgomery found morale at a low ebb, as if the Eighth Army was awaiting an inevitable defeat. At this first staff meeting, he made it clear that there would be no retreat from the Alamein Line, nor would there be gallant tank attacks without the support of other arms. Instead, he massed his artillery and armour behind the fortified line and waited.

Rommel was expected to go on the offensive around the full moon on 26 August. Montgomery judged that he would attack, as usual, to the south of the line. He would aim to break through and turn north to surround the Eighth Army, attacking it from behind, while a second column would drive on to take Cairo. It was make or break time for Rommel. Air and naval attacks on his supply lines meant that he had to take the Nile Valley then, or forever admit defeat.

So Montgomery laid a trap. There was a weak spot in the British defences. The gap between Deir el Munassib and Qaret el Himeimat was defended only by a single minefield. It was the perfect place for the Panzers to break through, wheel to the right and take the coast road. So behind it Montgomery prepared positions so that an attacking force would have to run the gauntlet between the very effective British 57mm anti-tank guns and dug-in tanks.

A delay in obtaining fuel meant that the attack did not go ahead until 31 August. From the beginning Rommel realized that he had lost the element of surprise. But two hours before

The popular Montgomery was known as 'Monty' to his men

his assault force of 200 Panzers, 243 Italian medium tanks and 38 light tanks was due to set off it was attacked by the RAF. Troops sent out in advance of the tanks to lift the British mines came under heavy fire from well dug-in troops. General von Bismarck, commander of the 21st Panzer Division, was killed by a mine, and General Nehring, commander of the Afrika Korps, was wounded in an air attack. Bayerlein, now promoted to general, took over.

The Panzers' progress was slowed by unexpected minefields and soft sand. This used up petrol and the column had to turn to the north prematurely, taking them directly towards the Alam Halfa Ridge. When the Panzers got within 1,000 yards (910 m) of the ridge, British tanks suddenly appeared on top of it. The ground below had been laid out with markers, so that the gunners could accurately judge the range and had every chance of hitting the Panzers first time.

Into the trap

The Panzers, on the other hand, had to stop to take accurate range findings, leaving them vulnerable. Nevertheless they managed to open a gap in the British line. But as they rushed forward to exploit it, they came under fire at a few hundred yards' range from concealed anti-tank guns. Taking heavy casualties, the Panzers were forced to withdraw at 1600. But they were hoping that the British would be tempted to follow them as they had so often before. Three thousand yards (2,730 m) back, they had their own line of anti-tank guns lying in ambush. But Montgomery's orders were specific. There would be no tank charges.

A sandstorm blew up, grounding the RAF and hampering the artillery but it lifted that night.

The RAF then employed one plane to fly in circles dropping flares, while others attacked the illuminated armour. The following day, fuel stocks were so low that only the 15th Panzer Division resumed the advance. British armour, again playing a purely defensive role, drove them back.

Rommel had now resorted to the very tactics that had failed the British. He was making unsupported tank attacks on artillery positions. Another offensive that afternoon failed. And still the British would not take the bait and chase the retreating Panzers into an anti-tank ambush. Instead, Montgomery slowly tightened a ring of steel around them, while they were bombed by the RAF day and night.

On the morning of 2 September, Rommel was visiting the Afrika Korps headquarters, which had already lost seven staff officers to British bombs, when he came under air attack. He threw himself in a slit trench, where he was showered by red-hot metal fragments.

An 8-inch (20-cm) splinter landed beside him, after piercing a metal shovel nearby. On their bomb runs, he noted, the RAF bombers flew in perfect formation – the way German bombers flew at party rallies at Nuremberg. And by the afternoon of 3 September, with the Panzers down to one issue of petrol – enough to take them 100 kilometres – Rommel ordered them to retreat.

Rommel wrote home to his wife on 4 September, 'We had to break off the offensive for supply reasons and because of the superiority of the enemy air force – although victory was otherwise ours.' He was, of course, whistling in the wind.

During the withdrawal, Rommel interviewed a distinguished prisoner of war, the commander of the 6th New Zealand Brigade, Brigadier Clifton. Clifton shamefacedly admitted to being taken prisoner by the Italians, but he had then told them that a huge formation of British armour was about to roll over the hill, and persuaded them to surrender to him.

They were taking the bolts out of their rifles, when a German officer happened along and stopped them.

Rommel complained to Clifton that his New Zealanders had repeatedly massacred prisoners of war and wounded Germans. Clifton explained that this was probably because there was a large number of Maoris in his brigade.

What impressed Rommel was that Clifton seemed absolutely certain of victory. In their conversations, Rommel remarked that the real danger to Europe lay in Asia. This was politically sensitive as Japan was Germany's ally. Later, when Clifton escaped by climbing out of a lavatory window, Rommel organized a huge manhunt. He was eventually spotted a couple of days later by two staff officers plodding across the desert with a jerrycan of water. Clifton was then sent to a prisoner-of-war camp in Italy where, Rommel said, he had escaped 'disguised as a Hitler Youth leader, complete with shorts and insignia, and in this garb had crossed the frontier to Switzerland'.

It seems that Clifton was actually in a merchant seaman's uniform and was apprehended at Como, just short of the frontier. He was then sent to Germany, but finally got away on his ninth escape attempt, even though he had been badly wounded on his eighth.

Instead of chasing the retreating Germans, Montgomery broke off the battle. This led

Rommel to think that Montgomery was a cautious man. In fact, Montgomery was simply sticking to his plan which called for a big offensive later on. Part of the plan was to keep the Germans' strength in the south. He let the Germans hold on to a strongpoint between two minefields at the southern end of the defensive line. A complicated plan of deception was also under way. Dummy supply dumps, dummy vehicles and even a dummy pipeline were laid in this sector and radio traffic was stepped up, giving the impression that an attack would be launched in the south early in November.

The real attack would be launched at the north end of the line, reversing the regular tactics. If Montgomery could break though in the north, he could come around behind the Germans, trapping them with their backs to the Qattara Depression.

The tanks and guns were moved to the north at night and massed around el Alamein itself, where they were carefully camouflaged. Long trenches were dug out into the desert to take the infantry across no man's land. These too were carefully concealed from German aerial reconnaissance. And as the preparations continued, the RAF stepped up its attacks on enemy airfields, effectively grounding the Luftwaffe.

The conventional wisdom of desert warfare was to take on the enemy's armour, then deal with the infantry. But Montgomery would only send diversionary forces against Rommel's armour at the south of the line. Meanwhile he unleashed a massive artillery bombardment in the north, first against the artillery positions there, then against the infantry. Montgomery's infantry would then pour out of their slit trenches to take on the dazed Germans. There would inevitably be vicious hand-to-hand fighting, but Montgomery reckoned his men would get the best of it. Then the armour would pour through the hole made by the infantry, systematically finish off the German infantry, then get into position at the rear to take on any remaining armour on ground of his own choosing. Even if he could not destroy the Panzers completely, without infantry, they could not hold ground and would have to retreat.

Meanwhile Rommel returned to Germany. His doctor had advised him to take a break, but he took the opportunity to report to Hitler and the High Command. He complained of the supply situation and explained that the British had learned to overcome the power of the Panzers with air attacks. The only way to defend against them was by reinforcing the Luftwaffe. Hermann Göring, head of the Luftwaffe, in particular made light of the Panzers' difficulties. When Rommel told him that British fighter-bombers were shooting up his tanks with American-made 40mm shells, Göring said, 'That's quite impossible. The Americans only know how to make razor blades.'

'We could do with some of those razor blades, Herr Reichsmarschall,' Rommel replied.

Hitler promised a considerable increase in supplies and said he would send forty of the new Tiger tanks, which carried an 88mm gun, had armour up to 10 cm thick and had a top speed of 38 mph (61 kph) even though it weighed 57 tons. These would be accompanied by 500 multiple rocket-projectors and carried on newly designed flat ferries whose shallow draft allowed torpedoes to pass underneath them and bristled with anti-aircraft guns.

'Rommel complained to Hitler the British had learned to overcome the power of the Panzers with air attacks'

On 23 October, the night of the attack, there was a full moon. This was vital as thousands of mines would have to be lifted to make a hole in the enemy's defences. The minefields were 5,000 to 9,000 yards (4,570–8,230 m) in depth and strengthened with booby-trap bombs and barbed wire. At 2140 hours the Second Battle of Alamein began when more than 1,000 guns along the whole line opened fire simultaneously on the German artillery. Twenty minutes later they switched their aim to the enemy's forward positions. As a huge curtain of dust and smoke rose over the enemy, the British infantry moved in with fixed bayonets to the skirl of the pipers.

The Germans resisted valiantly, but by 0530 hours the next morning two corridors had been opened and the armour began moving down them. Then things began to go wrong for the British. The infantry still had not made it all the way through the minefields when they were met with fierce resistance. This left the armour dangerously exposed. But by dusk the following day, one column of armour had made it through.

Missing man

On 24 October, Rommel's deputy General Stumme went missing on a visit to the front. First Field Marshal Wilhelm Keitel, head of the OKW (*Oberkommando der Wehrmacht*, the German Armed Forces High Command), then Hitler himself phoned Rommel at Semmering in the Alps where he was recuperating and asked him whether he was well enough to return to Africa. The next day, he boarded his plane. He returned to the fray knowing that his Panzers had less than a third of the petrol they needed to manoeuvre on the battlefield properly.

Rommel soon discovered that Stumme was dead. He had died of a heart attack when he had fallen from his car during a British attack. The situation was desperate. The troops were demoralized, the artillery did not have enough ammunition to bombard the British assembly points and the fuel shortage prevented any major movement. The 15th Panzer Division had made several small-scale counter-attacks, but had taken heavy losses from the British artillery and non-stop RAF attacks.

By the evening of 25 October, only 31 of their 119 tanks were serviceable.

Shortly before midnight on the 25th, the British succeeded in taking Hill 28, an important position in the northern sector. The 15th Panzer Division counter-attacked.

'The British resisted desperately,' said Rommel. 'Rivers of blood were poured over miserable strips of land which, in normal times, not even the poorest Arab would have bothered his head about.'

Rommel watched the action from the north, seeing load after load of bombs falling on his troops. The British held the hill. The German artillery had too little ammunition to prevent

Bonfire Night: vehicles silhouetted against the night sky by the flash of artillery fire during the 2nd Battle of El Alamein, 5 November 1942

them building their strength there. Later that afternoon, 160 British tanks broke out but, following a ferocious tank battle, they were forced back. However, Rommel reported that Alamein was becoming more an air battle than a tank battle, with British fighters shooting down slow-moving dive-bombers and forcing Italian planes to drop their bombs over their own lines, while German bombers pressed home their attack with heavy losses.

'Never before in Africa had we seen such a density of anti-aircraft fire,' said Rommel.

The morale of Rommel's men was sapped by continuous bombing and the supply situation got worse. The tanker *Proserpina* was sunk outside the harbour at Tobruk and there was only enough fuel to keep the supply traffic from Tripoli going for two or three more days.

'What we should really have done now was assemble all our motorized units in the north and fling the British back to the main defence line in a concentrated and planned counter-attack,' said Rommel. But they did not have the petrol to do it.

The other possibility was to draw the British into a free-wheeling tank battle a few miles to the west. In such a mêlée, the British would lose the advantage of their artillery and air force, as they would be in danger of hitting their own men. So Rommel risked withdrawing the 21st Panzer Division from the southern part of the line, even though he did not have enough petrol for it to return if the British attacked there.

At the same time, he wrote to Hitler saying that the battle was lost unless he received more fuel immediately. He had little hope that this would make any difference.

The 21st Panzer Division's move to the north was delayed by air attacks. The Sherman tanks now took to the battlefield and proved themselves to be far superior to Rommel's Panzer IVs. Under the cover of heavy artillery fire and smoke, the infantry would move forward clearing mines and obstacles. Then the Shermans would roll forward to within 2,700 to 2,000 yards (2,470–1,830 m) and open concentrated fire on Rommel's anti-tank and anti-aircraft guns, and his Panzers whose guns were unable to penetrate the Sherman's armour at that range. The British had seemingly inexhaustible supplies of ammunition and would loose off over thirty rounds at one target. The tanks were constantly replenished by armoured ammunition carriers. The tanks also carried observers who directed the artillery on to German strongpoints.

Lost cause

In the afternoon of 27 October, the 15th and 21st Panzer Divisions launched a counter-attack against Hill 28. They followed the British mode of attack. At 1500 hours the Stukas went in, followed by a concentration of all artillery in the area, and finally the armour moved in. It was met with powerful anti-tank defence from dug-in anti-tank guns and tanks.

'There is, in general, little chance of success in a tank attack over country where the enemy has been able to take up defensive positions,' wrote Rommel. 'But there was nothing else we could do.'

The British, it seems, had learned to take on the Panzers and win.

The Luftwaffe flew in 70 tonnes of fuel and more Panzer detachments were moved in to fill gaps in the line. But due to the continuing shortage of fuel, Rommel issued an order that was anathema to any Panzer commander. They were to make 'as little movement as possible'.

During the morning of 28 October, the British made three attacks along the north of the front. Each time they were thrown back by the Panzers, but at a heavy cost in tanks. The remaining armour was moved up from the southern part of the front and the whole of the Afrika Korps was now in the line. Meanwhile, the British were now preparing for another, decisive attack against a weakened enemy.

On the night of 28 August, after a tremendous artillery barrage, the 9th Australian Division drove a wedge down the coastal road. This was what Rommel was hoping for. If the British attempted to move around him to the north, he could cut their forces in two. So he moved his Panzers to the north. However, Montgomery did not follow up with a major attack down the coast and the Panzers' manoeuvre simply wasted more petrol.

The sinking of the *Proserpina*'s replacement, the *Louisiana*, meant that Rommel was forced to plan his withdrawal. This, he decided, could only be done successfully when the British attacked again. They would have to be fully engaged when he pulled his men out of the line, otherwise they would spot weak points and break through.

While he waited, the RAF repeatedly hit their positions and shot up their supply vehicles coming along the coast road. Although the fuel situation had eased, ammunition was getting low and again the artillery found itself unable to pour concentrated fire on British assembly points. So far the British had put only a few of their divisions on the front line and still had 800

tanks left. The Germans had 90; the Italians 140.

The expected British attack came on the night of 1 November, with thrusts on a narrow front either side of Hill 28. Massed British formations broke through the 15th Panzer Division to the south-west. Some 400 tanks were involved. German artillery observers reported that there were that many again waiting in reserve, while small groups of tanks and armoured cars started hunting down German supply units.

The next morning the Afrika Korps counter-attacked. But their Panzers were no match for the British tanks and many were lost. The parts of the 15th and 21st Panzer Divisions not already committed to the front pushed in on the British flanks, hoping to pinch off the wedge. A ferocious tank battle ensued.

The RAF concentrated on knocking out the Germans' 88mm anti-aircraft guns, which were now their only effective weapons against the British tanks. That day, though all available anti-aircraft guns had been brought up, there were only 24 of them. The artillery and troops from the southern sector of the front were brought up, along with every possible reinforcement. Even so the Germans' fighting strength was only a third of what it had been at the beginning of the battle, and the Afrika Korps only had 35 serviceable tanks left. Now was the time to withdraw.

Rommel knew that, after ten days of fighting, his men could not resist the next British attack. The rear installations had already left. Now the infantry were withdrawn. Montgomery had shown himself cautious, so Rommel hoped to get at least part of his infantry away safely. The mobile forces were heavily engaged though and he realized that much of it would be destroyed.

Fearing that the High Command did not understand the situation, Rommel sent his aide-de-camp Lieutenant Berndt to explain the situation to Hitler and beg him to give the Panzer Army total freedom of action. Rommel planned to fight a series of delaying actions to allow the

> **'Rommel sent his aide-de-camp to explain the situation to Hitler and beg him to give the Panzer Army total freedom of action'**

bulk of his army to get away. Hitler's response was to order Rommel to throw everything into the battle. His message concluded, 'Victory or death.' Rommel was stunned.

'For the first time during the African campaign, I did not know what to do,' he wrote.

The withdrawal was stopped while Rommel tried to persuade Hitler to change his mind. But the damage was done. The troops' morale collapsed. Meanwhile Montgomery waited and Rommel saw that he had had a chance to get his army away, but that chance was slipping.

On 4 November, 20 Panzers held off British attacks supported by 200 tanks. Rommel went

to see Kesselring, who explained that Hitler had given his order forbidding withdrawal because he was applying lessons he had learnt on the Russian Front. But Rommel came to believe that the order had been issued with propaganda considerations in mind. Those in power could not bring themselves to say to the German people, Rommel said, that el Alamein was lost.

While Rommel was away, the *Kampfstaffel*, the combat unit of his Corps HQ, was wiped out and General von Thoma captured. British armour was breaking through all along the front. In this case, Rommel believed, superior orders did not count. He had to save what could be saved. At 1530 he issued the order to retreat. A day had been lost and there was no chance of making an orderly withdrawal now. Anything that did not reach the coast road and head westwards with all speed was lost.

The following morning, far too late, the signal came from Hitler and the High Command authorizing the withdrawal.

Rommel withdrew his motorized forces to Fuka, 60 miles (96 km) to the west, where he set up his Panzer Army HQ and waited for the infantry. But soon they were forced by the RAF and British tanks to move on.

The 21st Panzer Division ran out of petrol and its immobilized tanks were destroyed by the British. Only four escaped. The rest of Rommel's Panzer Army was saved by a downpour on 6 and 7 November which turned the desert into a quagmire. The pursuing British 1st Armoured Division also ran short of petrol which prevented them overtaking the retreating column.

On 8 November, Rommel's Panzer Army received more bad news. A large Anglo-American force had landed in Algeria and Morocco, French North Africa. They would be able to attack Axis forces in Libya from the west. Rommel's Panzers were, as Rommel himself said, 'caught between two fires'.

To defend Rommel's rear against the Anglo-American force in Algeria, the Axis began pouring men into Tunisia. By the end of November 1942, their number had grown to around 25,000, including fresh reserve units from Germany, Italy and France, along with reinforcements desperately needed by the Afrika Korps. The troops were supported by 70 Panzers – 20 of which were the new Tiger tanks that Hitler had promised to Rommel.

Rearguard action

The men in Tunisia were originally under the command of General Nehring, the former commander of the Afrika Korps who had been convalescing in Tunis after being wounded. On 10 December, the formation in Tunisia became the 5th Panzer Army Command.

It was put under the command of the experienced Colonel-General Jürgen von Arnim, who had been moved from the Eastern Front. By January 1943, von Arnim had more than 100,000 veteran German troops guarding the mountain passes around Tunis. Meanwhile the Anglo-American force fought their way into Tunisia to find their way to the key ports of Tunis and Bizerte, once again, blocked.

Rommel had been back to Europe for consultations. He was told both by Hitler and Mussolini that he must hold a line against the British. Back in North Africa he ignored his orders, knowing his men did not have the strength to make a stand against a superior force. He had no supplies as any men and materiel that would have come his way were now being diverted to Tunisia. If he stopped to engage the British, he knew he would simply be outflanked and his entire Panzer Army would be lost. He evacuated Cyrenaica again, then pulled out of Tripolitania with the 15th Panzer Division fighting rearguard actions. But with just 36 tanks against the 650 the British brought up, there was little they could do. Libya was lost.

Rommel had already developed a plan to hold a line 120 miles (193 km) west of the Tunisian frontier, midway between Tripoli and Tunis. There, there was a narrow 12-mile (19-km) stretch of land between the sea and a chain of salt lakes and marshes known as the Chott el Jerid.

However, he was ordered instead to occupy the Mareth Line, an old French line of fortifications. Rommel objected as the Mareth Line could be outflanked, while the Akarit Line – his chosen defensive position between Chott el Jerid and the sea – could not. This time, though, he was forced to do as he was told.

When Montgomery reached Tripoli in late January 1943, he stopped to rest his troops and do essential repair work on his armour. This gave Rommel the breathing space to establish himself on the Mareth Line. He knew that he could not defeat Montgomery's veteran Eighth Army. However, he also knew that it would be some time before Montgomery would be able to bring up the artillery and aeroplanes he needed to overwhelm Rommel's Panzer Army without too much cost to himself. Rommel planned to hold the Mareth Line with a minimum of troops, then send a strike force against the inexperienced

Anglo-American force to his rear. His Panzers would destroy the untested and understrength American II Corps, then push along a mountain range called the Western Dorsal to the coast near Bône and knock out the Allied airfield there. After that, his strike force would double back to take on Montgomery. However, Rommel did not have the tanks to pull off this daring plan. But von Arnim did.

Unfortunately, Rommel did not get on with von Arnim, a Prussian aristocrat who did not trust Rommel's flair. Von Arnim refused to entertain such an audacious scheme. However, he would support a more limited attack to strengthen his position on the Eastern Dorsal, a mountain range to the south of Tunis. On 14 February, German dive-bombers attacked the 1st US Armoured Division guarding the town of Sidi Bou Zid in the Faid Pass. Then the tanks and infantry of the 10th Panzer Division quickly overran them, inflicting huge losses. The 21st Panzer Division, now up to strength again and under the command of the 5th Panzer Army, attacked from the south through the Maizila Pass. The defenders of Sidi Bou Zid stood no chance again the Panzers' veteran tank men. By noon they had been routed. The Americans quickly counter-attacked with a force of light tanks and infantry on half-tracks. This had been likened to the charge of the Light Brigade. The Americans lost over 2,000 of which 1,400 were taken prisoner, including General Patton's son-in-law, Lieutenant Colonel John Waters. Only 300 got out. Some 94 tanks were lost, along with 60 half-tracks and 26 self-propelled guns.

Rommel urged von Armin, who was in charge of the operation, to let the 21st Panzer Division push on that night and take Sbeitla. He did not give the go-ahead until the night of the 16th, resulting in a bitter battle for Sbeitla which the 21st eventually took the following day.

Rommel's combat group took Gafsa on 15 February without a fight as the Americans had withdrawn their garrison the previous day. The local populace greeted the Germans as liberators because the fleeing Americans had blown up their ammunition in the citadel without warning the people living in the neighbourhood. Thirty houses had collapsed on their occupants. Thirty dead had been dug out of the ruins and 80 people were still missing.

Rommel's new *Kampfstaffel* pushed on to Metlaoui to blow up the railway tunnel there. They also captured 200,000 tonnes of phosphate. Feriana was taken on 17 February, after stiff American resistance. The retreating garrison had set fire to their stores, but a dozen American armoured troop carriers with mounted or trailer 75mm guns were captured or destroyed. They then advanced on the airfield at Thelepte, where they found 30 aircraft on fire. The Panzers were back in business again, doing what they did best – making lightning thrusts into enemy-held territory.

The Americans were now falling back on Tebessa. Rommel wanted to go after them with the armour. He was convinced that a rapid thrust by the Panzers would push the Americans back into Algeria and delay any offensive they planned. But von Arnim did not approve of the plan and would not hand over the 10th Panzer Division which would be vital to its success. So Rommel went over his head. Kesselring approved the plan and sent it to Mussolini who was still, theoretically, in charge in North Africa. Il Duce needed a victory to bolster his political position and, on 19 February, Rommel got the authority to proceed – but the attack was not to be to the north-west to the communications centre at Tebessa, but northwards into the enemy's rear at Thala.

On the attack

The Afrika Korps began their attack on the Kasserine Pass in a rain storm. This was held by American troops, who occupied the high ground on either side of the pass.

The strike force commander, used to desert tactics, concentrated his attack in the valley, instead of deploying mountain troops to clear the hillside. Rommel drove up to take command and sent a combat group under General Buelowius around on a flanking attack.

The 21st Panzer Division was sent up the next valley to take Sbiba, but they were held up by the road which was waterlogged after the rains. Then they hit a minefield which was strongly defended by the 1st Guards Brigade.

Rommel believed that the Americans at Kasserine were weaker than the British at Sbiba and sent the 10th Panzer Division against the Americans. But when Rommel drove back to Afrika Korps headquarters to brief the commander of the 10th Panzers, General von Broich, he found that he had only brought half his force. Von Arnim had withheld part of it, including some newly arrived Tiger tanks, for his own purposes. Rommel then found that he had insufficient forces to overcome the Americans, who had been reinforced.

US Lieutenant Colonel Gore explained the confusion of that night. A rifleman was digging a slit trench and a tank came by, very nearly caving it in. He complained in the most vehement terms, only to find a revolver bullet whistling past his ear.

'The Germans shouted "Hands up – come out; surrender to the Panzers!" in good English,' said Gore. 'It was almost impossible to distinguish which were our tanks in the dark until a gunner scored a direct hit on the German tank so that it went up in flames. By the light of this fire nine German tanks were soon ablaze and their daring attempt was thwarted. No German motor infantry were in evidence, although for the rest of the night alarms were many and firing profuse.'

The Germans only took the pass when they brought up the new *Nebelwerfer* multiple rocket launchers, which were used for the first time in Africa. Heinz Schmidt, who led the attack, said that his men were exhilarated to have come up against Americans for the first time.

American armour was on the other side of the pass and the Eighth Panzer Regiment made a lightning attack on them, capturing twenty tanks and thirty armoured troop carriers, most trailing 75mm anti-tank guns. The troop carriers were soon going back over the pass, filled with American prisoners of war. Rommel drove up to inspect the captured equipment. He was impressed by how well equipped the Americans were and deduced that they had learnt a lot from the British, standardizing their vehicles and spare parts. Even better, Schmidt found that the Americans had abandoned some trucks full of rations and cigarettes.

Schmidt was then ordered by his commanding officer, Major Meyer, to take a company of Panzergrenadiers and some of the heavy

With the sun beating down on them mercilessly, Grenadier Guards advance over rough terrain near the Kasserine Pass, February 1943

Panzerjäger tank destroyers and advance down the road to Feriana, where American tanks had been seen. But as they approached the village they came under machine-gun fire. In Schmidt's words:

The rest of the battalion detrucked swiftly and we went in, infantry fashion, on a broad front. The sniping stopped. Out of the houses poured a number of Arabs – men, women and children, waving and shouting in the false jubilation which these people always accord any apparently victorious troops. Their sheikh recognized me as the officer in command and ran to me with outstretched arms. He gibbered words of greeting. But my right hand was on my automatic, just in case. He fumbled at me and tried to kiss my hands. When I pulled back in disgust, he grovelled on his knees and kissed my boots.

The Arabs then pointed out a minefield and warned them that American artillery had just pulled out. A number of heavy tanks, they said, were still on the far side of the village.

Schmidt continued:

The minefield was newly laid and the freshly turned soil betrayed the presence of each mine clearly. We picked our way through gingerly, with the sappers at our backs marking the track for the guns behind. Beyond the minefield the road began to climb again. I was rounding a sharp curve when I sighted a Sherman tank on the road ahead, within attacking range. I jerked the wheel in the driver's hand and the vehicle swerved sharply towards the left bank of the road. The detachment manning the gun immediately behind me was swift in taking their cue. In a matter of seconds they had jumped from their seats, unlimbered, swung round and fired their first shell, while the Americans still stood immobile, the muzzle of their tank gun pointing at a hillock half-right from us. Our first shell struck the tank at an angle in the flank. The tank burst into flames.

Further down the road, they ran into more tank and machine-gun fire. Schmidt deployed his anti-tank guns under cover and sent word back to Meyer. Fighting continued for an hour. Then ahead they saw thick columns of black smoke and heard explosions. Plainly the Americans were destroying an ammunition dump. Their tanks stopped firing and Schmidt's column continued its advance.

Schmidt described the conditions:

We went without sleep, without food, without washing, and without conversation beyond the clipped talk of wireless procedures and orders. In permanent need of everything civilized, we snatched greedily at anything we could find, getting neither enjoyment nor nourishment... The daily routine was nearly always the same – up at any time between midnight and 0400; move out of the lager before first light; a biscuit and a spoonful of jam or a slice of wurst, if you were lucky; a long day of movement and vigil and encounter, death and fear of death until darkness put a limit to vision and purpose on both sides; the pulling in of sub-units which had been sent out on far-flung missions; the final endurance of the black, close-linked march to the lager area; maintenance and replenishment and more orders – which took until midnight; and then the beginning of another 24 hours.

The British then fought a series of delaying actions along the road to Thala. The 10th Panzer Division reached Thala at around 1900 hours, overrunning a British battalion and taking around 700 prisoners. However, the 10th Panzers were soon forced out of Thala by the British 6th Armoured Division. Rommel believed that he could have held Thala and continued the offensive if he had the Tiger tanks that should have been with the 10th Panzer Division. When he requested them, von Arnim had told him they were under repair. Rommel found later that this was untrue and that von Arnim had kept them for his own offensive.

Disaster looms

American artillery was now taking its toll on Rommel's Panzers. The following morning he drove up to Thala again. He came to the conclusion that the Allied forces there had grown too strong for them to continue their offensive and they withdrew. Kesselring was delighted by the tactical victory at the Kasserine Pass and offered Rommel command of the Army Group. Rommel declined, knowing that von Arnim was Hitler's choice and, realizing that the situation was now untenable in North Africa, had no wish to take responsibility for another defeat. Even so, orders came from Mussolini that he was to head the unified command in Tunisia, Army Group *Afrika*.

Rommel's first action as Army Group commander was to pull the 10th Panzer Division back from the Kasserine Pass. Mussolini was not happy. But Montgomery was already assailing the Mareth Line with an attack on the 15th Panzer Division's rearguard on 20 February. However, the Panzers managed to get a close-up look at the competition. During the retreat, they captured a Sherman tank. This was considered so significant that a piece about it appeared in the March issue of *Die Wehrmacht*:

Through the streets of Tunis rolls an American Sherman tank – bouncing along on its mobile tracks, its engine rumbling, with captured ammunition in its gun barrels, and on board, its crew – the German scout patrol that captured it in the hills of Sbeitla on the foggy morning of 22 February. Down it travels from the hills through the sea of olive groves, headed towards the seaport of Sfax. It's a journey of some 210 miles (338 km), lasting four-and-a-half days, which testifies well to the overall march capacity of this steel colossus. The thing weighs about 31 tonnes. It was loaded on to a ship in the harbour while German fighter planes wheeled overhead in the clear sky of Africa, and not one enemy bomber dared intrude on this deadly zone. Now, after many intermediate stops, this star of American armament has arrived at its destination, a proving ground near Berlin, in the hands of German arms experts who are testing its combat efficiency and durability. Preliminary investigation in Tunisia had already revealed that this rolling steelmine is not a bad product. It was captured by a German Panzer regiment.

Rommel approved von Arnim's plan to outflank and destroy the Allied formations at Medjez el Bab, 40 miles (64 km) west of Tunis. The 5th Panzer Army attacked on 26 February. Again a lightning attack caught the enemy by surprise

and the Panzers made an easy breakthrough. But the enemy soon responded with ferocious counter-attacks. Then rain halted the assault.

Rommel was particularly displeased because the Tigers, which could have made such a difference at Thala, were thrown into an attack in a marshy valley where their principal advantage – the long range of their 88mm guns – could not be used. The heavy tanks got stuck in the mud and were pounded by shellfire. Of the 19 Tiger tanks that went into action, 15 were lost. Other tanks were driven into the narrow valleys in that part of Tunisia where they could be destroyed easily by artillery on the hillsides. Rommel cancelled the operation, but it was resumed by von Arnim after Rommel had been recalled from Africa.

Von Arnim's offensive delayed the 10th and 21st Panzer Divisions' return to the Mareth Line, allowing Montgomery to establish himself at Medenine, immediately in front of the German defensive positions.

Rommel's Panzer Army now had two choices. Either it could wait for the British to attack, and suffer a massive defeat, or attempt to gain time by attacking the enemy's assembly area. Rommel decided to send one Panzer division, the 21st, to attack Medenine, while the 10th moved to the south to counter any attempt the British might make to outflank them.

On the morning of 6 March, the German artillery, including a *Nebelwerfer*, opened up. But the attack soon came up against a strong defence line.

Assault after assault failed. Fifty-two German tanks were completely destroyed, while the British lost none at all and only one squadron

A heavily armoured Churchill tank in the Medjed el Bab area, 23–25 April 1943 – one was hit 80 times by the Germans but kept going

was engaged in the fighting. Even the Stukas proved ineffective due to the number of anti-aircraft guns the British had.

Rommel called off the attack at 1700. He reckoned that it had come a week too late. Montgomery had prepared his positions with remarkable speed. They were designed to prevent the fighting ever becoming fluid and, thus, giving the advantage to the Panzers.

Rommel knew that the position was now untenable. He promised Hitler that, if he were to remove his army and re-equip it in Italy, he would hold back the Allies when they inevitably invaded southern Europe.

When this was refused, he unveiled a plan to dramatically shorten the line from 400 miles (640 km) to 100 miles (160 km). He was told that he had more than enough troops to hold the area he currently occupied. But, he pointed out, the troops he had were not mechanized. They were not Panzer troops.

The amount of supplies he received was dramatically increased, but it was too late. The Allies had more supplies too – and vastly more than the Axis forces were receiving. When Rommel returned to Europe to explain the situation in person to Mussolini and Hitler, it was suggested that he take sick leave. He was back in his hospital bed in Semmering when his Panzer Army in Tunisia under von Arnim was overwhelmed.

Montgomery, as Rommel had predicted, outflanked the Mareth Line while simultaneously hitting it in the north.

The Germans managed to pull back to the Akarit Line, while the 10th Panzer Division held off an American attack to the rear that attempted to cut them off from the 5th Panzer Army. Rommel began insisting that his men be got out. His requests fell on deaf ears, though some of his best men including General Bayerlein and General Gause were flown to Italy.

On 6 May, the Americans at Medjez el Bab advanced, completely annihilating the 15th Panzer Division. And with no more arms or ammunition, the remaining Axis forces surrendered. The Allies had, at last, learnt how to fight the Panzers and win.

6. OPERATION BARBAROSSA:
THE PANZERS TURN EAST

When Heinz Guderian first heard that Germany was going to invade Russia he could hardly believe it. He had specifically warned against this in his book *Achtung – Panzer!* and Hitler himself had regularly criticized the German leaders in the First World War who had taken them into a war on two fronts. But now, before Britain had been invaded and subdued, he intended to go ahead with Operation *Barbarossa*: an attack on the Soviet Union.

Objection overruled

Guderian said he expressed his disappointment and disgust in the most vehement language, but General Halder, the chief of the army general staff, had calculated that Russia would be defeated in just eight to ten weeks. As well as condemning the plan to attack the Soviet Union on principle, Guderian criticized the plan in detail. It involved three army groups of approximately the same size attacking with diverging objectives. One

would go to the north-east, one to the east and one the south-east.

'No single clear operational objective seemed to be envisaged,' said Guderian.

When he pointed this out, it fell on deaf ears.

Guderian set about studying the campaigns of Charles XII of Sweden, who invaded Russia in 1708, and Napoleon I of France, who invaded in 1812. Both had been defeated and it became clear to Guderian that Germany was in no way prepared for such a vast undertaking. The problem was, he said, the swift victory that the Panzers had given the High Command in the west had 'eliminated the word "impossible" from their vocabulary'.

The first problem was that the German manufacturers could not produce the number of tanks required, so the Panzer divisions were equipped with French tanks that were in no

Top: A Panzer II patrols a Russian country road, summer 1941

Operation *Barbarossa*, 22 June 1941: the German invasion of the Soviet Union

in July 1941, a month after *Barbarossa*, the Germans got to see the superior Russian tank on the battlefield. It was the T-34.

Guderian was also afraid that the Russians could outproduce them. By 1941, Germany was producing 1,000 tanks a year, but as early as 1933 he had visited a Russian tank factory that was producing 22 tanks a day.

Once the Balkan campaign was brought to a swift conclusion, the preparations for *Barbarossa* got under

way suited to the conditions they were going to meet in eastern Europe. However, Panzer Is and IIs had mostly been replaced with IIIs and IVs.

The Russians had more tanks than the Germans, but they were relying on the superior performance of their tanks. Guderian, however, was doubtful. In the spring of 1941, Hitler had allowed a Soviet military commission to inspect the German tank factories and training schools. The Russian officers refused to believe that the Panzer IV was the heaviest tank the Germans had and insisted that, contrary to Hitler's orders, they were concealing their newest models from them. The conclusion that he drew from this was that the Soviets already possessed heavier tanks. And

way. Guderian set about training his troops, warning them that the campaign ahead of them was going to be far more difficult than anything they had experienced so far. For security reasons, he could not be more specific.

The three army groups used for the attack were to be Army Group North under Field Marshal Ritter von Leeb, who would attack from East Prussia, Army Group Centre under Field Marshal von Bock and Army Group South under Field Marshal von Rundstedt, which would attack from Poland. The plan was for these three army groups to break through the Soviet formations on the border, encircle and destroy them, while the Panzers raced forward deep into Russia to prevent the Soviets forming any new defensive fronts – just as they had done in Poland.

Guderian was to command Panzer Group 2, with General Hoth's Panzer Group 3 immediately to his north. These two groups came under Army Group Centre. Guderian's group was to cross the Bug – which now formed the border between the German and Soviet zones of Poland – at Brest-Litovsk, break through the Soviet defences and head for Smolensk. From there, he and Hoth were to turn north towards Leningrad.

Hold-up

The start of *Barbarossa* was delayed because the Bug and its tributaries were in flood well into May, due to a wet spring, and the ground nearby was swampy and nearly impassable, even by tank. Once the attack went ahead, the first task would be to take the citadel at Brest-Litovsk which was then in Russian hands. Having done this in 1939, Guderian knew that it could only be taken by tanks in a surprise attack. As this would not be the case this time, he asked that infantry be assigned to take the citadel while his tanks crossed the river either side of Brest-Litovsk.

On 14 June, Guderian joined the commanders of the Panzer Groups, Army Groups and Armies in Berlin. Hitler addressed them and explained his reason for attacking Russia. Britain could not be invaded so, to bring the war to an end, he

must win a complete victory on the Continent and to make Germany's position on the mainland unassailable Russia had to be defeated. Guderian and the other commanders listened to Hitler's speech in silence. There was no discussion. He left with a heavy heart. Soon after, he received an order saying that, in the event of excesses being committed against prisoners of war or civilians, the soldiers responsible would not automatically be tried and punished according to military law. In other words, they could murder, rape and loot as they pleased. Guderian said that he did not convey this order to his men as he felt that discipline might suffer as a result.

Back in Poland, he observed that the Soviets on the other side of the Bug were totally unprepared for an attack. They were making little progress with fortifications along their side of the river.

On 22 June 1941, Guderian went to his

A *Sturmgeschütz III* assault gun is mounted on a Panzer III crossing the Bug, 1941

The Germans construct a pontoon over the River Dnieper near Kiev

followed in an assault boat at 0650. His command staff with two armoured radio trucks, some cross-country vehicles and some motorcyclists arrived on the far bank at 0830 and they set off following the tank tracks of the 18th Panzer Division. Soon they reached the bridge over the River Lesna. Its capture was important, but when Guderian arrived the only people in sight were two Russian sentries. They made off. Two of Guderian's orderly officers set off after them, against Guderian's wishes, and were killed.

The leading tank company arrived at 1025 and crossed the bridge. Following was the divisional commander General Nehring, who would later see action in North Africa. Guderian stuck with the 18th Panzer Division until mid-afternoon, when he returned to his command post. Assessing the situation, he saw that the Russians had been taken completely by surprise. The bridges to the south of Brest-Litovsk had all been taken intact. To the north, the Panzers had built their own bridges. However, the citadel in Brest-Litovsk was still in Russian hands. It held out for several days, depriving the Germans of the road and rail bridges there.

By evening, the lead Panzers began to encounter some resistance. There was fighting

command post in an observation tower 9 miles (14 km) north-west of Brest-Litovsk. He arrived there at 0310 hours. Five minutes later the German artillery opened up. At 0340, the dive-bombers went in. Then at 0415 advanced units of the 17th and 18th Panzer Divisions began crossing the Bug. They had been equipped with waterproofing that had been tested for Operation *Sealion*, which allowed them to move through 13 feet (4 m) of water, so they simply forded the river. By 0445, the lead tanks of the 18th Panzer Division were across. Guderian himself

at Maloryta and Kobryn, and the 18th Panzer Division was involved in the first tank battle of the campaign at Pruzana. It was soon won and Guderian moved his group headquarters up to Pruzana the next day.

On 24 June, Guderian headed for Slonim, which had already been taken by the 17th Panzer Division. On the road, he ran into Russian infantry, who were locked in a firefight with a battery of the 17th Panzer Division, and some dismounted motorcyclists. Guderian joined in the fight, manning the machine gun in his armoured command vehicle. They succeeded in dislodging the enemy and drove on.

Narrow escape

At the headquarters of the 17th Panzer Division, he found the divisional commander General von Arnim, who would later turn up in Tunisia, and the corps commander General Lemelsen. They were discussing the situation when from behind a burnt-out truck Russian tanks emerged pursued by Panzer IVs. Seeing a group of officers, the Russian tanks opened fire on them. Guderian and the other generals were old soldiers and instinctively flung themselves on the ground. Two younger officers failed to do so and were wounded, one lethally. The Russian tanks succeeded in forcing their way into the town, but there they were put out of action.

Guderian had another lucky escape that day. While he was moving up to the front, his headquarters came under air attack. After he had reached the front he drove a Panzer IV across no man's land to the 18th Panzer Division, who he ordered to push on in the direction of Baranovicze. Guderian then returned to his

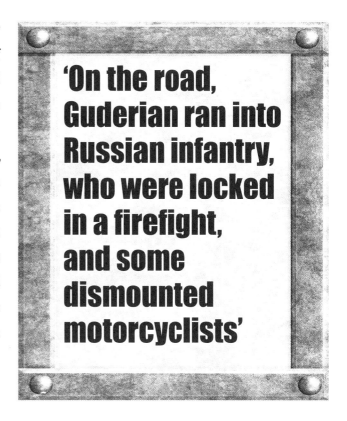

'On the road, Guderian ran into Russian infantry, who were locked in a firefight, and some dismounted motorcyclists'

command post. On the way, he came upon Russian infantry which had been brought up to the outskirts of Slonim on lorries. Guderian ordered his driver to drive full-tilt through the Russians who were so surprised they did not have time to loose off a bullet. But Guderian believed that they recognized him because, soon after, the Russian press announced his death. He informed them of their mistake by radio.

The left flank of Guderian's Panzer Group was threatened by Russians pouring back from Bialystok. Hitler had planned to encircle the Russians there and wanted the Panzers to turn back. But the High Command persuaded him to stick to the original plan and the Panzers raced on eastwards taking Vilna and Kovno. They paused for a moment while motorized infantry units came up to secure the rear areas before continuing their advance on Minsk in Belarus.

Hoth's Panzer Group 3 arrived in Minsk on 26 June. The 17th Panzer Division arrived the following day to find much of the city destroyed. In Army Group North, the 8th Panzer Division had succeeded in capturing Dünaburg in south-east Latvia and its bridges over the Dvina. In his book *Lost Victories* von Manstein said with obvious pride:

Before the offensive started I had been asked how long we thought it would take us to read Dvinsk (Dünaburg), assuming that it was possible to do so. My answer had been that, if it could not be done inside four days, we could hardly count on capturing the crossings intact. And now, exactly four days and five hours after H-hour, we had actually completed, as the crow flies, a non-stop dash through 200 miles (322 km) of enemy territory.

Meanwhile the infantry had succeeded in bottling up the bulk of Russian forces in the Bialystok area and the first stage of *Barbarossa* was almost over. Again Hitler wanted the Panzers to turn back and finish off the Russians in the Bialystok pocket; Guderian thought that this could be left to the infantry while the Panzers pushed forward to Smolensk. In the meantime, he arranged his Panzer Group in defensive positions, in case the Russians tried to break out. On 28 June, he moved his headquarters up to the old castle at Nieswiez, which had once belonged to the famous Radziwill family.

The previous occupants had been Russian officers, but in the attic he discovered a

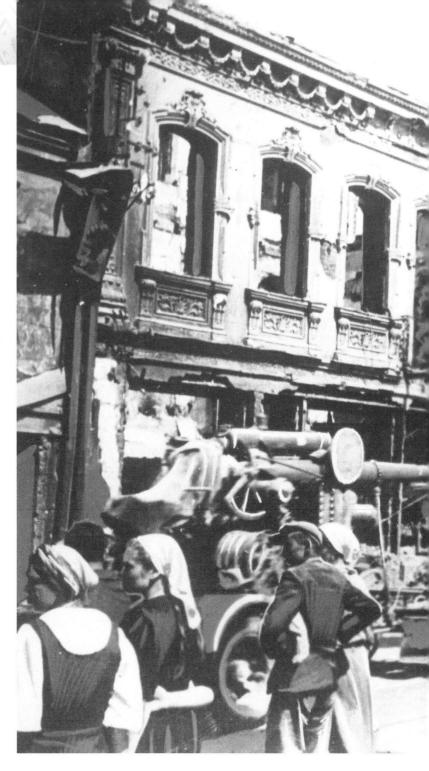

photograph of Kaiser Wilhelm, who had once joined a hunting party there. Later he moved up to Tolochino, which had been Napoleon's headquarters in 1812.

Taking to the air in a bomber, Guderian saw little chance of a Russian breakout and he and Hoth began moving detachments forward. On 30 June, the High Command ordered the Panzers to advance to take the crossings of the Dnieper on the borders of Russia itself. This had to be done

People in Minsk watch a German armoured column head past in an image that may have been touched up by the propaganda department

in a lightning attack as they could count on no support from the infantry, who were held up by fighting around the Bialystok pocket. But if the Panzers did not go ahead now, Guderian feared they would be held up for weeks. As it was, he was ordered to advance without the 17th Panzer Division which von Kluge wanted to hold back in case of a Russian breakout. Guderian did not agree with this order, he said, but he forwarded it to the 17th anyway. Mysteriously they did not

seem to receive it, and continued to advance with the group. Von Kluge was furious as a similar mishap had occurred in Hoth's Panzer Group. He suspected a conspiracy and threatened Guderian and Hoth with court-martial.

On 2 July, the 18th Panzer Division ran into trouble at Borissov on the River Beresina where they were attacked by Russian tanks. These were beaten off, but at considerable cost to the 18th. They had come up against the Russian

T-34 for the first time. The T-34 was arguably the best tank of the war; certainly, this was how von Kleist described it. Guderian himself regarded its arrival on the battlefield as 'very worrying'. It was fast, with a top speed of almost 35 mph (55 kph), was fitted with wide tracks which made it far more manoeuvrable in the Russian conditions than its German counterparts, and possessed an impressive 76.2mm gun. What set the T-34 apart, however, was its heavy armour, 70mm thick at the front, and ingeniously sloped in a way that made it practically impervious to German guns.

Falling-out

On 3 July, the Russians in the Bialystok pocket surrendered so the Panzers' entire attention could turn to the east. The following day XXIV Panzer Corps, led by the 3rd and 4th Panzer Divisions, reached the Dnieper, near Rogachev. But two days later the Russians crossed the Dnieper, near Shlobin, and attacked XXIV Panzer Corps' right wing. They were beaten off by the 10th (Motorized) Infantry Division. Radio intercepts indicated that the Russians were forming a fresh defensive front along the Dnieper and the Panzers were going to have to move quickly to cross the river before it was in position. Meanwhile the 17th and 18th Panzer Divisions were held up by heavy fighting involving an unusually large number of Russian tanks. At this point there was a disagreement about objectives between Hitler and the High Command. Von Bock and von Kluge also fell out, with neither wanting to take responsibility for the actions of the unruly Panzer Groups 2 and 3. The decision whether to cross the Dnieper therefore fell to Guderian.

He could see that defences were being built. The Russians maintained strong bridgeheads on the west bank of the river. Russian reinforcements were on their way and, once across the river, his Panzers would be vulnerable to flank attacks. On the other hand, it would take two weeks for the infantry to arrive. By that time the Russian defences would be considerably stronger, ending the mobile warfare they had enjoyed. Guderian's primary objective was Smolensk so he decided to take a chance and cross the river.

Guderian ordered the 17th and 18th Panzer Divisions to break off, but not before the 17th had destroyed 100 Russian tanks. All three Panzer corps under his command were to cross the Dnieper on 10 and 11 July. Preparations were to be made covertly and troop movements were to take place at night. Meanwhile Guderian organized air support and the Luftwaffe promised air supremacy in the area of the crossings.

However, Field Marshal von Kluge turned up at Guderian's headquarters on 9 July. When Guderian told him of his plans, von Kluge ordered him to cancel the operation and await the arrival of the infantry. Guderian said he could not do that. The preparations had gone too far to be cancelled. His Panzer corps were already massed at their jumping-off points and it was only a matter of time before the Russian air force attacked them. Besides, Guderian was convinced that the operation would succeed and said that it could decide the Russian campaign.

'Your operations always hang by a thread,' complained von Kluge. But he gave his approval.

The Dnieper crossing went ahead more or less as planned, though the 17th Division had met such opposition on the east bank south

A Russian T-34 – its sloped front armour and broad tracks made it hard to beat

his XLVI Panzer Corps around to the south. It met with fierce resistance and Guderian aimed to support them with his XLVII Panzer Corps. However, without telling Guderian, von Kluge had ordered the 18th Panzer Division to stay where it was. So the 17th Panzer Division, now under the command of General von Thoma, went alone, preventing a breakout.

Fierce fighting continued and, for a few days, the advance was halted. Intelligence reports indicated that the Russians were constructing a new defensive line to the east and Russian infantry broke into the Smolensk bridgehead. But on 26 July, Hoth finally managed to encircle them.

Tactical confusion

The following day Guderian flew back to Army Group headquarters for a meeting. He expected to be given orders to advance on Moscow, or at least Bryansk to the east. Instead he was told to turn to the south-west and then encircle eight to ten Russian divisions that were in the area around Gomel, back in Belarus. Guderian and the other officers at the meeting – indeed even the High Command – thought this was a mistake. It gave the Russians time to set up new defensive formations to the east and prevent them reaching Moscow.

But Guderian's more immediate concern was the capture of Roslavl, an important crossroads and communications centre to his right. This

of Orsha that it withdrew and made another crossing at Kopys, behind the 29th (Motorized) Panzer Division. Some of the bridges had been damaged by air attack, but Guderian got all his troops across and ordered the advance to continue throughout the night of 11 July to take maximum advantage of the element of surprise.

During the crossing of the Dnieper, Guderian's headquarters played host to a number of VIPs, including Hitler's principal adjutant Colonel Schmundt. It became clear to Guderian the High Command still had no idea what was going on or what resistance they faced, but nevertheless they gave Guderian his head. The Panzers reached Smolensk on 15 July, taking it the following day. The day after that Guderian was awarded Oak Leaves to his Knight's Cross. He was only the fifth man in the Wehrmacht to receive this decoration.

The Russians began to counter-attack Smolensk from the north-east and the city was badly damaged by shellfire. Hoth began to encircle the enemy there, while Guderian sent

would give him an unhindered route to the south-west, as Hitler ordered, but it also opened the way to the south and east. To take Roslavl he was given several more divisions. These were to be formed into Army Group Guderian, an autonomous force that was no longer under the command of the Fourth Army. Guderian was flattered by the rapturous reception he got from the new troops under his command and met up with Lieutenant Colonel Freiherr von Bissing, who he had shared a house with in Berlin-Schlachtensee for many years.

The attack was to begin on 2 August, but on 29 July Hitler's principal adjutant turned up again, bearing the Oak Leaves for Guderian's Knight's Cross. During discussions Schmundt revealed that Hitler had changed his mind once again about his objectives. Leningrad and the Baltic were on the list again. So was Moscow. And Hitler was considering an attack on the Ukraine, but he had not made up his mind about that yet. Guderian urged Schmundt to advise Hitler to push on to Moscow and the heart of Russia. He should avoid operations like the Gomel encirclement that involved losses without being decisive. He also begged Schmundt for the new tanks he needed to bring the Russian campaign to a speedy conclusion.

Bombing the wrong side

The attack on Roslavl went ahead as planned. It would begin with a flanking manoeuvre by motorized infantry divisions, while the 3rd and 4th Panzer Divisions moved on the town itself. There was little serious opposition from the enemy, but the Luftwaffe mistakenly bombed the advancing German troops, causing heavy

'The Luftwaffe mistakenly bombed advancing German troops... one bomb fell within 16 feet of Guderian's car'

casualties. One bomb fell within 16 feet (5 m) of Guderian's car, but he was unhurt. By mid-afternoon the 3rd Panzer Division had taken the bridge and captured a Russian battery. By the time Guderian got back to his headquarters that night, the town was theirs though fighting continued.

On 4 August, Guderian was ordered back to Army Group headquarters for a conference with Hitler. Schmundt, von Bock, Hoth and the chief of the operations department, Colonel Heusinger, were also there. Guderian, von Bock and Hoth all urged Hitler to advance on Moscow, but he had decided that the industrial area around Leningrad should be the next objective. After that, he thought they should take the Ukraine. If Germany was to continue the war, it would need the Ukraine's raw materials and grain that grew there. Then they had to move against the naval bases in the Crimea to prevent Soviet aircraft carriers carrying out operations against the Romanian oilfields. But he still hoped to be in Moscow by winter.

Guderian listened to what Hitler had to say, then pointed out that, if any more large-scale tank operations were going to be carried out that year, he would need new tanks and tank engines; the current ones had become very worn by the dust thrown up on Russia's unmetalled roads.

Hitler eventually promised to send 300 new engines to the Russian Front, which Guderian said was totally inadequate. And there would be no new tanks. The current production was to be retained to equip new formations Hitler was setting up. Guderian complained that he could only cope with the Russians' numerical superiority in tanks if his losses were made good. According to Guderian, Hitler replied: 'If I had known that the figures for Russian tank strength which you gave in your book [*Achtung - Panzer!*] were in fact true, I would not, I believe, ever have started this war.'

Strength in numbers

In *Achtung - Panzer!* Guderian had given the Russian tank strength in 1937 as 10,000, although he had seen intelligence reports putting it as high as 17,000. Even then he had problems getting the lower figure past the censor. The Germans had begun *Barbarossa* with just 3,200 tanks.

Despite what Hitler had said, on his flight back Guderian decided to make preparations for an attack on Moscow. But when he landed he discovered that, while he had been away, the Panzers had lost control of the Moscow road. Guderian went forward and ordered his commanders to resume their positions on the Moscow road. In his headquarters, he told his

'Hitler eventually promised to send 300 new tank engines to the Russian Front which Guderian said was totally inadequate'

staff to prepare to advance on Moscow, believing that Hitler would change his mind. Meanwhile the High Command requested that Guderian send Panzers to attack Rogachev on the Dnieper. This was 125 miles (200 km) behind his front line and Guderian refused.

By 8 August, the Battle of Roslavl was finally won. Some 38,000 Russian prisoners had been taken, along with 200 tanks and 200 guns. Intelligence confirmed that there was no enemy for 25 miles (40 km) ahead in the direction of Bryansk. To secure their right flank, XXIV Panzer Corps attacked the enemy in the Miloslavitchi area of Belarus. Women came out on to the battlefield with bread and butter and eggs, and Guderian said that they refused to let him move until he had eaten – though he acknowledged that this friendly attitude disappeared when the military administration was later replaced by Nazi 'Reich commissars'.

However, this victory at Miloslavitchi was a

tactical error. Although Guderian had cleared the way to make an attack on Moscow, his move to the south gave the High Command a fresh excuse to order the XXIV Panzer Corps back to Gomel. Soon the whole of his force was to move southwards and, on 23 August, Guderian was called to another conference at Army Group where he was informed that Hitler had indeed changed his mind. But now the objective was neither Leningrad nor Moscow. It was the Ukraine and the Crimea. This, Guderian and the other officers present were told, was Hitler's 'unalterable resolve'.

Guderian expressed doubts that his armour was capable of taking Kiev, the capital of the Ukraine, and then turning back to take Moscow. This could necessarily involve a winter campaign. He pointed out that his XXIV Panzer Corps had not had a single day for rest and maintenance since the beginning of *Barbarossa*. Von Bock suggested that Guderian go to the Wolf's Lair, Hitler's headquarters in East Prussia, and speak to him personally. But when he touched down in East Prussia Field Marshal von Brauchitsch forbade him to bring up the subject of Moscow. So when Guderian met Hitler he merely detailed the poor condition of his Panzers. Hitler asked if they were capable of making another great effort. Yes, replied Guderian, 'If the men are given a major objective, one that each individual soldier will immediately see as important.'

'You mean Moscow, of course,' said Hitler.

'Now you mention it… ' said Guderian. And he went on to spell out why they should push on to Moscow, rather than turn to the south towards Kiev. He explained that, as well as being a great road and rail hub, Moscow was the heart of Russia. Taking it would sap the Russian people's will to fight. On the way to Moscow he would smash what was left of the Russian army. Afterwards it would be easy to take Kiev as it would be impossible for the Russians to reinforce their garrison. He spoke of the enthusiasm of his Panzer troops to press on to Russia's capital. Besides, his formations were facing eastwards and pulling back his advanced units to make an attack to the south would subject their vehicles to more wear and tear. Moving on to Moscow was the only way that the Russian campaign could be won within the timetable set by the High Command – or even that year. Militarily that was the primary objective: everything else was subsidiary.

Seize Kiev!

Hitler listened to all this without interrupting. Then he spoke once more of the bread basket that was the Ukraine and how aircraft carriers from the naval bases in the Crimea could deprive them of the Romanian oilfields. He complained that his generals never understood the economics of war. Hitler was adamant. Kiev was the next objective. Guderian flew back to his Panzer Group with orders to move towards the Ukraine on 25 August. He subsequently found out that orders to that effect had been drawn up two days before his meeting with Hitler.

Guderian had got an assurance from Hitler that his Panzer Group would not be split up. Nevertheless Army Group Centre removed XLVI Panzer Corps from his command and put it in reserve. This left Guderian only two Panzer corps – XLVII and the exhausted XXIV – for the attack on Kiev.

On the morning of 25 August, Guderian was on his way to the 17th Panzer Division to lead the advance when he drove down a sandy track. The sand thrown up knocked out his command vehicles, a number of lorries and some motorcycles. He duly had to wait two hours for replacements. This, he decided, was not a good omen.

When he reached the headquarters of the 17th Panzers, he saw that they were understrength; nevertheless, the advance was to go ahead. The following day, he moved forward to an artillery observation post to watch the dive-bombing of the Russian positions on the other side of the River Rog. The bombing did not do much damage, but it did make the Russians keep their heads down and Guderian's men crossed the river without casualties. However, the Russians spotted the staff officers in the observation post and mortared, wounding five officers including Major Büsing who was sitting next to Guderian. Guderian himself had another lucky escape.

On 26 August, Russian resistance stiffened and Guderian requested the return of his XLVI Panzer Corps. This was denied. His Panzer Group was then delayed by the necessity of attacking forces on its flanks. But by 31 August, the 4th Panzer Division had crossed the Dresna on its way south. Again both the XXIV and XLVII Panzer Corps were experiencing heavy counterattacks on their flanks and Guderian felt that they did not have enough strength to continue the attack. Again he asked for reinforcements. With the XLVI Panzer Corps, the 7th and 11th Panzer Divisions and the 14th (Motorized) Infantry Division, he said, he could bring the Kiev campaign to a swift conclusion. He was

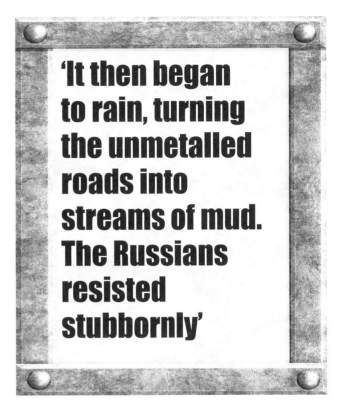

'It then began to rain, turning the unmetalled roads into streams of mud. The Russians resisted stubbornly'

given two infantry regiments. It then began to rain, turning the unmetalled roads into streams of mud. The Russians again resisted their advance stubbornly. Only dive-bombers seemed to make any dent in their resistance. Then Guderian got lucky. Captured documents indicated a gap in the Russian line. The 3rd Panzer Division, under Lieutenant General Model, went to look for it.

When Guderian returned to his headquarters on 4 September, he got a telephone call telling him that the High Command was dissatisfied with the operations of his Panzer Group. Even though, since the beginning of the advance on 25 August, they had taken 120 tanks, 155 guns and 17,000 prisoners. The XXIV Panzer Corps had taken another 13,000 men. The High Command were particularly angry that, instead of heading directly south, as ordered, the XLVII Panzer Corps were on the eastern bank of the Dresna. Despite the fact they were within sight of victory there, they were ordered to return to the west bank. Meanwhile, far to the north, after a dizzying dash to the Baltic, Panzer Group 4 were preparing to assault the outer defences of Leningrad.

Guderian was with the 4th Panzer Division when XXIV Panzer Corps crossed the Seim. Then when he returned to his headquarters he discovered that Model had found the gap in the Russian line. But as he had no reserves to exploit Model's success, Guderian decided that the only thing he could do to help was join the 3rd Panzer Division behind the Russian lines himself.

The 3rd Panzer Division had bypassed the town of Konotop which had an important railway station where the Panzers could be supplied. The 4th Panzer Division went to take it, while Guderian drove off in pursuit of the 3rd. On the Seim bridge, he was attacked by Russian bombers and he was shelled by Russian artillery on the road, but again he emerged unscathed. Already the road was littered with vehicles that had got stuck in the mud and trucks that were supposed to be pulling guns were pulling other trucks.

Model had taken the enemy completely by surprise at Romny. Along the north side of the town, the River Romen had provided a natural defensive line, which the Russians had reinforced with wire entanglements and anti-tank ditches. The 3rd Panzer Division had simply run over them and taken the town. When Guderian arrived, there were still enemy stragglers in the gardens and it was only possible to drive through the town in an armoured vehicle.

The Panzers were also subjected to air attacks. Bad weather to the west kept the Luftwaffe on the ground, while the weather was good enough to the east for the Red air force to take to the air.

Konotop had fallen, along with Borsna to the west and, militarily, things were going well. But the torrential rain made the going difficult. Colonel General von Kleist's Panzer Group 1 with Army Group South had been unable to reach its objective due to the condition of the roads. Air reconnaissance was impossible and ground reconnaissance got stuck in the mud. Nevertheless XXIV Panzer Corps pushed as best they could towards von Kleist's Panzer Group 1 to close the Kiev pocket which contained the remains of five Russian armies.

Objective achieved

On 15 September, Guderian flew back to Army Group headquarters once again, this time to discuss the advance on Moscow and the final destruction of the Red Army. The following day, Guderian moved his headquarters up to Romny which, he recalled, had been the headquarters of Charles XII of Sweden before his defeat by the Russians at the Battle of Poltava in 1708. On 19 September, Kiev fell and five Russian armies were bottled up on the steppes outside it. Guderian's Panzers resisted a ferocious push from the Russians in the east, trying to break into the pocket. Panzer Group 4 had found it impossible to break into Leningrad and had left it under siege while they turned south.

On 23 September, the Panzers began regrouping for their advance on Moscow. Panzer Group 2's assembly area was to the north of Gluchov giving the most advanced units a drive of 50 miles (80 km). The main offensive was to begin on 2 October, but Guderian requested that his Panzers be allowed to start on 30 September. He

Bogged down in a muddy field near Kiev, a German supply lorry is rescued by tracked vehicles more suited to the terrain, 1941

wanted to start as early as possible, before the weather got any worse, and for this he would get the concentrated support of the Luftwaffe for the first two days. Meanwhile, on 26 September, the Russians outside Kiev surrendered and 665,000 men were taken prisoner. Guderian considered this a tactical success, but a strategic disaster. It led even Guderian to underestimate the remaining Russian formations' will to fight.

At last Panzer Group 2 were given 100 new tanks, but 50 of them had been misdirected to Orsha and missed the start of the advance. And there was still a shortage of fuel. Guderian thought that the Army Group's deployment, concentrating all the armour in the centre of the line, was a mistake. It was better, he believed, to put two well-rested Panzer divisions on the flanks.

Once again the attack took the Russians by surprise and XXIV Panzer Corps raced ahead. However, Russian heavy tanks were soon in

evidence when they surprised two infantry battalions and captured their vehicles. On 1 October, XXIV Panzer Corps took Sevsk and succeeded in breaking through the enemy front. As Guderian followed up behind he saw the road was littered with shot-up vehicles, showing just how effective the Panzers' surprise attack had been. That day the XXIV Panzer Corps advanced 85 miles (137 km).

The following day, after ferocious fighting, a complete breakthrough was made and the Russian Thirteenth Army was thrown back to the north-east. The 4th Panzer Division took Kromy, reaching a metalled road that led to Orel, a major road and rail hub, which they took the next day. The surprise there was so complete that the trams in Orel were still running when the Panzers rolled in and in the streets were abandoned crates filled with tools and dismantled machinery that was to have been evacuated to the east. Meanwhile the XLVII

Panzer Corps headed for Bryansk. Panzer Group 4 surrounded the Russian forces to the north of Viasma, while Panzer Group 3 took a bridgehead over the Dnieper near Cholm.

By 4 October, elements of XXIV Panzer Corps were on the road to Tula. The 3rd and 18th Panzer Divisions were heading for Karachev. And the 17th Panzer Division were building a bridgehead across the Nerussa so they could advance to the north. The next day they were on their way to Bryansk. Again the speed of the advance was phenomenal. Guderian took to using an aircraft to visit his forward units, to save spending long hours bumping over bad roads. This had its downside. Even airfields in the rear that were now occupied by the Luftwaffe were subjected to Russian bombing.

Problems pile up

On 5 October, Guderian's Panzer Group 2 became the Second Panzer Army. However, it began to run into difficulties. The 4th Panzer Division were badly mauled by Russian T-34s south of Mzensk, resulting in huge casualties. The superiority of the Russian heavy tanks was becoming apparent and the rapid advance on Tula that Guderian had been planning was abandoned.

Nevertheless on 6 October, the 17th Panzer Division took Bryansk and its bridges over the Desna. That meant supplies could be brought up easily along the road and railway that ran from Orel to Bryansk. Victory was within their grasp, but that night the first snow fell.

'The roads rapidly became nothing but canals of bottomless mud, along which our vehicles could only advance at snail's pace and with

great wear to the engines,' said Guderian. He asked for winter clothing, but was told not to make further unnecessary requests of this type. Requests for antifreeze were similarly ignored.

Despite the poor weather, the High Command considered that Moscow could now be taken. The Second Panzer Army was to advance from the south through Tula, while Panzer Group 3 came in from the north. Orders were issued that took no account of the conditions. Even the metalled roads were now a series of bomb craters and the advancing Panzers were met by fresh formations of T-34s. These could only be knocked out by the short-barrelled 75mm guns of the Panzer IVs if they were hit from the rear. Even then the shell had to hit the grating above the engine to be effective. It required enormous skill to get such a shot in. The Russians too had developed a new tactic. They made a frontal assault on the tanks with infantry while sending their tanks against the flanks. The T-34s were now turning up in greater numbers, driven straight to the battlefront from the production line by women factory workers.

Guderian began to notice that the morale of his men was being worn down by the Russian successes in battle. But this did not seep through to Army Group headquarters who continued to make over-optimistic plans. As vehicles became stuck in the snow, the order came to take Kursk, 285 miles (460 km) south of Moscow, to complete the encirclement of what remained of the Red Army. But, by this time, conditions were so bad that wheeled vehicles could only move if they were towed by tracked vehicles. Tanks did not have the appropriate chains or couples and rope had to be dropped from aircraft.

The 4th Panzer Division got caught up in heavy street fighting in Mzensk. Support was slow in coming because of the mud and T-34s inflicted heavy losses on the Panzers.

'Up to this time we had enjoyed tank superiority,' said Guderian, 'but from now on the situation was reversed.'

He wrote a report saying that it was no longer possible for his Panzers to make rapid advances. He also asked for a commission consisting of representatives from the Army Ordnance Office, the Armaments Ministry, tank designers and tank manufacturers to come to his sector of the front to see T-34s on the battlefield and talk to the men who had to fight them. In the meantime, he asked for the rapid production of an anti-tank gun powerful enough to knock out T-34s.

While Guderian's Second Panzer Army was halted at Dmitrovsk by snow and mud, things continued to go well in the south. In the battle for the Sea of Azov the Sixth, Ninth, Twelfth and Eighteenth Russian armies were destroyed, 100,000 prisoners were taken and 672 guns and 212 tanks captured, and the way was open to the Crimea and the lower Don. Around Kharkov, though, progress was slowed by the appearance of more T-34s which regularly threw the First Panzer Army on to the defensive, though Kharkov itself eventually fell on 24 October.

Delaying tactics

As the Second Panzer Army advanced on Odessa, it was held up by the retreating Russians who were holding positions near to a bridge. Captain Georg von Konrat was ordered to clear the road with three tanks – Sea Rose 1, 2 and 3 – and two

German troops break cover and run for shelter behind armoured personnel carriers in the streets of Kharkov, 1941

"'The Russians were firing half blindly, sending out shell after shell in one continuous bombardment'"

armoured cars – Sea Rose 4 and 5. He decided to use an encircling manoeuvre through a forest. Von Konrat wrote of the affair:

We moved rapidly out through the trees and on to the field, immediately starting to pick up speed. At first, I could see nothing because of the smoke, but then, suddenly, we were through and into the open field, in sight of the Russian guns. Jochum, my driver, yelled: "We're doing 55." "See if you can make it 65," I roared back. Two seconds later we made our first turn, shooting out to the left in an eighty-degree twist and heading full tilt for the Russian guns. They were blasting at us non-stop, but before we could line up again we were off to the right and heading at an angle for the river. Then we went left again and back towards the turn-off. The Russians must have thought we had gone crazy or that we were trying to cut them off from their retreating forces.

We made another sharp turn back towards the river and this time I jammed the lid of the turret shut – just in case one of those grenade throwers hit bull's eye. If we had to go out, I didn't want it to be over something as measly as that. We turned left again, 55 degrees, dodged towards the forest and then were off again on a right-hand tangent before the guns had a chance to aim. The Russians were going berserk. I had my periscope up and was watching them.

Two Russian 76mm infantry guns were set up at the end of the road where they could command the field and were well protected from hits. And there were more heavy guns in the trees on the other side of the road.

Everything else was too well covered to be visible. But I had seen enough. I could have split my side watching their barrels turning frantically about. They were firing half blindly, sending out shell after shell in one continuous bombardment, but none even half-hopeful of aiming the right way.

But it was not just the Russians who were having a problem aiming:

Dita was having the same trouble and I could hear an unending stream of curses issuing from the gun turret.

Both sides were firing wildly when the Panzers closed within 50 metres, so they dashed back and forth randomly so that the Russians could not work out any pattern.

Five seconds later, we were off again to the right and back towards the river.

The Russians now had an old Katyusha rocket launcher doing her bit, spraying the field with lollipops. The sky was a mass of exploding shells. I could see the infantry digging in ahead of the guns, so we charged them this time, machine-gunning and shelling madly. They dropped their spades with the first burst and went rushing back to the road and out of sight. I was grinning like a madman. I think we all were. We careered off again, then right, then left, backwards, forwards, left, right, and off again. The tank heeled about wildly lurching off in another direction almost before it had regained its balance from the last zigzag. At times I thought we had been hit or lost our tracks, the way Jochum was throwing the poor tank around. My stomach felt turned inside out and I almost fainted with the sudden, violent jolts. I did not even dare to think what was going on in my lungs. Only the excitement kept me conscious… Dita had now given up his cursing. The gun turret was lifting so much that even when he was lucky enough to find the barrel pointing in the right direction, we had turned again by the time he fired and the shells went completely wild, whizzing over the Russians' heads into the trees, into the ground, anywhere and everywhere. We kept it up hoping madly that each turn wouldn't be the unlucky one, the one where we drove straight into a shell.

The other Panzers came charging in. But the Russian infantry were massing again.

I ordered my driver to race back towards them. Otherwise, they could jump on my other tanks and throw grenades down the turrets. "Right into them for a hundred metres next turn!" I yelled. Jochum did not answer. He didn't have time to. With a sharper spin than ever to the left, the tank seemed to keel over. But it steadied itself on the edge and righted itself again. Now the gun turret was steady and Dita was grinning. He could shoot directly into the Russian gun positions, while our machine guns cross-fired into infantry, sending them flying.

Von Konrat ordered the tank in again. This time Jochum seemed to lose control and overrun the road itself.

If the Russians weren't laughing with glee, they were shivering in their boots, I could see men flying out and leaving their guns in all directions as our tanks roared down on them full tilt.

At the last minute, Jochum turned and the tank raced back off across the field to safety, leaving the Russian infantry positions shattered. However, the Russian guns were still firing at von Konrat's other two tanks. He continued:

Ordering Jochum to spin round completely to the south, I threw open the lid of the turret and stuck my head out so I could see more clearly. At the same time, I clung on to the sides for grim death. The Russians had no idea what was happening out on the field anymore. We hadn't gone in, we hadn't retreated. We had just played cat and mouse with them like kids at a Sunday school picnic...

He charged them again but, just as he was drawing level with Sea Rose Two, he saw the armoured car Sea Rose Four 'just one great roaring flame'.

Now we were completely surrounded by Russian guns and Dita had our gun turret turning to the left and right and firing continuously at everything. Sea Rose Two came quickly back on to the main road and the three tanks moved down it in line, our machine guns cross-spraying to keep the infantry off. We moved down towards the turn-off, gradually silencing every gun in the area. None of them was powerful enough to knock out a tank.

As they rolled on towards Odessa all they saw was burning vehicles and infantrymen fleeing towards the sea. But they were running out of ammunition:

It was becoming hard for me to think clearly. I felt sick – I felt lousy. All I wanted to do was to get the hell out of Russia, Odessa, and everything to do with it, and lie on a nice soft bed and sleep.

He braced himself against the side of the tank and ordered his tanks to turn around. Sea Rose Two was to head back to the forest to find out what had happened to Sea Rose Five, while he and Sea Rose Three would head back up the road with their machine guns firing to left and right as they drove through the Russian artillery positions again.

While we were among them they could not fire for fear of blowing each other up, so all they could do was scatter – all except for one Russian officer. We drove the tank straight at him but he did not budge. Alone on the empty road, he stood waiting unflinchingly for us to roll over him. I never felt so much for a Russian before. Just before we reached him, we turned and drove past him and down the bridge road. I did not look behind but I knew he would still be there. As soon as we turned, Dita swung his gun around and loosed off our final shell. Then we raced for the river at top speed.

By this time the infantry lines had reformed. Von Konrat cursed that he had used up his last shell when he came across a Russian anti-tank gun. They shot it up with their machine guns. Sea Rose Three still had a shell and blew it out of existence.

Sea Rose Three then reported that it had found Sea Rose Five. *Fähnrich* (officer cadet) Olle then told von Konrat that the armoured car was a red mass of fire, and that he was heading back to the river.

Von Konrat concluded that it must have got ahead of the tanks, or that it had been caught by a gun they had missed – but he consoled himself with the thought that his men may have got out. Returning to the German lines, he told his commanding officer of his high-speed attack across the field.

I saw that, [said Major Horst] and I nearly died laughing too. Those Ruskies must have used up half the ammunition in Odessa lighting up the sky like fairyland for you – while you did exhibition dancing underneath.

Von Konrat agreed that he had had some fun.

When the Second Panzer Army resumed its advance on Tula, it found that the road disintegrated under the weight of the tanks. The Russians had blown the bridges and laid minefields on either side of the roads. To make progress, the Germans had to lay corduroy road, made from felled trees, for miles on end. On top of that, they were running short of petrol. The High Command then came up with the idea of sending the Second Panzer Army south-east towards Voronezh where Russia forces were massing. This presented the Panzers with another problem: no road led there. As this plan was therefore out of the question Hitler ordered 'fast-moving units to seize the Oka bridges to the east of Serpuchov' just 60 miles (96 km) south of Moscow itself. But, given the conditions, there were no 'fast-moving units' any more. The Orel–

'On the night of 3 November, there was a frost. This made the going easier, but it also brought a new problem – cold'

Tula road had now disintegrated completely and the maximum speed vehicles occasionally achieved was 12 mph (19 kph). The Second Panzer Army had been told to take Tula by a *coup de main*, but it found itself held up 2 miles (3.2 km) outside the town by heavy Russian anti-tank defences. Heavy artillery could not be brought up because of the state of the road. Front line troops had had no bread issue for over a week and the 3rd Panzer Division had to be supplied by air.

Unsuitable conditions

Guderian decided to bypass Tula, crossing the Shat to the south-east at Dedilovo. But progress was slow because of the huge wear and tear the conditions inflicted on the vehicles. He then decided that motorized troops could not be deployed until there was a frost. Elements of the XXIV Panzer Corps reached Dedilovo on 1 November. A Russian column moved in from the south to attack the Panzers stalled outside Tula, and was thrown back by LIII Army Corps.

On the night of 3 November, there was a frost. This hardened the ground and made the going easier. But it also brought a new problem – cold. By 7 November, men were reporting cases of frostbite. Meanwhile to the south, Kursk had fallen to the XLVIII Panzer Corps and the First Panzer Army was attacking Rostov-on-Don. But around Tula the XXIV Panzer Corps had gone on the defensive.

On 12 November, Guderian flew back to Army Group headquarters for a conference. He received orders for his Second Panzer Army to take Gorki, 400 miles (644 km) from Orel and 250 miles (400 km) to the east of Moscow. One of his staff officers pointed out that it would be

German troops dig out a Panzer IV stuck in snow as they begin to appreciate the true nature of the task that lies ahead of them, 1941

a miracle if they made another 30 miles (48 km).

'This was not the month of May and we were not fighting in France,' said Guderian.

When Guderian returned to the front the following day, he flew into a snowstorm. The temperature dropped to –8°F (–22°C): 40 degrees of frost. Due to frostbite, the combat strength of the infantry was down to 50 men from the usual 200 per company and the tanks were immobilized. They could not climb the ice-covered slopes because their tracks did not have the right calks (tapering metal pieces that dug into the ground) and they did not have more than one day's supply of fuel.

Telescopic sights froze up and fires had to be lit under the tanks to start their engines as the fuel froze in the pipes and the oil in their sumps began to solidify.

Food was another problem. The Russians had tried to burn the silos, but a lot of grain had been rescued. However, as the railways had now been knocked out, it was difficult to get bread through to the men.

Running repairs could be made to the tanks as factories that had not been stripped of their machinery were quickly put back at work. But even anti-Communists among the populace were not pro-German. One old Czarist general told Guderian:

If only you had come twenty years ago we would have welcomed you with open arms. But now it's too late. We were just beginning to get on our feet and now you arrive and throw us back twenty years so that we will have to start all over again. Now we are fighting for Russia and in that cause we are all united.

Despite the conditions, the Second Panzer Army began a slow advance, sometimes covering as many 6 miles (10 km) a day, but usually only 3 (5 km). The commission to examine the T-34s arrived on 20 November. The following day the First Panzer Army took Rostov-on-Don, though the retreating Russians had blown the bridges over the river.

Guderian flew back to Army Group headquarters on 23 November to request that his orders be changed as the Second Panzer Army plainly could not reach the objectives it had been assigned. Von Bock was sympathetic, but the High Command would not change its mind and Guderian was told the advance must continue.

Winter bites

The ill-clad, half-starved Panzer troops began to come up against well-fed, warmly attired Siberians, fully equipped for winter fighting, and began to suffer heavy casualties. On 27 November the Russians began to counter-attack at Rostov. The Second Panzer Army met strong Russian forces on the Tula–Aleksin road. However to the north, the 2nd Panzer Division had reached Krasnaya Polyana, 14 miles (22 km) from Moscow. But that was the height of the advance. The following day, the Russians re-entered Rostov and the First Panzer Army evacuated. As a result the commander of Army Group South Field Marshal von Rundstedt was sacked and replaced by Field Marshal von Reichenau.

Guderian moved his headquarters up to Yasnaya Polyana, the country estate of Leo Tolstoy, to begin his encirclement of Tula. There were two houses at Yasnaya Polyana. Guderian allowed the Tolstoy family to stay on in one of them, the Castle, while he occupied the Museum. After the war, the Soviet authorities accused the Germans

of vandalizing the Tolstoy estate. Guderian insists that none of the furniture was used or damaged, and none of the books or manuscripts touched. They burnt wood from the forest and made their own furniture out of planks. He even says he visited Tolstoy's grave to pay his respects, but found that the Russians had laid land mines around it.

On 2 December the 3rd and 4th Panzer Divisions broke through, but were halted by a blizzard the following day. The roads became treacherous. On the way back from visiting his forward troops, Guderian's command vehicle drove into a chasm cut in the clay soil by the autumn rains and now concealed by snow. There was no way of extricating it. But on the far side, he came upon a signals truck that took him back to his headquarters.

On 4 December the temperature fell to –31°F, (–35°C), on 5 December to –36°F (–38°C) and the tanks were immobilized. Guderian had no alternative but to break off his attack and, for the first time in the Russian campaign, pulled his men back to a defensive line. The whole of the German line was frozen with General Reinhardt's Third Panzer Army just 20 miles (32 km) from the Kremlin. The Wehrmacht just stopped where it was, not in properly prepared or fortified positions where they could have sat out the winter. They were exposed, not just to the weather, but to attacks by the Russians who were better prepared for the conditions.

'I would never have believed that a really brilliant military position could be so buggered up in two months,' Guderian wrote in a letter home on 8 December. 'If a decision had been taken at the proper time to break off and settle down for the winter in a habitable line suitable for defence, we would have been in no danger.'

But danger there was. On 8 December, after the attack on Pearl Harbor, Japan joined the war. Fatefully, on 11 December, Hitler declared war on the United States. However, Japan did not reciprocate and declare war on the Soviet Union, so all the Russian troops out in the Far East were brought back to face the Germans. The Panzers' fluid, fast-moving war was over, for the time being. In the Russian winter, the tanks were sitting ducks.

Guderian drove for 22 hours in a blizzard to meet Field Marshal von Brauchitsch in Roslavl and begged to be allowed to pull back to fortified positions so that he could close a gap in the line and asked that his request be conveyed to Hitler. Von Brauchitsch did so and was sacked, and Hitler phoned Guderian to tell him not to give up an inch of land. The withdrawals that Guderian had already started were to be halted. The Russians began to break through, though frostbite was causing more casualties than gunshot wounds, and Guderian decided that he must fly back to speak to Hitler personally who, after the dismissal of von Brauchitsch, had appointed himself Commander in Chief of the army.

Cold reality

On 20 December, Guderian arrived in East Prussia. He conferred with Hitler for 5 hours, with two breaks of half an hour each. Guderian knew that he stood in lonely opposition to the High Command and, for the first time, he noticed an unfriendly look in Hitler's eye.

Guderian began by describing the pitiful state of the army and, once again, suggested withdrawing to a fortified line prepared along the Rivers Susha and Oka.

'No, I forbid it!' yelled Hitler. 'They must dig in where they are and hold every square metre of land!'

Guderian pointed out that they could not dig in as the ground was frozen to a depth of 2 metres in most places and their entrenching tools made no impression.

'In that case they must blast craters with the heavy howitzers,' said Hitler. 'We had to do that in the First World War in Flanders.'

But Guderian pointed out that they had neither the guns nor the ammunition to do this, and they were experiencing cold much more severe than anything Hitler had experienced in western Europe. Even to drive a stake into the ground to hold a telephone wire required high explosives. But Hitler would not be shaken. He insisted that the army followed orders and stayed where it was.

Guderian continued to argue the point, saying that taking up positional warfare on unsuitable terrain, as they had in the First World War, would result in the loss of officers, non-commissioned officers and the men suitable to replace them.

'This sacrifice will be not only useless but irreparable,' he said.

'Do you think Frederick the Great's grenadiers were anxious to die?' asked Hitler. 'They wanted to live too, but the king was right to ask them to sacrifice themselves. I believe that I too am entitled to ask any German soldier to lay down his life.'

Guderian said that it was one thing to risk your life for your country, quite another to throw it away uselessly. Hitler then accused Guderian of spending too much time with his troops. If he

as there were no trains to take it forward. When he had asked for it to be brought forward by truck in September and October his request had been refused. Now it was too late as the roads were impassable.

Hitler sent for the Quartermaster-General who confirmed that this was true. But the only result of this was that the propaganda minister, Joseph Goebbels, ran a campaign to collect winter clothes for the soldiers on the Eastern Front. But that was all it was – a propaganda campaign. Nothing that was collected reached the front.

Hitler then turned the tables on Guderian. He complained that Guderian had too many men in the supply columns and not enough carrying rifles at the front. Guderian said that

A cyclist stops near a poster of Hitler and an appeal for 'winter charities' in Stuttgart

stood back a bit more, Hitler said, he would see things more clearly. Guderian explained that this was hard to do when he lost more men from frostbite than from gunfire because they were still clothed in summer uniforms and the winter boots, vests, gloves and woollen hats they needed were either non-existent or hopelessly worn out.

'That is not true,' yelled Hitler. 'The Quartermaster-General told me that the winter clothing had been issued.'

Guderian agreed that it had been issued, but it had never arrived. It was stuck on Warsaw station

this was because the trucks that had broken down had not been replaced and transporting adequate supplies forward using local transport such as sledges took a great deal more men. Nothing could be done to change the situation until the railways were running again.

'It was difficult to make Hitler grasp this simple fact,' said an exasperated Guderian.

Guderian had seen a newsreel of von Brauchitsch showing Hitler around an exhibition in Berlin of the equipment available to troops on the Eastern Front. The problem was that they did not have any of these things. The armaments minister, Dr Fritz Todt, then presented Guderian with two trench stoves he had built for Hitler. They were to serve as models for the troops who should build them themselves with materials available.

After dinner, Guderian suggested that officers who had experience of frontline fighting in the winter war be posted to the general staff as he felt that the messages he sent to the High Command were being misunderstood and misinterpreted. Hitler gruffly refused. And as Guderian left the conference room, knowing his conversation with Hitler had been a failure, Hitler turned to Keitel and said, 'I haven't convinced that man.'

Hitler's message

Guderian returned to the front and went around his Panzer Army, trying to explain Hitler's decision to his men. Naturally, the Russians lost little time exploiting Guderian's position. On 24 December, they took Livny. That night they took Chern, encircling the 10th (Motorized) Infantry Division. When Guderian reported the situation, von Kluge accused him of evacuating Chern the day before. Guderian then ordered his Second Panzer Army to withdraw to the Suska–Oka Line, in direct contradiction to Hitler's orders. On 26 December, Guderian was relieved of his command by von Kluge.

Back in Berlin, Guderian found that a number of fellow officers were sympathetic and felt that he had been treated unjustly. But at the time, there were a great number of arbitrary sackings going on as Hitler tried to find someone to blame for the fiasco in the east. This purge was not done without protest. When Colonel-General Hoepner was sacked after saying that the fault lay with the 'civilian leadership', Hitler also stripped him of his right to wear his uniform or decorations, stopped his pension and took away his house. But Hoepner ignored these orders, saying they were illegal, and lawyers for the High Command told Hitler that he could not issue such orders without a formal disciplinary hearing, which would undoubtedly have found in Hoepner's favour. Hitler grew angry and pushed through a new law in the Reichstag on 26 April 1942, giving him the right to change the law by decree without reference to the Reichstag. Hitler had finally taken the absolute powers of a despot.

Hearing of the Hoepner case, Guderian asked a military court of inquiry to investigate his conduct. Hitler turned down this request, refusing to give reasons for doing so. By this time Guderian was showing the strain, and his wife was ill, so they went for a four-week cure at the spa at Badenweiler.

In September, when Rommel was planning to return to Germany due to ill health, he telegraphed from North Africa, saying that he had proposed to Hitler that Guderian deputize for him in his absence. The request was denied. Guderian decided to move out of Berlin and he and his wife began looking for a house near Lake Constance and in the Salzkammergut, an area often referred to as the 'Austrian Lake District'. When Hitler heard of this, he said that Guderian came from East Prussia and should return there. As he had a Knight's Cross with Oak Leaves, he would be given a small parcel of land in that region. So Guderian put away his field grey uniform and prepared to start a new career as a gentleman farmer.

7. SOVIET SUPERIORITY

Even though he was now a civilian, Guderian kept abreast of the war. During the offensive of July and August 1942, the Caspian oilfields were captured, the Volga – Russia's great maritime artery – was cut and Stalingrad was destroyed as an industrial centre. However, to Guderian, these moves made no sense: Hitler was going after military and ideological objectives without first destroying the enemy's armed forces. Those in the military who had the temerity to point this out were sacked and their powers taken by Hitler, who nursed a growing distrust of leading figures in the army.

However, one of the things that Hitler did get right, in Guderian's opinion, was to concentrate much of his energies on the development of new weapons, taking especial interest in the development of a new tank to take on the Russian T-34. The officers at the front had suggested that German tank manufacturers make a straightforward copy of the T-34, but the designers would not hear of it. They pointed out that it would not be easy to mass produce the T-34's aluminium diesel engine quickly and shortages of raw materials made it difficult to copy the Russians' steel alloys. Instead they would concentrate their efforts on the 57-tonne, five-man Tiger tank that was already in production and designed a lighter Panther tank, around 45 tonnes. Both had one main turret-mounted gun and two 7.92mm machine guns. The design of the Panther was submitted to Hitler in January 1942. He ordered 600 a month to be made.

Chaos and confusion

However tank production was in turmoil. Chassis were being diverted to the artillery to make self-propelled guns. New hollow-charge shells showed better armour penetration and Hitler believed that the days of the Panzer were coming to an end. This perception was not shared by Albert Speer who had taken over as minister for armaments and war production when Dr Todt died in an aeroplane accident. In March, the

Top: A fresh delivery of Panther tanks to challenge the T-34

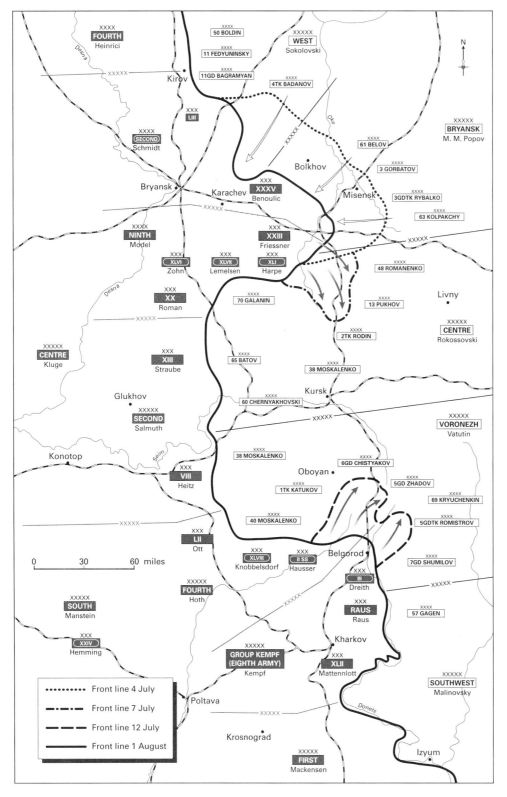

the next spring. As a result of this renewed push in tank design and production, car manufacture was halted.

Speer told Hitler that 85 Tiger tanks would be available by October 1942 and a further 135 by March 1943. In April, Hitler insisted that 75mm and 80mm guns be fitted to the Tigers and Panthers and new shells were to be designed. And 12 Panzer IVs with 80mm frontal armour were ordered for a putative operation against Malta which never came off.

In May 1942, Hitler approved the MAN Company's Panther design. The production of Panzer IIIs was increased to 190 a month, the construction of flat cars able to carry very

The Battle of Kursk, the largest tank battle in history, which took place in July and August 1943

designer of the Tiger tank, Professor Ferdinand Porsche, and the armaments manufacturer Krupp were told to start work designing a 100-tonne version. A prototype was required by heavy tanks was begun and an air-cooled diesel tank engine was to be designed. In June he ordered that the front armour of the Panzer IV be increased to 80mm, and that a consideration

The highly effective Panther, with a design much influenced by the T-34

Tigers. Initially, Hitler wanted them to be deployed against Leningrad in the summer of 1942, then he said he wanted them for operations in France in September: it seems he was already expecting a full-scale Allied landing following the raid on Dieppe that August. As the Tiger was electrically powered and its engine air-cooled, it seemed the appropriate weapon for North Africa. But its range was only 30 miles (48 km). That would have to be increased to 90 if the Tiger was going to be any use in the desert.

of 100mm be made. Similarly, the question of whether the Tiger's frontal armour could be increased to 120mm should be investigated. Porsche's Tiger tank's belly armour was increased to 100mm and guns were to be upped to 100mm, and the Panther also got 100mm frontal armour. Eventually this race to gigantism led Hitler to order the design of a monster tank weighing 1,000 tonnes.

New orders were issued quicker than the manufacturers could react. Panzer IIIs were to be re-equipped with 75mm cannon. All Panzer IVs returned to the factory for repair were to be given long-barrelled guns and an enquiry was set up to see how quickly a new 88mm cannon capable of penetrating 200mm of armour could be fitted to the Tigers. These changes slowed the production of the

Speeding up production

Tank production reached 800 units in September 1942, including fifty Tiger and 600 Panther tanks. However, 600 guns built on tank chassis were also produced and production began to swing in their favour. It seemed to Guderian

The 57-tonne Tiger tank was invulnerable to all but the best-aimed shells

that armaments production was turning from offensive to defensive weapons. To increase the production of self-propelled guns, unhardened steel was used, which, the troops began to complain, made them very ineffective as weapons.

As the Battle of Stalingrad intensified, there was a call for more effective assault guns. Their calibre was increased to 75mm and the thickness of the frontal armour to 100mm. Heavy infantry guns were mounted on Panzer IV chassis and some of the Tigers then under construction had their revolving turrets replaced by 88mm cannon and 200mm of frontal armour added. These were the Tiger 'Ferdinands', and 'Elefants'. It was acknowledged that the current generation of tanks was no good for the kind of street fighting they were experiencing in Stalingrad, but modifying tanks that were already in production created numerous variations

and made supplying spare parts a nightmare.

The first Tigers went into action in September 1942 against the advice of tank experts. Since the 1920s, Guderian and others had propounded the theory that new weapons should be held back until they can be used in sufficient numbers to win a significant victory. The British, he said, had wasted the surprise effect of the introduction of their tanks by deploying them too soon and in too small a number. Ignoring this, Hitler committed a handful of Tigers in swampy forest outside Leningrad. It was totally unsuitable tank terrain as they had to drive single-file down a forest track. This allowed Russian anti-tank guns to attack them from the side, causing heavy casualties and halting the advance. And the Russians now knew about the Tiger tank and the element of surprise was also lost.

Below: Crew members lie dead after a tank fight near Stalingrad

During the struggle for Stalingrad, German troops set up their mortar in the shadow of an abandoned Soviet T-34

A German soldier advances past a burning Soviet tank, probably a T-34, somewhere in the south of Russia

The only really effective tank available to the Germans at that time was the Panzer IV. Production had just reached 100 a month. But Hitler decided that more assault guns, infantry guns and mortars should be mounted on Panzer IV chassis.

Meanwhile, Panther chassis were to carry 88mm assault guns. Guderian considered that tank production was moving in quite the wrong direction. However, he did approve of the decision to arm the Tiger with an 88mm flat-trajectory gun, rather than a heavier calibre gun with a lower muzzle velocity. The flat-trajectory gun was better for fighting enemy tanks, which was the Tiger's primary purpose. Tiger production was increased, reaching 25 a month in November. Meanwhile the production of assault guns climbed to 100 a month. It reached 220 a month by June 1943, after production capacity had been increased by stopping the production of Panzer IIIs. Production also began

to favour light field howitzers, with a low muzzle velocity but a high trajectory. These were good for infantry support, but were of little use against hostile tanks.

Standing firm

That winter the Tigers performed well at Stalingrad. They simply sat on a defensive line, firing without moving, while the Russian T-34s attacked and were blown to bits in the minefields the Germans had laid 30 metres in front of their positions. It has been said that this tactic was adopted more by accident than design. The German tanks would not start when the temperature dropped to –45°F (–43°C). But the Tigers stood like fortresses, seemingly impervious to anything that was thrown against them.

In the final days of the Battle of Stalingrad, one Tiger became a kind of metal pillbox. It had been used by one of the regimental commanders of the 24th Panzer Division and was connected to divisional headquarters by field telephone. Five Panzergrenadiers took refuge in it during a Russian advance. They slammed the turret shut as the Russians sped by and soon found themselves completely cut off 1.2 miles (2 km) behind the front line. There was food inside the tank. Both its main gun and machine guns worked and there was plenty of ammunition for both. One of the Panzergrenadiers turned the handle of the field telephone and asked divisional headquarters what they should do.

'Stay where you are,' they were told.

They stayed there for a week until a Russian patrol stumbled upon them. A Russian infantry company was sent in but when it got within 50 metres of them, they opened fire and drove them off. Twenty-four hours later the Russians resumed the assault, with tanks. Again they were repelled and the Panzergrenadiers were able to report to divisional headquarters that they had knocked out three T-34s. More T-34s, mortars and artillery were brought up to take what the Russians were calling 'Command Post 506'.

The Panzergrenadiers phoned up again and

The *Elefant*, an 88mm gun mounted on a Tiger chassis

asked what they should do now. They were told to 'remember what the Russians did when they were pinned down in the silo'.

This was cold comfort. The Russians caught in one of Stalingrad's grain silos, they knew, had fought on until they had run out of ammunition. When they called their commander and complained of lack of food, they were told that they would not feel hunger if they fought harder. Shortly before they were annihilated, their commander told them, 'The Soviet Union thanks you: your sacrifice has not been in vain.'

Germany did not thank the five Panzergrenadiers in Command Post 506. The metal pillbox was attacked with flame-throwers and they were never heard of again.

Despite the problems with supplying spare parts the production of multiple versions caused, in January 1943 Hitler ordered that new Tigers should

A self-propelled German gun, the *Jagdpanther*, based on the Panther

be fitted with 150mm frontal armour, 80mm side armour and a long 88mm gun. He also ordered that Porsche's 100-tonne Maüschen or Mouse tank go into production at ten units a month, although it did not even then exist as a wooden mock-up. Mass production should start at the end of the year and a 128mm, perhaps even a 150mm, gun should be fitted.

Even more bizarre was the Rammtiger, which Hitler envisaged knocking down walls in Stalingrad and ramming enemy tanks into submission. Auxiliary fuel-carrying vehicles were to be supplied, smoke mortars carried, and helicopters should be designated to direct artillery and tank battles.

Then there was a new heavy field howitzer called the Lobster and an 88mm self-propelled gun on a Panzer IV chassis. The production lines producing the Panzer II and Czech T38 tanks were to be turned over to the production of self-propelled guns. Ninety new Porsche Tiger 'Ferdinands' were to be produced, and Panthers and Panzer IVs were to be given new metal 'aprons' to protect their vertical surfaces, tracks and wheels from the Russian infantry's new anti-tank weapon.

Ill-conceived plans

At the same time, Speer was told to increase tank production. But with all the versions he was supposed to produce, he could not match the output of the Russian tank factories who kept on turning out one single successful tank: the T-34.

A column of SS *Das Reich* tanks, including Panzer IVs and VIs (Tigers), in a wood near Kirowograd in northern Russia, 1943

The general staff took a hand and produced a plan to simplify tank production. It envisaged turning all capacity over to the production of Tiger and Panther tanks. Hitler accepted the proposal. However, it would mean the end of the production of the Panzer IV while the production of Tigers was only up to 25 a month. Guderian believed that this plan would have handed victory to the Russians long before the Western Allies could have made an amphibious landing. But then a surprising thing happened. On 17 February 1943 the telephone rang and Guderian was summoned to Supreme Headquarters in Vinnitsa in the Ukraine for a meeting with Hitler.

By this time, the situation for the Third Reich was dire. The entire Sixth Army had been lost at Stalingrad. Rommel was fighting on two fronts in North Africa. And at the Casablanca conference, in an unguarded remark at a press conference, President Roosevelt had called for nothing less than the unconditional surrender of Germany.

In a preliminary meeting, Hitler's chief adjutant Schmundt, now a general, explained the position. The general staff and the armaments ministry were at loggerheads and the Panzers had lost confidence in the High Command. They were asking for someone with practical knowledge of armoured warfare to be given control of their branch of the service. Consequently Hitler was offering Guderian the position of inspector-general of armoured troops.

Guderian said that he would only accept the job if he was not subordinate to the chief of the army general staff, but answerable only to Hitler himself. He also needed the appropriate authority to deal with the armaments ministry

'On 17 February 1943 the telephone rang and Guderian was summoned to the Ukraine for a meeting with Hitler'

and the Army Ordnance Office, and control of the tank training units of the army, the Waffen-SS and the Luftwaffe. That afternoon, he was summoned to see Hitler who gave him the authority he needed and confirmed him in the post. They withdrew alone together to Hitler's study. There was a copy of *Achtung – Panzer!* on Hitler's desk and he said that he had been re-reading Guderian's pre-war writing. It was now time, he said, for Guderian to put his theories into practice.

After talks with Goebbels and Speer, Guderian visited Daimler-Benz at Berlin-Marienfelde and the Alkett Company at Spandau to get an idea of how the tank manufacturing industry was performing. Then he drew up plans for the establishment of new divisions of Panzers and Panzergrenadiers, which were re-equipped motorized infantry divisions, for the rest of 1943 and 1944.

On 9 March, Guderian returned to Vinnitsa to

tell Hitler of his planned reorganization of the Panzers. He pointed out that it was better to have a few strong divisions than numerous weak ones as ill-equipped divisions tended to have a higher proportion of wheeled vehicles which were a burden to command and supply and also blocked roads. To launch large-scale attacks in 1944 – which they would have to do if they were to win the war – Panzer divisions would have to be reorganized so that they contained four tank battalions and the strength of each division must not drop below 400 tanks, otherwise its combat efficiency was lost. At this point Guderian read an article by Liddell Hart to Hitler to back his argument.

Maximizing resources

Due to the need to supply replacements to the armies in North Africa and Russia, it would only be possible to create or fully re-equip one tank battalion a month. As a large number of assault guns were being made, it was also proposed that another battalion equipped with light assault guns be created each month and incorporated into the Panzer divisions. Rather than stopping the production of Panzer IVs, this should be increased, which Guderian thought he could do without hurting the production of Tigers and Panthers. New models needed to be thoroughly tested and perfect, and their crews given more training. They should also be supplied with artillery observers.

Guderian returned to his old maxim that success on the battlefield could only be achieved on the right terrain with the proper concentration at a decisive spot. That meant that secondary theatres of war must not be supplied

with new tanks. Units there should rely solely on captured equipment. All tank units were to be concentrated in Panzer divisions under commanders who were expert at armoured warfare. New formations should not be set up, as that dispersed equipment and experienced men. Armoured assaults were only to be carried out on suitable terrain for tanks. New equipment – particularly Tiger and Panther tanks, and heavy assault guns – should be held back until they could be used in sufficient numbers and Panzer divisions should not be used in a defensive role as that delayed them being reformed and re-equipped ready for a new attack.

A T-34 unapologetically barges past a stranded Panzer

Anti-tank defence should concentrate on the deployment of assault guns as other anti-tank weapons were useless against the T-34s. Assault-gun battalions and anti-tank battalions should be amalgamated. Heavy assault guns, which were primarily tank-killers, should be concentrated on the major battle fronts. Secondary battle fronts would have to make do with reserve equipment.

Guderian pointed out that armoured reconnaissance units had not been used much on the Eastern Front, but they had been effective in the desert. If they were to launch a great offensive in Russia in 1944, they would need them there too. They would need a sufficient number of 1-tonne armoured troop-carrying vehicles, which were currently under construction. They would also need armoured cars capable of speeds of up to 35 to 45mph (56 to 72 kph). No such vehicle was being made and Guderian asked permission to consult with Speer about producing one. An updated 3-tonne armoured troop-carrier was also needed for the Panzergrenadiers. He also asked the assault artillery to be put under his command, along with Hermann Göring Division, and the assimilation of army and Waffen-SS motorized divisions into the Panzer Army.

After prolonged discussion, Guderian's plan was approved – except for his request to take over the assault artillery, backed only by Speer. Finally, Hitler said, 'You see, they're all against you. So I can't approve either.' Guderian considered this a tragic mistake.

Guderian made a tour of the Tank School at Wünsdorf and more tank factories. On 19 March he watched a demonstration of Porsche's Tiger Ferdinand and the Panzer IV equipped with the armoured 'apron'. The Tiger Ferdinand, he noted, carried just an 88mm cannon and no other guns – making it useless for fighting at close quarters. Guderian could not share Hitler's enthusiasm for this behemoth, but 90 of them had already been built, so he formed a Panzer regiment with two battalions of 45 Ferdinands each. However,

Guderian did think that the armoured 'aprons' for the Panzer IVs and Panthers would prove useful.

Guderian was also given a demonstration of the 800mm 'Gustav' railway gun.

'What do you think of that?' asked Hitler. 'Dr Müller [of Krupp's] has told me that the "Gustav" could also be fired at tanks.'

'It could be fired at them,' said Guderian. 'But it could never hit one.'

Dr Müller protested. But Guderian simply asked him, 'How can you fight tanks with a gun that takes 45 minutes to reload?'

On 29 March, Guderian flew out to the headquarters of Army Group South to meet Field Marshal von Manstein who had just recaptured Kharkov with his armoured formations.

There he caught up with his old friend Hoth, commander of the Fourth Panzer Army. Then he went on to the front to talk to the Panzer commanders about their experiences with their new Tiger tanks.

When he returned to Germany, Guderian went to see Speer and Hitler to ask for the production

A *Stug III*: after 1943, self-propelled guns were mass-produced to save money and time

of Tigers and Panthers to be increased. He also visited SS leader Heinrich Himmler about integrating the Waffen-SS into his command as Hitler had agreed. Himmler refused to countenance such a thing and made it clear that he and Hitler were intent on building a private army, which would be used if the Wehrmacht ever turned against him. This was not so far-fetched. Guderian had already been approached by men plotting a *coup d'état* to rid Germany of Hitler and make peace with the Allies.

Hopeless cause

When the situation in Tunisia deteriorated, Guderian asked that tank crews – particularly the commanders and technicians who now had years of experience behind them – be flown out, especially as a large number of older tanks were being returned to Italy empty. The request was denied and valuable new tanks, including the newest Tiger battalion, were being shipped to North Africa to be thrown away in what was now an increasingly hopeless cause.

Guderian visited von Rundstedt in Paris, then moved on to Rouen. His plan was to examine the Atlantic Wall to assess its defences against tank landings, but before he could do that he was summoned back to Munich to discuss plans for a summer offensive in Russia. The chief of the army general staff, General Zeitzler, had prepared a plan to use the new Tiger and Panther tanks to envelop and destroy a large number of Russian divisions in a salient to the west of Kursk. Model argued against this as air reconnaissance photographs showed that the Russians had prepared strong defences there in anticipation of a German pincer movement and

withdrawn most of their mobile force from the salient. Guderian backed Model, pointing out that any such attack would certainly result in a heavy loss of Panzers, just at the time when they should be building up a model reserve to counter the expected Allied landings in the west. It also relied heavily on the use of Panther tanks, which were still suffering from teething troubles that were unlikely to be put right in time. Speer agreed. But von Kluge favoured Zeitzler's plan. There was still bad feeling between Guderian and von Kluge. Later Schmundt showed Guderian a letter in which von Kluge proposed challenging Guderian to a duel and asking Hitler to be his second. Hitler made it clear that he did not want the duel to take place.

Guderian had planned for a new offensive in Russia in 1944 and he asked Hitler why he wanted to attack in the east in 1943.

Keitel said, 'We must attack for political reasons.'

'How many people do you think even know where Kursk is?' asked Guderian. 'It's a matter of profound indifference to the world whether we hold Kursk or not.'

Hitler said Guderian was quite right. Whenever he thought of another attack in the east, his stomach turned over.

Panzer IV production increased and, by April 1943, German manufacturers were producing 1,955 tanks a month. Anti-aircraft defences were stepped up around the tank factories and Guderian suggested that they be moved, but Speer's assistant Herr Saur pointed out that the Allied bombers were concentrating their attacks against aircraft factories and would only attack

Right: Soviet troops advance in the Kursk 'bulge'

the tank plants when the destruction of the aircraft industry was complete.

On 1 May Hitler inspected a wooden model of the Mouse, designed by Professor Porsche. It was to be armed with a 150mm cannon and would weigh 175 tonnes. By the time the changes Hitler wanted were added, it would weigh 200 tonnes. But, like the Ferdinand, the display model did not carry machine guns for close-quarters fighting. Nevertheless everyone else admired the gigantic machine.

Turning tide

Guderian visited his Panzer units and, finally, made a tour of the Atlantic Wall. He was not impressed. When he returned to Berlin, he discovered that the High Command had decided to send the 1st Panzer Division – the first to be equipped with Panthers – to Greece, in case the British made a landing in the Peloponnese. Guderian was outraged that his strongest reserve should be sidelined in this way. But Keitel insisted they were sent and Hitler backed him. It was only

then that one of Guderian's tank officers who had been sent on a reconnaissance mission reported that the narrow mountain tracks and bridges in Greece were not wide enough to take Panthers. Guderian also opposed sending the Panthers to Russia until the problems with their drive and track suspension were overcome.

In June Guderian had a meeting with Rommel in Munich, where they discussed the lessons of the North African campaign. By this time Tunis was lost and Rommel was coming to believe that the day of the Panzer was over. On 10 July the Allies landed in Sicily and on 25 July Mussolini was deposed and imprisoned. It seemed likely that the new Italian government would switch sides, leaving the German homeland vulnerable to attack from the south. But Germany was unable to turn their defences that way because, belatedly, the attack against the Kursk salient had gone ahead. Seven Panzer and two Panzergrenadier divisions had gone in from Orel to the north and one Panzergrenadier and ten Panzer divisions went in from Belgorod in

Soviet troops survey a landscape of wrecked military hardware and battered vehicles in the aftermath of the Battle of Kursk, 1943

the south. What followed was the largest tank battle in history, involving some 6,000 tanks, 4,000 aircraft and 2,000,000 troops.

Guderian visited both fronts and was shocked at the inexperience of the raw recruits fighting there. The equipment was not performing well either. The 90 Porsche Tigers, which were with Model's army to the north, ran short of ammunition. With no machine guns they could not suppress enemy infantry: if they reached the enemy artillery with no infantry support, they were defenceless. Casualties were huge and Model's attack bogged down after 6 miles (10 km). In the south, the attack went better, but it did not succeed in closing off the salient or force the Russians to withdraw.

On 15 July, the Russians began a counter-attack and, on 4 August, Orel had to be evacuated. The same day Belgorod fell. The Russian advance continued and Kharkov was in Russian hands by 23 August.

The Battle of Kursk marked the end of the German offensive capability on the Eastern Front. Large numbers of men were lost, along with their equipment. All the reorganization and

re-equipment of the armoured forces undertaken by Guderian was wasted. It was now doubtful whether the Panzers had enough tanks to hold the Eastern Front, let alone take on the British and Americans if they landed in the west.

After his journey to the Russian Front, Guderian became ill. He was convalescing with his wife in Upper Austria when they heard that their house in Berlin had been bombed. Hitler then made good his promise of giving them a country home. They moved to Deipenhof in the Hohensalza district, where Guderian's wife remained until the Russians arrived in 1945.

While Guderian was in Russia, an attempt was made to halt the production of Panzer IVs and turn the capacity over to building assault guns. The tank turrets, it was proposed, were to be used on pillboxes along the Atlantic Wall. Guderian then had a disagreement with Hitler over the production of anti-aircraft tanks. Guderian wanted them equipped with quadruple 20mm guns which were readily available; Hitler wanted twin 37mm guns which were not. This slowed production once more.

In October 1943, Hitler inspected a wooden

model of the Tiger II, which the Allies called the King Tiger. This was even heavier than the Tiger I and, at 68 tonnes, the heaviest tank to go into service with the Wehrmacht. In action, it was highly successful; however, only 484 were ever made because that month saw the beginning of Allied bombing of the German tank factories. More tank production capacity was lost when, in December 1943, factories stopped making the Czech 38-tonne tank and switched production to tank destroyers – recoilless guns mounted on Czech tank chassis. Defensive weapons were now urgently needed.

Shambles

By the second half of October, the Russians were crossing the Dnieper and in early November they captured Kiev. Hitler launched a counter-offensive to retake Kiev, but it was a shambles. The 25th Panzer Division were called in from France.

The 25th Panzer Division had been formed the previous year in Norway under General von Schell. He had been a colleague of Guderian's in the defence ministry between 1927 and 1930, working on the problems of transporting troops by motor vehicle. He then went to the US where he studied Ford's production techniques. When he returned to Germany, Hitler made him under-secretary of state for transport, but when he tried to persuade the motor industry to adopt new American methods of production he ran into opposition. This damaged Hitler's confidence in him and he was sent to Norway. There he rallied the occupation troops and, with Guderian's help, raised a Panzer division. This was then moved to France, but in October 1943 it was ordered to send 600 of its new vehicles to the 14th Panzer Division on the Eastern Front. As the plan was for the 25th Panzer Division to stay in France for some time, it could make do with inferior French tanks. Before the division had got used to these changes, or even been fully equipped, it was transferred to the Eastern Front. Before they went, Guderian inspected them and reported that their departure should be delayed by at least four weeks so that the division could be re-equipped and complete its training. He was overruled.

Guderian sent them a Tiger battalion, though the battalion was not fully equipped and had no commander. Even so, the 25th had just 30 Panzer IVs and 15 Tigers in all. The anti-tank battalion was light one company of assault guns.

The Russian Josef Stalin II tank which was developed from the heavy KV series

The anti-aircraft battalion was missing a battery. The engineer battalion was missing a bridging column. The artillery regiment had just changed from captured Polish guns to German 100mm guns and light field howitzers, while one battalion moved off without their guns.

On 29 October, the 25th Panzer Division was loaded on to trains and taken east, but no one was sure where it was to disembark. The tracked vehicles and the wheeled gun tractors and armoured troop-carrying vehicles were unloaded at two separate drop-off areas three days' march apart. They then set off towards the assembly area without establishing wireless or telephone communications and commanders had to drive between them to deliver orders.

Before the 25th Panzer Division had been fully assembled at its assembly point, it was ordered into action at Fastov with a number of other units that had been hastily thrown together. Partisans had blown the bridges on the route they were told to take. They bumped into a retreating column of demoralized Luftwaffe personnel. Rain fell and the tracked vehicles got separated from the wheeled column. Before they reached Fastov, they heard from retreating troops that it had fallen. Then they bumped into Russian T-34s. The Panzergrenadier regiments quickly retreated, but one was halted and ordered to dig in. The Russians attacked and destroyed their transports during the night. Von Schell had to ride to the rescue and managed to break through the encircling enemy tanks.

Some elements of the 25th reached the headquarters of XLVII Panzer Corps at Biala Zerkov, 20 miles (32 km) from Fastov. Others fought on, reaching the outskirts of Fastov itself. But they were unable to dislodge the heavy enemy forces there. Soon after, the 25th were ordered to hold a 25-mile (40-km) front, where it was attacked and practically destroyed by an overwhelmingly superior force. The casualties were so high that Hitler and the High Command wanted to disband the division altogether. Later it was rebuilt from scratch. Such tactics do not win battles and soon the Russians were outside Vinnitsa.

Costly decision

As the Germans fell back on the Eastern Front, Hitler maintained a bridgehead across the Dnieper at Nikopol for economic reasons. He wanted to exploit the manganese found there. This bridgehead was extremely costly in terms of casualties. It would have made more operational sense, Guderian pointed out, to pull back and form the Panzer divisions up into a

took a hand, suggesting that Panzer divisions be withdrawn from the front.

While they were being built up to strength again, they would be on hand to fight in the west if needs be.

The proposal won the High Command's approval but the orders they sent to the army groups were equivocal. They said that understrength Panzer divisions should be withdrawn 'as soon as the battle situation made it possible'. Naturally, in the eyes of the army commanders, the intense fighting meant that the battle situation never made it possible.

However, by D-Day – 6 June 1944 – Guderian had ten Panzer and Panzergrenadier divisions ready in the west.

As the war dragged on, Guderian came to believe that the Panzers were wasted in the east. Mobile warfare now favoured the Russians. He believed that the reconstruction of a heavily fortified line of defence along the old frontier between the German and Russian sectors offered the best form of defence. He suggested this to Hitler one day over breakfast.

'The heavy casualties suffered on the Eastern Front left the High Command with no coherent plan'

mobile reserve, but whenever Hitler heard the word 'operational' he lost his temper.

With the 25th Panzer Division sent to the east, Guderian set about creating a mobile defence force on the Western Front in case the Allies invaded. He moved all the demonstration units from the tank schools to France and formed them into the Panzer-*Lehr* (Panzer Teaching) Division. Its commander was General Fritz Bayerlein who had been Guderian's first operations officer in Russia and had then gone on to distinguish himself in North Africa.

The heavy casualties suffered on the Eastern Front left the High Command with no coherent plan to build up forces in the west for the invasion they were sure would come in spring 1944. Guderian again

Perhaps the most powerful tank of the war, the 68-tonne King Tiger was hard to kill

Hitler said:

Believe me, I am the greatest builder of fortifications of all time. I built the West Wall; I built the Atlantic Wall. I know what building fortifications involves. On the Eastern Front, we are short of labour, materials and transport. Even now the railways cannot carry enough supplies to satisfy the demands of the front. So I cannot send trains to the east full of building supplies.

Guderian disagreed. He said that the only railway bottleneck was at Brest-Litovsk. In Poland there were plenty of materials and labour. But Hitler's real concern was that, if he built an East Wall, his commanders at the front would retreat to it. He was still determined that not an inch of ground should be given up.

'I can't understand why everything has gone wrong for the past two years,' he often said to Guderian.

'Change your methods,' said Guderian. He was ignored.

Even Rommel had changed his mind about tactics. Meeting Bayerlein at Hitler's headquarters in East Prussia in July 1943, he said that Germany had lost the initiative.

He told Bayerlein:

We have just learnt in Russia that dash and over-optimism are not enough. There can be no question of taking the offensive for the next few years, either in the west or the east, so we must try to make the most of the advantages that normally accrue to the defence. The main defence against the tank is the anti-tank gun. In the air we must build more fighters and give up all idea of

bombing. I no longer see things as black as I did in Africa, but total victory is now, of course, hardly a possibility.

All this was before the Battle of Kursk had ended in disaster. Bayerlein asked how Rommel saw defence in practical terms. Like Guderian, Rommel thought that they should withdraw to a prepared defensive line. If they could prevent the Western Allies creating a second front, then he thought the Russians could be defeated. He said:

If we can only keep the Americans and the British off for two more years to enable us to build up centres of gravity in the east again, then our time will come. We'll be able to start drawing blood from the Russians once more, until they allow the initiative to pass once more back to us. Then we'll be able to get a tolerable peace.

Hitler had told Rommel that Germany would be producing 7,000 aircraft and 2,000 tanks a month by the beginning of 1944. But the key to victory, he thought, lay with the anti-tank gun.

'Remember how difficult we found it to attack the British anti-tank screens in Africa,' he told Bayerlein. 'It needed first-class, highly trained troops to achieve anything at all against them.'

Rommel had made a careful study of the position in Russia and concluded that the Russian soldier was stubborn and inflexible.

He will never be able to develop the well-thought-out, guileful method with which the Englishman fights his battles. The Russian attacks head on, with enormous expenditure of material, and tries to smash

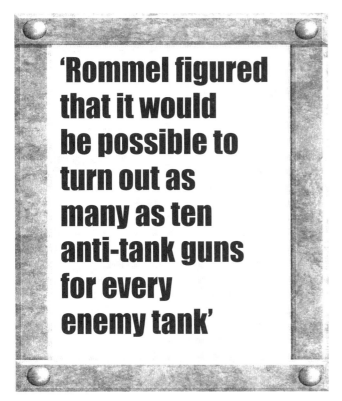

'Rommel figured that it would be possible to turn out as many as ten anti-tank guns for every enemy tank'

his way through by sheer weight of numbers. If we can give the German infantry divisions first fifty, then a hundred, then two hundred 75mm anti-tank guns and install them in carefully prepared positions, covered by large minefields, we shall be able to halt the Russians. The anti-tank guns can be quite simple; all that is necessary is that they should be able to penetrate any Russian tank up to a reasonable range and at the same time be usable as an infantry gun.

Fresh hope

While there was no chance that Germany could keep pace with the Russian output of tanks, they could compete in

anti-tank guns. Rommel figured that it would be possible to turn out as many as ten anti-tank guns for every tank. He envisaged the Russians attacking a heavily mined sector where there was an anti-tank screen some 6 miles (10 km) deep. 'For all their mass of materiel,' he said, 'they would bog down in the first few days and, from then have to gnaw their way through slowly.'

In the meantime, the Germans would deploy more anti-tank guns behind their screen.

'If the enemy makes 3 miles' (5 km) progress a day, we'll build 6 miles (10 km) of anti-tank screen and let him run himself to a standstill,' Rommel said. 'We'll be fighting in the cover of our positions; he'll be attacking in the open.'

And while the Germans would be losing anti-tank guns, the Russians would be losing tanks, which were far more costly to replace.

'To move the guns we can use Russian horses or anything else we can lay our hands on. That's what the Russians do and we must adopt their methods.

The Joseph Stalin II tanks would become a target for the numerous new anti-tank guns

Fighting in the Crimea in December 1943 – the Red Army landed on the peninsula with the intention of forcing out the Germans

'Once it becomes clear to the troops that they can hold their ground, morale will go up again… Our last chance in the East lies in equipping the army thoroughly for unyielding defence.'

But no one was listening.

The year 1944 started with fresh attacks by the Russians who could now deploy T-34s in overwhelming numbers. In the Ukraine the Germans faced 63 tank formations backed by 101 rifle formations. Two attacks in January and a third at the beginning of March pushed the Germans back across the Bug.

In April the Crimea, with the exception of Sebastopol, found itself in Russian hands. Sebastopol fell in August.

To the north, the situation was not quite so dire. But the siege of Leningrad was finally lifted on 27 January 1944, after 900 days.

8. TIGERS IN NORMANDY

When von Arnim took over in North Africa, Rommel had found himself disgraced. He was bitter in his criticism of the High Command and Hitler himself, which came as a shock to his son Manfred who was then a committed member of the Hitler Youth. However, a few days before the fall of Tunis, Rommel received a phone call ordering him to report to Hitler's headquarters. Seeing Hitler's political and military leadership up close led to his final disillusionment with the Nazi Party, his son said.

Bleak outlook

When he arrived in Berlin, he was greeted by Hitler who looked pale and shaken.

'I should have listened to you before,' he said. 'But I suppose it is too late now. It will soon all be over in Tunisia.'

A few days later it was announced that the Army Group Afrika had surrendered. Later Rommel drew comfort from the fact that his Panzer troops were the prisoners of the Western Allies, rather than being sacrificed in the senseless slaughter on the Eastern Front. But at the time, the loss of his men in Tunisia left a deep scar.

While Guderian had never wanted a war with the Russians, Rommel had never wanted a war with the West. By 1943, Rommel had come to believe that the war was unwinnable. Hitler thought so too, Rommel confided to his family, but his enemies would not make peace with him. The Allies demanded unconditional surrender, and as British and American bombers filled the skies over Germany, Hitler whipped himself up into a pathological impotent hatred.

'If the German people are incapable of winning the war,' he told Rommel one night in July 1943, 'then they can rot.'

The best were already dead, according to Hitler. If he was to be beaten, he would fight for every house. Nothing would be left. The German people must die heroically – it was 'a historic necessity'.

Top: The US landings in Sicily, Operation *Husky*

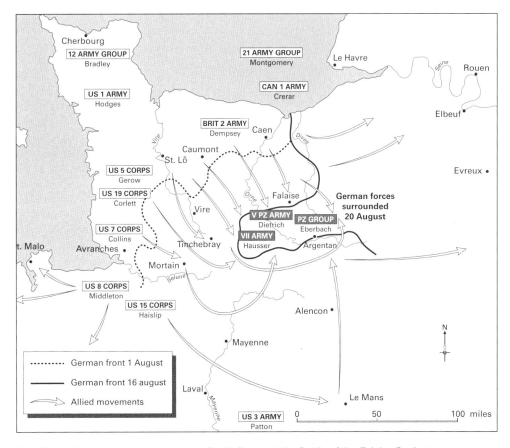

The Allied advance through Normandy after D-Day, and the Battle of the Falaise Pocket

'Sometimes you feel that he is no longer quite normal,' said Rommel.

Even so, Rommel had been brought up in the tradition of the German officer and he was deeply imbued with the idea that he must obey a superior without question. But his commitment to the Nazi ideal was shaken. When Manfred told his father that he wanted to join the Waffen-SS, his father told him that it was out of the question.

'I don't want you serving under the command of a man who carried out mass killings,' he said. It was plain that Rommel meant Himmler.

In Rommel's conversations with Bayerlein in East Prussia about how to defeat the Russians, he made one thing clear.

'The west is the place that matters,' he said. 'If we once manage to throw the British and Americans back into the sea, it will be a long

time before they return. If we can make their efforts fail, then things will be brighter for us.'

On the morning of 10 July 1943, when British and American forces landed in Sicily, Rommel was in line to be Commander in Chief in Italy, but the Luftwaffe had blocked his appointment. However, a British disinformation campaign now led Hitler to believe that the British were planning to make landings in Greece and Rommel was made Commander in Chief, South-east, with command over all the German and Italian forces in the Balkans.

Sicily was defended by four divisions of Italian infantry and six coast guard divisions, none of whom wanted to fight. Also present were the 15th Panzer Division, recently constituted after the debacle in North Africa, and the Panzer Division *Hermann Göring*. The 15th had just sixty tanks, while the *Hermann Göring* had 100 tanks, including 17 Tigers. They pushed the Americans back to the beaches, but the Allied build-up could not be halted and the XIV Panzer Corps had to be brought in to hold the line.

Fearing that the capitulation of Italy would leave the precious Tigers stranded there, Guderian requested that they be withdrawn

resistance of the Panzers allowed the Germans to pull out 100,000 men and 9,800 vehicles, including 50 tanks, before the Allies landed on the Italian mainland at the beginning of September. Italy was not natural tank country and Rommel thought that the German forces should pull back to a defensive line in the Apennines. But Hitler would not hear of it. Instead he sent the LXXVI Panzer Corps, which included the 16th and 26th Panzer Divisions, to repel the landings. But Panzers were not strong enough to fight off the Allies. At Salerno, the 16th Panzer Division was allotted a 30-mile (48-km) sector to defend. They inflicted heavy casualties, but never had any hope of pushing the British and Americans back into the sea.

Indecision

Italy switched sides on 13 October 1943 and Rommel supervised the disarming of the Italian troops. In mid-November, Hitler decided that Rommel should take over as commander in chief in Italy. But while the orders were being sent, he changed his mind. Instead Rommel would go to Normandy to oversee the defences there. The Panzers fought on in Italy though, first holding the Gustav Line 60 miles (96 km) south of Rome. This was broken at the end of May in 1944. Tigers and Panthers were also deployed on a second defensive line, 200 miles (320 km) to the north. But largely they were used as mobile gun emplacements. The Panzers were not cut out for this kind of static, defensive warfare in mountainous terrain.

They were also outclassed and outnumbered on the Eastern Front. But the Western Allies still had nothing that could match the Tiger tank and, in the west, after the D-Day landings, the

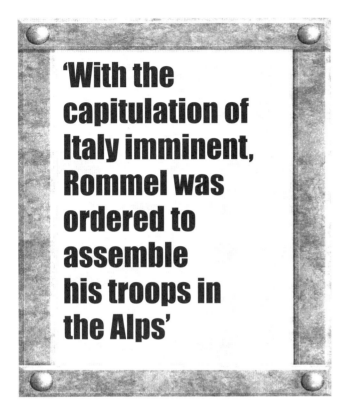

> 'With the capitulation of Italy imminent, Rommel was ordered to assemble his troops in the Alps'

to the mainland. Göring said, 'But Tigers can't pole-vault across the Straits of Messina, General Guderian. You must realize that.'

'If you have won air supremacy over Sicily as you say,' replied Guderian, 'the Tigers can come back from Sicily the same way they went in.'

Two weeks after the Allied invasion of Sicily, Mussolini fell from power. Rommel was not unhappy to see the back of him.

'It suits us in some ways, of course, to have only one big man running Europe,' he wrote to his wife.

With the capitulation of Italy imminent, Rommel was ordered to assemble his troops in the Alps, ready to drive into Italy. Rommel was ordered to cross the Brenner and take the Alpine passes, but he found the new Tigers did not work well on concrete roads. One overturned; another caught fire.

Overwhelming Allied air superiority forced the Germans to withdraw from Sicily. The tenacious

British bren-carriers coming ashore near Salerno in 1943 from a US Navy tank-landing ship, later sunk by the Germans off Cherbourg

Panzers still stood a chance of pushing the great Allied invasion force back into the sea. Instead, Rommel was to experience his last great defeat at the head of a Panzer Army.

Guderian was also involved in the defence of Normandy. In February 1944, he had toured the area and realized that the task of defending France against an invading army would be all the more difficult because the Allies had total superiority at sea and in the air. This was brought home forcefully to Guderian when he was out on a tank training exercise.

'Whole formations of hostile aircraft manoeuvred above our troops,' he said. 'There was no telling when the bomb bays might open to discharge their loads on the training area.'

In meetings with Field Marshal von Rundstedt and General von Geyr, it was decided that the defence of France depended on preparing adequate reserves of Panzers and Panzergrenadiers. To be effective, these must be positioned far enough inland so that they could easily be moved to the main invasion front, once it had been recognized.

The French road network would need to be repaired and they would have to prepare alternative river crossings, with underwater bridges and bridges of boats, as the Allies would be sure to bomb the bridges. And for the Panzers to achieve sufficient speed and concentration, they would have to move only at night.

Back at Supreme Headquarters, Guderian studied the plans drawn up by the High Command and found that the Panzer divisions that were the principal reserve were to be stationed very near to the coast. That meant that they could not be withdrawn and deployed elsewhere quickly if the landing did not come in the expected place. Guderian pointed this out to Hitler, who said, 'The present arrangement was suggested by Field Marshal Rommel. I don't like to give contradictory orders over the head of the field marshal on the spot without having heard his opinion first. Go back to France and discuss the matter with Rommel.'

In the west, as in the east, Rommel no longer believed that victory could be gained by mobile warfare. Like Guderian he saw the difficulties that Allied air superiority caused the Panzers. But he also saw that the German armaments industry could no longer keep pace with the Allies' output of tanks, guns, anti-tank guns and other vehicles.

Bombarding London

Rommel believed that the invasion would come across the Straits of Dover to the Pas de Calais, because this was where Hitler intended the V1 sites to be. These were flying bombs, the forerunner of modern cruise missiles that were to be launched against London in June 1944. The Germans were also building large guns in the Pas de Calais that would be able to bombard London. Once these long-range attacks were launched they would take such a toll on London that the Allies would have to attack via the quickest route. Rommel believed that these long-range attacks should be launched when the weather in the Channel was bad. The invasion force would then either have to sit in England and watch London be destroyed, or risk trying to cross the Channel in adverse weather conditions.

After inspecting the Atlantic Wall in December 1943, Rommel had concluded that it was too thinly held to hold off a concerted attack and would be quickly penetrated. He said:

We know from experience that the British soldier is quick to consolidate his gains and then holds on tenaciously with excellent

support from his superior air arm and naval guns. The enemy will probably succeed in creating bridgeheads at several different points and in achieving a major penetration of our coastal defences. Once this has happened it will only be by the rapid intervention of our operational reserves that he will be thrown back into the sea. This requires that these forces should be held very close behind the defences.

Rommel argued that if the Panzers were held well back inland, it would take too long to bring them up, allowing the Allies to establish a foothold. They would also be very vulnerable to air attack as they made their way to the front.

By comparison with the British and Americans, the troops holding the Atlantic Wall were badly armed and poorly trained. The only way to defeat the Allies, he concluded, was to abandon mobile warfare completely. What was needed was a mined and fortified zone extending 5 or 6 miles (8–9 km) inland from the coast, with small gaps in it to counter-attack through. Again he was applying the lessons he had learned with his Panzers in North Africa.

'We have learnt with our engagements with the British that large minefields with isolated strongpoints dispersed within them are extremely difficult to take. Moreover, mined zones of this kind lend themselves particularly well to garrisoning by auxiliary troops or reserve formations' – which was practically all they had in the west as all the crack units had been sent to the Eastern Front. He recommended deepening the defences immediately and asked for some 200 million mines to be sent to France.

He organized the construction of twenty million in France itself. But only just over four million had been laid by D-Day.

Rommel now envisaged a stationary role for his Panzers. Tanks were to be dug in as strongpoints in these minefields. The enemy landing force making its way from the beaches, or airborne troops infiltrating from behind, would have to cross these minefields under the Panzers' guns.

Preparing a reception

He also oversaw the laying of obstacles along the foreshore and in the rear to defend against airborne landings. Ten-foot stakes fitted with captured shells were designed to inflict heavy losses on paratroopers or troops landing in gliders. Meanwhile Rommel found himself a billet in the château that once belonged to Madame de Pompadour at Fontainebleau, where he stayed with the two dachshunds presented to him by the Organisation Todt, who were building the fortifications along the Atlantic Wall. They howled at night because, Rommel thought, they were homesick for their previous owner.

Rommel grew fearful of the situation on the Eastern Front and in Italy. He was also worried that his only son Manfred was now leaving home to join the army. On 27 April 1944, he wrote home to his wife saying, 'Guderian is due here this afternoon.'

Guderian was on his way from the tank depot at Camp de Mailly, which was completely destroyed by an Allied air raid. Fortunately General von Geyr had moved much of the equipment out of the depot and scattered it throughout the nearby villages and woods. But once again, Guderian had been given a vivid demonstration of the effects of Allied air power.

In their discussion, Rommel said that he did not even think that it would be possible to move Panzer and Panzergrenadier divisions at night. And he rejected the arguments advanced by Guderian and von Geyr that a Panzer reserve needed to be kept inland. Guderian pointed out that, as the Allies had overwhelming superiority in the air and at sea, the only way to win was to destroy the enemy in a large-scale Panzer operation on land. Rommel thought this was impossible.

He maintained that the secret of using armour was to concentrate all its strength at the right spot. He had already decided that the Allied landings would be north of the Somme in Pas de Calais, so his Panzer force was concentrated there, rather than in two mobile groups, one north and one south of Paris, as Guderian and von Geyr suggested.

'On all these points Rommel's views coincided with those of Hitler, though on different grounds [wrote Guderian].

'Hitler had remained a man of the 1914–18 trench-warfare epoch and never understood the principles of mobile operations. Rommel believed that such operations were no longer possible because of the enemy's air superiority. Small wonder that the Commander in Chief, West [von Rundstedt] and I found that Hitler turned down our proposals for the redistribution of our motorized formations, on the grounds that Rommel had more recent experience of battle than either of us.'

Rommel dismissed the ideas of Guderian and von Geyr because their experience came from the Eastern Front. Fighting the Western Allies,

Rommel believed, was fundamentally different.

Rommel told Fritz Bayerlein:

Our friends from the East cannot imagine what they're in for here. It's not a matter of fanatical hordes being driven forward in masses against our line with no regard for casualties and little recourse to tactical craft. Here we are facing an enemy who applies all his native intelligence to the use of his many technical resources, who spares no expenditure of material and whose every operation goes its course as though it had been the subject of repeated rehearsal. Dash and doggedness alone no longer make a soldier, Bayerlein. He must have sufficient intelligence to enable him to get the most out of his fighting machine.

Rommel was aware of the irony of the situation.

'At one time they looked on mobile warfare as something to keep clear of at all costs,' he said, 'but now that our freedom of manoeuvre in the west is gone, they're all crazy for it… The day of the dashing cut-and-thrust tank attack of the early war years is past and gone – and that goes for the east too.'

Dissenting voices

Rommel had problems with his own staff officers who were inclined to Guderian and von Geyr's view that mobile warfare was still possible and did not believe that the enemy's air force could exercise so great an influence over what happened on the ground.

However, Rommel persisted in his belief that the only hope lay in concentrating the Panzers on the coast.

'If in spite of the enemy's air superiority, we succeed in getting a large part of our mobile defence into action in the threatened coastal defence sectors in the first few hours, I am convinced that the enemy attack on the coast will collapse completely on the first day,' he wrote to General Jodl on 23 April 1944. He went on to say that his only real anxiety was these mobile forces, which had not yet been put under his command, as promised, and were too widely dispersed to play any part in the battle for the coast. The situation did not improve.

On 6 June 1944, there were ten Panzer and

Tiger E belonging to the *Adolf Hitler* SS Division, Normandy 1944

Panzergrenadier divisions in France. Four – the 2nd, 21st, 116th and 12th SS Panzer Divisions – were under Rommel's command. The 1st SS, Panzer-*Lehr* and the 17th SS Panzergrenadiers were in reserve and under the personal control of Hitler, while the 9th, 11th and 2nd SS Panzer Divisions were in the south of France ready for any invasion along the Mediterranean coast.

'This dispersal of strength ruled out all

possibility of a great defensive victory,' said Guderian. 'But apart from that, events took the most unsatisfactory course imaginable.'

Firstly Rommel was not in France on D-Day. He was on his way to a conference with Hitler in East Prussia and he had stopped off in Germany to visit his wife on her birthday. He had left orders that the 21st Panzer Division, which was nearest to the Normandy beaches, was not to counter-attack without his permission. Hitler had gone to bed late and could not be disturbed when first news of the invasion came. Without his permission, the Panzers in reserve could not be released. And, still fearful of a Mediterranean landing, the three Panzer divisions in the south of France stayed where they were and did not begin moving north.

However, the Panzer-*Lehr* Division did receive orders to advance, which it did so in daylight, despite the enemy's air superiority. But with Rommel away, there was no one in command who knew anything about tank tactics and it was ordered to make a frontal attack in an area in range of the Royal Navy's guns.

'Thus Germany's sole possible military force for defeating the invasion was prematurely ground down,' wrote Guderian.

The Panzer-*Lehr* took enormous casualties which could not be made good as, after 22 June, the Eastern Front threatened to collapse and all available replacements were sent there.

Things did not get better when Hitler awoke. He was not convinced that the attack on the Normandy beaches was the main landing and refused to release the Panzer reserves. However the 21st Panzer Division did manage to frustrate Montgomery's plan to take Caen on the first day.

When Rommel returned to France he found, as predicted, it was impossible to bring up the Panzers because of the danger of enemy air attack.

'Even the movement of minor formations on the battlefield – artillery going into position, tanks forming up, etc – is instantly attacked from the air with devastating effect,' he wrote on 10 June. He believed the Allies were flying 27,000 sorties a day, though Liddell Hart put the maximum at just over 10,000. It was not just the tanks that were in danger. On 10 June the staff of Panzer Group West was put out of action by a bombing raid.

Total confusion

On 16 June the 9th Panzer Division was at Avignon, the 11th Panzer Division was in the Bordeaux area, the 116th Panzer Division was still on the coast well to the north near Dieppe and the 2nd SS Panzer Division *Das Reich* was fighting guerrillas in southern France. The 2nd Panzer Division had been sent into action, but piecemeal. And the 9th *Hohenstaufen* and 10th *Frundsberg* SS Panzer Divisions had been brought across from the Eastern Front. But, again, their strength was being wasted in frontal attacks within the range of the Allies' naval guns and they fell into a trap set for them by Montgomery, committing seven of the nine Panzer divisions into the Caen sector to face the British and Canadians, allowing the Americans to the west to break out.

On 17 June Hitler came to France for a conference with Rommel and von Rundstedt at Soissons. Rommel suggested pulling back the Panzer divisions that were currently engaging

D-Day: US troops from the First Division wade ashore on Omaha beach – defences were unexpectedly strong and many lives were lost

the enemy and assembling them to the south, so that they could attack the enemy's flank out of range of the naval guns. It was also suggested that Hitler visit the front and speak to the commanders there, as Churchill had on the Allied side a few days before. The following morning, an errant V-1 landed near Hitler's headquarters. He left for Germany immediately, dismissing Rommel's proposal and saying that victory would come by 'holding tenaciously to every yard of soil'.

Rommel and Guderian met one last time in Berchtesgaden, Hitler's retreat in the Obersalzberg on 29 June at a conference for the commanders on the Western Front. Guderian said:

'I again received the impression that I had gained at his headquarters at La Roche-Guyon the previous April – that as a result of the enemy's air supremacy Rommel no longer believed mobile defence was possible.' This seems to have been Hitler's view too. The principal matter discussed at the conference was the strengthening of the Luftwaffe and anti-aircraft defences. Göring promised to supply 800 planes, but only 500 crews were available. There were to be attacks on enemy shipping and Hitler ordered, 'The immediate provision of 1,000 jet fighters from new production, in order to achieve air superiority over a limited area for at least a few days a week.'

In reality, the jet fighters were not ready for use. Although 1,988 Messerschmitt 262s were built before the end of the war, they saw little action.

Rommel came right out and asked Hitler how he envisaged the war could still be won. He expected to get fired. Instead von Rundstedt was sacked and von Kluge was brought in from the Eastern Front to take over as Commander in Chief in the West. He immediately criticized Rommel's handling of the Western Front.

On 5 July 1944, Rommel wrote to von Kluge saying, 'The rebuke which you levelled at me at the beginning of your visit, in the presence of my Chief of Staff, to the effect that I, too, "will now have to get accustomed to carrying out orders", has deeply wounded me. I request you to notify me what grounds you have for making such an accusation.'

A copy was forwarded to Hitler.

Rommel also requested that the 12th SS Panzer Division *Hitlerjugend* be moved to the area around Lessay-Coutances so that it could counter-attack the enemy in the Cotentin Peninsula. In a 14-point memorandum he complained that none of the Panzer divisions were in the positions that he had requested before the invasion and concluded by saying, 'Only unified, close-knit command of all services, after the pattern of Montgomery and Eisenhower, will vouchsafe final victory.'

The future US president General Dwight D. Eisenhower was in nominal command of the Allied invasion after heading the Anglo-American invasion of French North Africa. He had since directed the landings in Sicily and Italy. Rommel's old adversary Montgomery was the Allied commander on the ground in Normandy. He too had seen action in Sicily and Italy.

After a tour of the front, von Kluge quickly conceded that Rommel was right.

Armour and motorized troops could only be moved at night or in bad weather, although, with sufficient anti-aircraft defence, small armoured groups could go into action in daylight.

However, the Germans had managed to hold on to Caen, stopping the British breaking out to the east and making a dash for Paris. But Montgomery was about to do something about that. On the night of 7 July, the RAF dropped 2,300 tonnes of bombs on Caen, destroying much of the city. Largely they missed the German defensive positions but the raid raised the British troops' morale. Many of the bombs had time-delay fuses that were set to go off as the British and Canadians attacked at 0420 hours the following morning, supported by another huge bombardment. The bombing and shelling practically wiped out the 12th SS Panzers. As the British and Canadians moved into Caen, Montgomery then ordered the Americans on his right flank to push southwards. The British then started Operation *Goodwood*. Following another carpet bombing of the city, they would push on through Caen, then engage the Panzers in the open tank country to the east of the city and keep them away from the American breakout.

Rommel strafed

On 17 July Rommel's car was shot up by a British fighter. He was flung from the car and cracked his skull. After a period in hospital, he returned to Germany to convalesce. During that time, he changed his mind about the desirability of the *coup d'état* that some officers in the army were planning. He had not favoured the removal of Hitler when Germany was only fighting on the Russian Front as it might have precipitated a collapse of the front, leaving the Russians streaming across Europe. But now the British and Americans would be able to stop them.

A US-built Sherman tank advances cautiously for fear of lurking Tigers

Until the end of June, most officers in the army still thought that they could hold off any British and American invasion long enough for new weapons – jet planes, new tanks and the much-vaunted secret weapons – that would swing the war back in Germany's favour. And if they had repelled the invasion, they thought the Western Allies would have dropped the requirement for unconditional surrender, made peace and, possibly, even joined in fighting the Russians on the Eastern Front, rather than see the whole of the Continent fall to Stalin and communism.

But now that the Western Allies had secured a bridgehead in France that could not be dislodged, the only way to make peace was to get rid of Hitler. On 20 July, General Claus von Stauffenberg attempted to blow up Hitler in his headquarters in East Prussia. The attempt failed. Stauffenberg was summarily executed that night. Rommel was also implicated, but allowed to take his own life.

After the assassination attempt, Hitler appointed Guderian chief of the general staff.

However, he was denied any authority to make decisions. Hitler had to approve everything in detail. When he proposed that he be given the authority to make decisions in all but the matters of most fundamental importance, Keitel and Jodl opposed him. Then he asked Hitler whether he could have a word in private with him about this matter. His request was denied. So Guderian became a front-row spectator at the destruction of the Panzer Army he had spent over twenty years of his life creating.

The situation in the east was dire. Army Group South had been holding its own in the Ukraine, but to the north the Russians had broken through on 12 July and by 21 July they had reached Brest-Litovsk on the Bug. Twenty-five divisions of Army Group Centre had been lost, while Army Group North was in full retreat from the Gulf of Finland. Guderian suggested that all the divisions being held in reserve in Romania be brought in to plug the gaps in the line. Hitler agreed. The Germans then evacuated the Baltic states, shortening the line and the Russian advance was halted along the Vistula. The Germans had the impression, at the time, that it was their defence that stopped the Russians. In fact, they halted because there was an uprising in Warsaw led by Poles who supported the government in exile in London. The Soviets wanted this uprising to be suppressed by the Germans to rid Poland of the remaining pro-Western sympathizers so that it would be easier to install a new pro-Soviet regime.

On 18 July, the Canadians liberated Caen. The British armour moved on to the east of the city only to find German resistance heavier than expected. On 20 July, while Montgomery was announcing the success of Operation *Goodwood*, the British armour was halted by German anti-tank guns. In the ensuing battle 413 tanks – 36 per cent of the British Second Army's armour – was destroyed. The British had progressed just 7 miles (11 km) at a rate, Eisenhower said, of a thousand tons of bombs a mile.

Stout resistance

Despite the destruction of the British armour, Montgomery's overall strategy worked. The Germans committed the Fifteenth Army's last armoured division, the 116th Panzer Division, to the Caen section, leaving America's four armoured divisions and 13 infantry divisions facing just two armoured divisions and seven infantry divisions. However when the American armour advanced it met fierce opposition from the 1st and 9th SS Panzer Divisions astride the Caen–Falaise road. The advance had to be called off after twenty-hours. On 25 July, a new offensive began with saturation bombing, which destroyed all of the Panzer-*Lehr*'s tanks and killed two-thirds of its men. After three days of rapid advance, the Second Armoured Division – 'Hell on Wheels' – broke through into open country. The remaining Panzers were pulled out of the Caen area and sent to close the gap, but they could only move slowly due to lack of fuel. By this time, Hitler had realized that no attack was coming on the Pas de Calais and he released Panzer reserves who moved westwards.

On 3 August Hitler ordered that Panzers holding the line between the River Orne and the town of Vire be replaced with infantry

The aftermath of US air force attacks on German columns, Falaise

divisions, freeing the armour to push westwards to Avranches and cutting in two the American forces under General Patton breaking out to the south. But instead of heading for Brittany as originally planned, Patton circled around to the south-east, outflanking the Panzers that Hitler was sending against Avranches.

By this time the German army was falling apart. However, when the Panzers turned and fought they often showed a tactical superiority, and their technically superior tanks could bring an Allied advance grinding to a halt. As they pulled back inland where the countryside was flatter, the fighting became more mobile, which suited

Right: Badly damaged Tiger I and Panzer IV at Villers Bocage

the Panzers. This was the kind of warfare they were used to. However, there had been another breakthrough in warfare that the Panzers knew nothing about.

The British codebreakers at Bletchley Park had broken the German military codes. So when Panzer commanders sent their orders by radio, the British could listen in and it became impossible to concentrate sufficient Panzers to mount a counter-attack without attracting an air strike. Fuel was running low, resulting in tanks having to be abandoned, and ammunition was scarce, particularly for anti-tank guns.

Somehow Hitler mustered 185 tanks and threw them at the American VII Corps in Mortain. This was exactly the kind of armoured attack that Rommel had said was doomed, given the Allies' air power. No one, with the exception of Hitler, had any faith in the plan. The commander of

the 116th Panzer Division had to be replaced when he refused to join the attack. Although British codebreakers gave the Allies a few hours' warning of the attack, the Germans managed to take Mortain and, briefly, held the high ground to the east of the town. But by the evening of 7 August, 40 of the 70 German tanks spearheading the attack had been destroyed and the armoured column ran out of fuel after just 5 miles (8 km). Meanwhile Patton was speeding through France and by 8 August had taken Le Mans.

That same day, Michael Wittmann, Germany's Panzer ace, was killed. During the war he had knocked out 138 tanks and 132 anti-tank guns, along with countless half-tracks and soft-skinned vehicles. On 12 June, at the head of four Tigers and one Panzer IV, he had held up the entire British 7th Armoured Division at Villers Bocage, destroying 25 British tanks and knocking out

numerous infantry carriers. Although eventually ambushed in the narrow streets and his Tiger put out of action by an anti-tank gun, he and his men escaped on foot.

Death of a German hero

On 8 August, he was not so lucky though. At St Aignan-de-Cramesnil, south of Caen, his three remaining Tigers came up against the Shermans of the 1st Northants Yeomanry. The Tigers outclassed Shermans, but the Northants Yeomanry had a Sherman Firefly, which was fitted with a British 17-pounder gun. This was the only gun the Allies had capable of penetrating the Tiger's heavy armour, though it had to be closer than 1,000 metres.

Colonel Tom Boardman, second in command of A Squadron, said:

When the Tigers were about 1,000 yards (910 m) from us and broadside on to us, I told 3 Troop and my gunner to fire. The Firefly did the damage, but our 75mms helped and must have taken the track off one, which started to circle out of control. They shot back at us, putting the Firefly temporarily out as its commander was hit on the head. However, at the end of a very few minutes there were three killed Tigers and as nobody was seen to bale out, presumably the crews were killed.

In 1983, Wittmann's identity disc was discovered, along with assorted shreds of uniform and bone found in the area and it has now been established that Wittmann and his three Tiger tanks were the victims of Number 3 Troop, A Squadron, 1st Northamptonshire Yeomanry.

Exhausted young German conscripts are taken into custody

On 9 August, Hitler ordered the stalled Panzers to hold their position where they, along with the rest of the army, could easily be encircled. Briefing Hitler on 15 August, Guderian said ruefully, 'The bravery of the Panzer troops is not enough to make up for the failure of the other two services – the air force and the navy.'

While the British and Canadians pushed south-east, cutting off the German retreat, Patton was told to turn northward, closing the trap. The two jaws of the pincers closed around Falaise, with the Canadians taking the town on 16 August. The German Seventh Army and their Panzer support were now caught in a pocket.

Their only way out was through the 12-mile (19-km) gap between Falaise and Argentan. The Germans were not unduly worried by this encirclement. Panzer groups had been surrounded before on the Eastern Front and had fought their way out. The Soviets, however, had not possessed the air power that the Allies used to pound the trapped armour.

Hitler decided to make a counter-attack against

Right: The French army returns to France amid much jubilation

the Americans at Argentan and assembled Panzer Group Eberbach, under General Eberbach. But by the time it was in place, it had just 45 tanks and 4,000 men. Meanwhile Field Marshal von Kluge, commander of Army Group B, went missing after his car was attacked by a fighter-bomber. Worse news was to come. On 15 August, the Allies made landings in the South of France, tying up further Panzer reserves there.

On 16 August von Kluge reappeared at his headquarters in Normandy and reported that the Falaise Pocket could not be held. Hitler finally agreed to a withdrawal but it was too late. The following day a renewed push by the Canadians and the Americans closed the Falaise gap to just a few hundred yards and, despite fierce fighting, on 20 August, it was closed altogether. Von Kluge was sacked. Hitler believed that, in the

time he had been missing, von Kluge had been in contact with the enemy. Summoned to the Wolf's Lair, he committed suicide. Model replaced him, but there was little he could do. Eberbach managed to extract some of his Panzers from the Falaise Pocket. Those that remained were pulverized by Allied bombing. Resistance ceased on 22 August. Some 10,000 German soldiers were dead and 50,000 had surrendered. Only 20,000 escaped. They left behind 7,700 wrecked or abandoned vehicles in the pocket, not including 567 tanks or self-propelled guns, along with 950 abandoned field guns. The remnants of the eight Panzer battle groups who had escaped could only muster seventy tanks and 36 field guns between them. They fled for the German border which was now being fortified by women, old men and young boys.

9. LAST GASP IN THE ARDENNES

The Panzers were going to have one last chance to show what they could do. Although the German army was in full retreat on all fronts, the situation was not completely hopeless. Even Hitler realized that victory was no longer within his grasp. But he thought that if one decisive battle went in his favour he might be able to force the Allies to the negotiating table.

In early September Montgomery's attack on the bridge at Arnhem had proved 'a bridge too far' and Hitler realized that the Allies with their over-extended supply lines could still be halted, especially if they were denied the ports of northern Europe. He still had hopes of being able to persuade the British and Americans to negotiate a separate peace, and then combine with Germany to crush the Red Army.

Last-gasp strategy

The plan was to collect the remaining strength of the German army and throw it at the place where the British and American forces met in an area that was only lightly defended. A sweeping attack would sever the Americans' supply lines and cut off the British in Belgium and Holland, where they could be encircled and destroyed. Hitler planned the operation for mid-November, so that he would have time to move his forces back to the Eastern Front, ready for the anticipated Russian winter offensive. The operation was called *Wacht am Rhein* (Watch on the Rhine) and it would put at risk twenty German divisions. If it succeeded it would weaken the Western Allies and shatter their hope of total victory, drop their insistence on unconditional surrender and open peace negotiations. If it failed, there would be no stopping the Anglo-American army.

Hitler and his closest aides planned the operation in secret. When von Rundstedt, who had recently been reinstated as commander in the west, heard about it he was horrified. He and Model proposed a more modest objective: an offensive that stopped at the Meuse and sought only to defeat the Allied forces that lay to the east of the river between Aachen and Liége. Guderian said simply that the forces available 'lacked the

Left: The Shermans of the 74th Tank Battalion helped rout the 1st Panzers

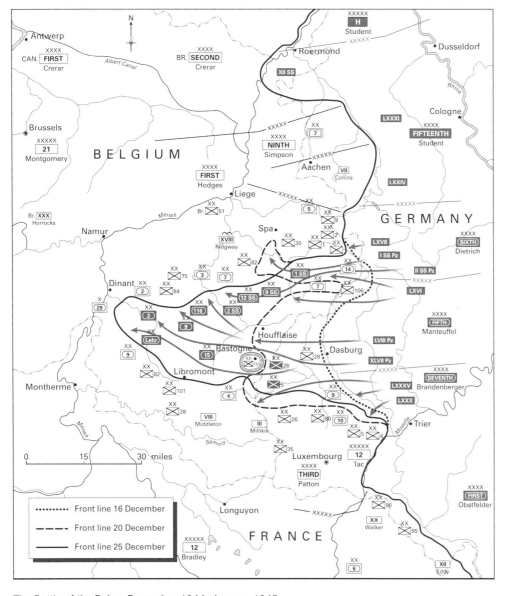

The Battle of the Bulge, December 1944–January 1945

on large numbers of men in 1940. Now, although the British were running short of recruits, the Americans had the limitless numbers they could call on. By the fourth day of the offensive, US reserves had doubled the number of men in the Ardennes to 180,000.

Hitler was persuaded to change the name of the operation from *Wacht am Rhein* to *Herbstnebel* (Autumn Mist) and delay the attack from 25 November to 10 December, then to 16 December to build up enough armour for the offensive.

mobile strength necessary for carrying out its difficult assignment'. But Hitler turned down von Rundstedt's proposal and insisted on his more grandiose plan.

It had taken 2,500 tanks to overrun France in 1940. Now, against far superior forces, Hitler planned to send just 1,420. More, they were short of fuel and would have to provision themselves by capturing American gasoline on the way. The Germans had enjoyed air superiority in 1940. Now the Allies ruled the skies. With no Eastern Front to worry about the Germans could call

Spearheading the breakout would be the Fifth Panzer Army under General Hasso von Manteuffel and the newly formed Sixth SS Panzer Army under Colonel-General Joseph 'Sepp' Dietrich. They would be supported by the 7th Army under General Erich Brandenberger who would protect the armour's southern flank. The Panzers would attack on a 90-mile (145-km) front from Echtnernach in the south to Monschau in the north. The Fifth Panzer Army would be in the centre, the Sixth on the right, where the main effort would be. Consequently Dietrich's

Sixth Panzer Army was given the best-equipped Waffen-SS units.

To blunt any counter-offensive, a hand-picked force of English-speaking Germans would be sent behind Allied lines wearing American uniforms and carrying American weapons. They would disrupt the Allied forces by switching signposts and misdirecting traffic. They would be commanded by SS Colonel Otto Skorzeny, who had recently headed the daring raid to rescue Mussolini from his mountain prison.

Hitler moved his headquarters from the Wolf's Lair in East Prussia to the Eagle's Lair near Bad Neuheim in the Rhineland, where he could direct the offensive personally. Luck, he thought, would be with him as he had been there in the Eagle's Lair in 1940 when the Panzers had crushed the Allies in France. But those around him said that he was getting increasingly out of touch with reality.

In November, while preparations were under way, the Allies had breached Germany's 'West Wall' frontier defences and had taken Aachen, the first German town of any size to be seized by the Allies. However, despite Arnhem, the Americans were beginning to show signs of hubris. The sector Hitler planned to hit was manned by just four divisions of the US VIII Corps, under Major-General Troy Middleton, spread thinly. They were the 4th and 28th Divisions, who had just been pulled out of the line to recuperate after heavy fighting, and the 9th Armoured Division and the 106th Division, who had never been in action before. Either side of the Ardennes front were the inexperienced and understrength First, Third and Ninth Armies of General Omar Bradley's Twelfth US Army Group. It was a palpable weak spot between the main American thrust into Germany to the south and the British thrust through Holland to the west.

However, despite the fact that the Germans had attacked in precisely this way in 1870 and 1940, army intelligence ruled out a German attack in this area. The hapless troops of the Twelfth were about to be attacked by three German armies, 25 divisions in all, 11 of them armoured.

Von Rundstedt sent a message to his men. It read, 'Soldiers of the west front. Your great hour has arrived. Large attacking armies have started against the Anglo-Americans. I do not have to tell you anything more than that. You feel it yourselves. We gamble everything. You carry the sacred obligation to give everything to achieve things beyond human possibilities for our Fatherland and our Führer.'

The final gamble

At 0535 hours on 16 December, 2,000 guns opened up in the Ardennes. The offensive took place during a period of bad weather when the Allied air forces were grounded and the Germans quickly developed a salient 50 miles (80 km) deep in the American lines. Churchill quickly dismissed the German winter offensive as 'the Battle of the Bulge', a name he had, however, already given to the 1940 Ardennes offensive. This time, though, it stuck.

Skorzeny's troops in American uniforms went in first. They fooled few, and most of them ended up in front of a firing squad. The Seventh Army were held up not far from their starting point, but the Panzers did better. The Sixth SS Panzer Army struck through what was called the Losheim gap

German soldiers in the Ardennes counter-offensive – at first they made excellent progress but it was ultimately doomed to failure

> **'The offensive was stalled, but Hitler refused von Rundstedt's suggestion that part of Dietrich's SS Panzers be moved north'**

and made significant gains, which they could not exploit due to lack of fuel. Von Manteuffel's Fifth Panzer Army swept through the 28th and 106th Divisions and penetrated deep into the enemy's positions with the foremost armoured units, the 2nd and 116th Panzer Divisions, reaching points close to the River Meuse, with elements of the 2nd Panzer Division actually reaching its bank. However, this was not exploited.

Units from the 6th SS Panzer Division were not switched to follow up the 5th's initial success and the advance was hampered by narrow, ice-bound roads.

The Fifth Panzers had another problem. The supply route ran through the town of Bastogne, which was held by the 101st Airborne Division under Brigadier-General Anthony McAuliffe. He found himself completely surrounded. When he was asked to surrender, he replied famously: 'Nuts.' The 101st held out for six days, supplied by air.

By 19 December, the offensive was stalled, but Hitler refused von Rundstedt's suggestion that part of Dietrich's Sixth SS Panzers should be moved north to support von Manteuffel's Fifth Panzers who had made rather better progress. Hitler wanted the SS to have all the glory. However von Manteuffel's main force halted 6 miles (10 km) short of the Meuse, the weather cleared and the Allied air forces took to the air again.

At a meeting at Verdun on 19 December, Eisenhower remained resolutely upbeat, telling his generals, 'The present situation is to be regarded as one of opportunity for us and not disaster. There will be only cheerful faces at this conference table.' The outcome of the meeting was to shift Patton's Third Army 150 miles (240 km) north to the left flank of the salient, while the recently promoted Field Marshal Montgomery would attack the northern side with some of Bradley's troops temporarily assigned to his command.

Although on 21 December the Fifth Panzers took the town of St Vith, von Rundstedt felt the advance had run out of steam and, on 22 December, he asked Hitler's permission to withdraw. It was refused.

Guderian said:

Even by 22 December it was plain that a less ambitious objective should have been chosen. A sensible commander would on this day have remembered the looming dangers on the Eastern Front which could only be countered by a timely breaking-off of this operation in the west that was already, from the long view, a failure. However, not only Hitler, but the High Command and particularly the Armed Forces Command

Staff could, during those fateful days, think of nothing save their own Western Front. The whole tragedy of our military leadership was revealed once again ... in this unsuccessful Ardennes offensive.

On Christmas Day, the Sixth SS Panzer Army suffered a crushing defeat and the following day Bastogne was relieved, at the cost of 3,900 American dead and 12,000 Germans. The Americans had lost 150 tanks in the action, the Germans 450. The Americans could afford to lose tanks. Thousands more were on their way from the States, while the Germans had few left and their tank factories now faced nightly bombing.

German atrocities had inspired the raw American troops to fight with renewed determination. The man largely responsible was General Jochen Peiper, who commanded 140 tanks and a battalion of motorized infantry. He was in the spearhead of the German offensive. At Honsfeld, his men shot 19 GIs and robbed their bodies. At an airfield near Bullingen, Peiper forced captured Americans to refuel his tanks. Afterwards, he shot them. Eight more US prisoners of war were killed at Lignueville. A hundred American prisoners were machine-gunned in Malmédy. Twenty, who miraculously escaped the slaughter, were found hiding in a café. It was set on fire and those who ran out were machine-gunned.

Final reckoning

Hitler thought that news of these massacres would demoralize the American troops. In fact, it gave them a first-class incentive to fight back and he was forced to order a withdrawal. By early January 1945, the front line was almost back where it had been before the Ardennes offensive had begun. Reviewing the casualty figures, Hitler claimed that Operation *Herbstnebel* had been worth it. The Germans had lost between 60,000 and 100,000 men, the Americans around 43,000 and the British, who played only a minor part in the action, 1,400. The Americans had also lost 733 tanks, the Germans 600 and an enormous number of guns and other equipment had been

US troops advance on Malmédy – Hitler thought that the massacres there would demoralize US troops but they served to spur them on

After their initial success, German troops inspect some captured US equipment in the Ardennes, but the tide was to turn against them

lost. But as the Allied air forces were now intent on the complete destruction of German cities by merciless bombing, the Germans could not replace their equipment. America's factories remained undamaged. The Battle of the Atlantic had already been lost. The sea lanes were no longer menaced by U-boats and German bombers. Liberty ships were steaming across the Atlantic carrying countless new tanks and guns. Hitler had thrown away his final strategic reserve and gained just six weeks' time to prepare the defences on the Rhine.

Finally, Hitler allowed the Sixth Panzer Army to be withdrawn. Six Panzergrenadiers seized the opportunity to desert and the commander of their battalion issued this order of the day:

Traitors from our ranks have deserted to the enemy... These bastards have given away important military secrets...

Deceitful Jewish mud-slingers taunt you with their pamphlets and try to entice you into becoming bastards also. Let them spew their poison! We stand watch over Germany's frontier. Death and destruction to all enemies who tread on German soil. As for the contemptible traitors who have forgotten their honour, rest assured that they will never see home and loved ones again. Their families will have to atone for their treason. The destiny of a people has never depended on traitors and bastards. The true German soldier was and is the best in the world. Unwavering behind him is the Fatherland. And at the end is our Victory. Long live Germany: Heil to the Führer!

Right: Remagen Bridge, which the Germans attempted to destroy

In the early weeks of March 1945, the US First and Ninth Armies reached the Rhine and a unit of the First Army found the railway bridge at Remagen intact and only lightly defended. It had not been blown up as Hitler had ordered and the Americans swept across it on 7 March.

Clean sweep

On 22 March Patton's Third Army established a bridgehead near Nierstein, ready for a drive across southern Germany. To the north Montgomery's 21st Army Group had also reached the Rhine and halted while the western bank was cleared. On the other side of the river were five divisions of Hitler's paratroopers, with just one Panzer division and one Panzergrenadier division as a mobile reserve. At dawn on 24 March, these were attacked by the US 17th Airborne and the British 6th Airborne, armed with bazookas – hand-held rocket launchers that meant infantrymen and airborne troops could now take on a tank. Some 1,696 transport planes and 1,348 gliders from 11 air bases in southern England and 17 bases around Rheims, Orléans, Evreux and Amiens dropped 21,700 men, 600 tonnes of ammunition and 800 guns and vehicles on the east bank of the Rhine.

This massive airborne fleet was protected by a close escort of 889 fighters. Meanwhile, more troops poured across the river in an amphibious assault called Operation *Plunder*.

Once a bridgehead was established 1,000 fighter bombers of the 2nd Tactical Air Force arrived to provide close air support and attack the Panzers on the ground. Some 3,789 German prisoners were taken and the 84th Division practically annihilated. The Panzers in the west were no more.

10. PANZER KAPUT

Things were going little better in the east. On 20 August 1944, the Red Army launched an attack against Army Group South Ukraine. Part of the front was held by Romanian troops who deserted in large numbers. Some turned their guns on the Germans. Others fled across the River Danube and closed the crossing places, leaving the Germans to the mercy of the Russians. Sixteen divisions were completely destroyed.

The situation worsens

By 1 September the Russians had fought their way into Sofia, the capital of Bulgaria. The king, a Nazi sympathizer, died in mysterious circumstances and the 88 Panzer IVs and 50 assault guns that the Germans had delivered to equip two anti-Bolshevik Bulgarian divisions were lost. German troops in Bulgaria were imprisoned and Bulgaria switched sides. Hungary also tried to make contact with the western powers. The military leaders then went over to the Russians. Hitler installed a new fascist government in their place, though it made little difference. And in Slovakia, partisans began stopping trains and killing any German soldiers they found on board. However to the north the First Panzer Army under General Heinrici, the Third Panzer Army under General Rauss, after Model was transferred to the west, and the Fourth Panzer Army under General Balck held the Russians back on the Vistula.

As Germany's main effort was now in the west, Guderian was ordered to stabilize the Eastern Front. The autumn promised to be mild and the frosts delayed, so it seemed likely that a Russian winter offensive might be put off until the New Year. Guderian planned the construction of strongpoints along the front and, by mid-December, had pulled all the Panzer and Panzergrenadier divisions out of the line to form a mobile reserve. But 12 understrength divisions was not an adequate reserve to hold a front 725 miles (1,160 km) long.

Top: A convoy of Soviet tanks helps 'liberate' Bucharest, Romania

Guderian's plan was to establish a major line of defence well camouflaged 12 miles (19 km) behind the line they were holding. As soon as the Russian artillery started the barrage that heralded an attack, everyone, save a rearguard, would pull back. The barrage would then be wasted as it would fall on positions already evacuated. The well-prepared assault would be fruitless and the Russians would simply run up against another line of defence where they would have to begin their preparations all over again. When Guderian submitted this plan to Hitler, he lost his temper. Hitler refused to accept the loss of 12 miles of territory without a fight and ordered that the second line be prepared just 1 or 2 miles (1.5–3 km) behind the front. This, Guderian said, was First World War thinking.

The fortifications themselves were well prepared, but the Ardennes offensive left the 'Great Defensive Line' poorly defended. Worse, Guderian said, was Hitler's order for the reserves to be held near the front. This meant that when the great Russian tidal wave came, it simply swamped both the defensive lines and the reserves. Hitler blamed the men who built the fortifications and claimed that he had always favoured a 12-mile gap between the defensive lines rather than a gap of 1 or 2 miles.

'Who was the halfwit who gave such idiotic orders?' he asked.

Guderian pointed out that it was Hitler himself who had made the decision. Hitler called for the minutes of the autumn planning meetings to be brought. But he broke off reading them after a couple of sentences.

The atmosphere in Hitler's headquarters became more and more otherworldly. Hitler

'Hitler ordered that the second line be prepared just 1 or 2 miles behind the front. This, Guderian said, was World War I thinking'

insisted that he was the only one there with real front-line experience, though he had not visited the front line once during the Second World War. His ego fed on the flattery of party officials, particularly Göring and von Ribbentrop. And he resolutely refused to learn from others. He told Guderian:

There is no need for you to try to teach me. I've been commanding the Wehrmacht in the field for five years now and in that time I have had more practical experience than any of the gentlemen of the general staff could ever hope for. I have studied Clausewitz and Moltke and read all the Schlieffen papers. I'm more in the picture than you are.

But all that experience could not stop the Russians. By 5 December they had reached the outskirts of Budapest and by Christmas Eve they had encircled the city.

Red Army troops take to the streets of Budapest, 1945. The siege of Budapest was one of the bloodiest battles of the Second World War

The odds lengthen

When it became clear on 23 December that the Ardennes offensive was a failure, Guderian begged for the attack to be called off and for the remaining forces to be switched to the Eastern Front. He reckoned that the Russian winter offensive would start on 12 January and he calculated that the Russians had a superiority of seven to one in tanks, 11 to one in infantry and twenty to one in guns. That gave them an overall superiority of 15 to one on the ground and twenty to one in the air. Guderian reckoned that German soldiers could still triumph with odds of five to one against them. But with these odds victory was impossible.

Guderian believed that the only hope was to build up a large Panzer army in the area around Lodz and, when the Russians broke through, fight a war of movement, a Panzer war – 'for this was a type of battle in which the German commander and soldiers, despite the long war and their consequent exhaustion, were still superior to the enemy,' he said.

On 24 December Guderian visited Hitler's headquarters for a conference. When he presented his report about the situation on the Eastern Front, Hitler refused to believe his figures on the estimated strength of the enemy and said that he doubted that the Russians would attack at all. Meanwhile, he was in the grip of self-delusion. He ordered the formation of Panzer brigades consisting of just two battalions – the usual strength of a regiment – and anti-tank brigades of just one battalion.

Jodl opposed Guderian's request for forces to be switched to the east. He wanted more attacks in the west, believing that the British and Americans could be halted if the Wehrmacht went on the offensive in Alsace. Guderian pointed out that the production from the factories in the Ruhr had been halted by enemy bombing. If they lost the industrial area of Upper Silesia to the Russians, they would no longer have the weapons-making capacity to continue the war. His request was denied and Hitler further weakened the Polish front by ordering Reinhardt's reserves to Budapest to lift the siege of the city. So two of the 14 and a half Panzer and Panzergrenadier divisions assembled to take on the Russian winter offensive were sent to a secondary front.

On New Year's Eve, Guderian went to Hitler's headquarters to ask for reinforcements once again. This time he had a preliminary meeting with von Rundstedt, who informed him that there were three divisions on the Western Front and one division in Italy that he could have. They were already by railway stations, ready to be transferred.

When Guderian got to see Hitler, Jodl opposed the movement of forces to the Eastern Front once again, saying that there were no units available. Guderian contradicted him and when Jodl asked where he had got the information from, Guderian replied that it was from von Rundstedt, Commander in Chief of the Western Front. Jodl could say no more and Hitler approved the transfer of the four divisions. However, instead of sending them to Poland where they were needed, he sent them to Hungary.

At a meeting on 9 January, Guderian again begged Hitler to strengthen his mobile reserve, but when he showed Hitler the enemy dispositions and strengths, Hitler claimed that they were the work of an idiot and ordered the man who prepared them locked up in a lunatic asylum. Guderian pointed out that they had been prepared by one of his very best officers and he would not have presented them if he had not agreed with them.

'So you had better have me certified as well,' he said.

Again Hitler refused Guderian's request for a strengthening of his Panzer reserve.

'The Eastern Front has never possessed such a strong reserve as it does now,' said Hitler. 'It is all your doing and I thank you for it.'

Guderian replied, 'The Eastern Front is a house of cards. If the front is broken at one point, the rest will collapse. Twelve and a half divisions are far too small a reserve for such an extended front.'

As Guderian left, Hitler said, 'The Eastern Front must help itself and make do with what it has got.'

This sent a chill though the Prussian Guderian: when the Russians broke through it was his homeland that would be lost.

On 12 January, huge numbers of men and tanks began pouring over the Vistula into the Russian bridgeheads. The following day the Russian Third and Fourth Guards Tank Armies broke though south of Warsaw. Meanwhile the offensive in Alsace had stalled. Over the next few days, the Russians attacked along the entire line and the front began to disintegrate.

Guderian kept Hitler informed of the worsening situation by phone and by 15 January

Hitler began interfering. Over Guderian's head, he ordered the transfer of the *Grossdeutschland* Panzergrenadier Corps from East Prussia to the area around Kielce. Guderian protested that this was done too late to stop the Russian breakthrough at Kielce and it weakened the defences in East Prussia at the very time they were coming under attack.

In the bunker

On 16 January, Hitler returned to the partly bombed Chancellery in Berlin to be nearer to the Eastern Front. He now decided that the Western Front should go on the defensive to release troops to fight in the east. He also decided that they must hit the southern flank of the Russian spearhead and Hitler ordered Guderian to send the Sixth Panzer Army to Hungary. It was necessary, Hitler said, to hang on to the oil fields in Hungary, otherwise there would be no fuel for the Panzers.

General Nehring's XXIV Panzer Corps was stemming the Russian attack around Kielce, but the XLVI Panzer Corps had to pull out of the Warsaw area when it risked being encircled. It was supposed to go south to stop a Russian breakthrough that would cut East and West Prussia off from the rest of Germany. But the Russians threw it back on to the north bank of the Vistula and began their dash on the German border unhindered.

The German garrison in Warsaw now risked being cut off. Guderian told Hitler that they should be withdrawn, but he grew angry and insisted that Warsaw be held at all costs. But the garrison commandant had little artillery and only four infantry battalions with limited combat experience. It would have been impossible for them to hold the city and the commandant withdrew his garrison despite Hitler's orders not to. Hitler was furious and spent the next few days investigating the loss of Warsaw rather than devoting himself to more pressing matters. When Hitler ordered the arrest of members of the general staff, Guderian said that he alone was responsible for the loss of Warsaw, so it was he who should be arrested, not his staff. Nevertheless Hitler had three of Guderian's staff arrested at gunpoint. Guderian again insisted that he was the one whose conduct should be investigated, so ending up subjected to lengthy interrogations at a time when he should have been concentrating all his efforts on the battle for the Eastern Front. Two of his staff were then released, but instead of returning to their staff duties were sent to command regiments on the Eastern Front. Three days later one of them was killed. The third member of Guderian's staff was sent to a concentration camp, which he later swapped for an American prisoner of war camp.

On 18 January, the Germans in Hungary attacked in an attempt to lift the siege of Budapest. They fought their way through to the banks of the Danube. But that same day the Russians entered the city, so the effort had been wasted. Nevertheless Hitler sent the Sixth Panzer Army to Hungary in an attempt to hold the Russians there.

On 20 January, the Russians first set foot on German soil. Guderian's wife, who had been under constant surveillance by the local Nazi Party, was then allowed to leave and flee to the safety of Guderian's headquarters, half an hour before the first shell landed in Deipenhof.

The Russian onslaught could not be resisted. Hitler began to accuse his Panzer commanders of treason. Guderian tried to calm him, but Reinhardt and Hossbach were relieved of their commands.

The Russians had now mastered the art of Panzer warfare. They advanced rapidly, bypassing strongpoints and outflanking fortified lines – though most of the fortifications in the east had been stripped to build the Atlantic Wall. Germany's only hope now was that the Western Allies would realize what the rapid Russian advance might mean for the future of Europe and sign an armistice. Guderian said that he proposed to the German foreign minister von Ribbentrop that he open negotiations for an armistice on at least one front – preferably the Western. Von Ribbentrop told Guderian that he was a loyal follower of Hitler and he knew that the Führer did not want to make peace.

'How would you feel if in three or four weeks the Russians were at the gates of Berlin?' said Guderian.

'Do you believe that that is possible?' asked a shocked von Ribbentrop.

When Hitler heard of this, Guderian too was accused of treason, though he was not arrested. Hitler had few enough able officers left.

Guderian proposed a plan that would give them some breathing space. They should form a new army group specifically to hold the centre of the line. Guderian suggested that its commanding officer should be Field Marshal Freiherr von Weichs, a commander in the Balkans. Hitler approved Guderian's plan for the creation of a new army group, but gave its command to Himmler. Guderian was appalled. Himmler was not a military man. He was a politician, the head

'Hitler approved Guderian's plan for the creation of a new army group but gave its command to Himmler. Guderian was appalled'

of the SS. He was also chief of police, minister of the interior and Commander in Chief of the Training Army, any one of which positions might be thought a full-time job. But Hitler was insistent. Guderian tried to persuade him at least to give Himmler von Weichs' experienced staff. But Hitler, who was now wary of all his generals, ordered Himmler to choose his own staff. Himmler surrounded himself with other SS leaders who were largely, in Guderian's opinion, incapable of doing the jobs they had been given. SS Brigadenführer Lammerding was his chief of staff. Previously the commander of a Panzer division, Lammerding had no idea of the duties of a staff officer. The new army group was to be called Army Group Vistula, though the Russians had crossed the Vistula months before.

Hitler set up new 'tank destroyer' divisions. These consisted of men issued with anti-tank grenades and bicycles. Somehow they were expected to stop the huge armies of T-34s that were now driving westwards. And by this time 16-year-old boys were being conscripted into the army.

'Hitler became so enraged that the veins on his forehead stood out and members of staff feared he might have a heart attack'

By 28 January, Upper Silesia was in Russian hands. Speer wrote to Hitler saying, 'The war is lost.' Hitler now cut Speer completely and refused to see anyone alone in private, because they always told him something he did not want to hear. Hitler began demoting officers on a whim, and brave soldiers denounced by party members found themselves in concentration camps without even the most summary investigation. Guderian found that more and more of his day was spent listening to lengthy monologues by Hitler as he tried to find someone to blame for the deteriorating military situation. Hitler often became so enraged that the veins on his forehead stood out, his eyes bulged and members of staff feared that he might have a heart attack.

On 30 January, the Russians attacked the

Second Panzer Army in Hungary and broke through. Guderian proposed evacuating the Balkans, Norway and what remained of Prussia and bringing back all the Panzers into Germany for one last battle. Instead Hitler ordered an attack and on 15 February the Third Panzer Army under General Rauss went on the offensive. In overall command of the offensive was General Wenck. But on the night of the 17th, after a long briefing by Hitler, Wenck noticed that his driver was tired and took the wheel, only to then fall asleep himself and crash into the parapet of a bridge on the Berlin–Stettin highway. Wenck was badly injured and, with him in hospital, the offensive bogged down and never regained its momentum.

In March, Rauss was summoned to the Chancellery and asked to explain himself. Hitler did not give him a chance to speak. After he had dismissed Rauss, Hitler insisted he be relieved of his command. Guderian protested that he was one of the most able Panzer commanders. Hitler said that he could not be trusted because he was a Berliner or an East Prussian. It was then pointed out that Rauss was an Austrian, like Hitler himself. Even so he was relieved of his post and replaced by von Manteuffel.

Himmler's Army Group Vistula did little to halt the Russian advance and Guderian eventually suggested that Himmler be replaced. On 20 March, Hitler agreed. He was replaced by a veteran military man, Colonel-General Gotthard Heinrici, who was currently commanding the First Panzer Army in the Carpathians. Under his command was the Third Panzer Army under von Manteuffel.

Guderian continued to come up with

suggestions of how the Russian advance could at least be slowed. But after one final falling-out with Hitler, he was ordered to take convalescent leave of six weeks. He left Berlin on 28 March intending to go to a hunting lodge near Oberhof in the Thuringian Mountains, but the rapid advance of the Americans made this impossible. Instead he decided to go to the Ehenhausen sanatorium near Munich for treatment of his heart condition. Warned that he might invite the attentions of the Gestapo, Guderian arranged to be guarded by two members of the Field Police.

Marshal Georgy Zhukov led the Russian advance on Berlin – by this time the Germans had no chance of beating invading forces

The defence of Berlin was left in the hands of General Heinrici, an expert in defensive warfare. On the eve of the Soviet attack, he had pulled his front-line troops back so that Zhukov's massive bombardment fell on empty positions. The Ninth Army had dug in on the Seelow heights, blocking the Berlin road. Zhukov's men eventually overwhelmed the Seelow line with sheer weight of numbers, but then they came up against more German defences, reinforced by General Karl Weidling's 56th Panzers, and were halted. It was still the Panzers who stiffened the resistance. On 20 April, Marshal Konstantin Rokossovsky's 2nd Belorussian Front attacked von Manteuffel's Third Panzer Army.

Days of reckoning

The Ninth Army began to disintegrate. When Zhukov got close enough to Berlin to start bombarding the city with long-range artillery, the situation became hopeless. Berlin was defended by the Hitler Youth and elderly men from the *Volkssturm* (Home Guard). To the end Hitler maintained that a relief column of Tiger IIs was on its way and SS-Obersturmführer Babick, battle commandant of the Reichstag, was at his map planning for the arrival of these King Tigers. Gerhard Zilch, an NCO with the 3rd Heavy Flak Battery, gave this account:

Babick was still bubbling over with confidence. He thought he was safe in his shelter. SS sentries were posted outside. Others guarded the corridors of the Reichstag and the King Tigers, our finest weapon, were apparently just around the corner. He had divided his men into groups of five to ten. One group was commanded by SS-Untersturmführer Undermann, or something like that: I did not quite catch his name. He was posted to the Ministry of the Interior – 'Himmler's House' – south of the Molke bridge, with the bridge itself in his line of fire. Then an SS subaltern, about 19 years old, came to Babick and reported that Undermann and his men had come across some alcohol and that they had got roaring drunk. He had brought Undermann with him and he was waiting outside. Babick roared, "Have him shot on the spot!" The subaltern clicked his heels and marched out. Moments later, there was a burst of machine-gun fire. The boy returned and reported that the order had been carried out. Babick put him in charge of Undermann's unit.

The Soviets drew the noose tighter and 15,000 Russians guns began to pound the city, Hitler dropped all pretence of running things and announced that he would commit suicide before the Russians arrived. Meanwhile the forty or fifty left in the cellars of the Reichstag began looking for hiding places. On 30 April, Hitler and Eva Braun, the mistress that he had married the previous day, committed suicide.

'At dawn on 1 May, we heard over our portable radio that the Führer had "fallen in battle for the Reich capital" with his wife at his side,' said Zilch. 'Goebbels and his family had gone the same way. We were our own masters at long last.' At midnight on 8 May 1945, the war in Europe was over.

Right: A Soviet soldier hoists the red flag over the Reichstag, Berlin

AFTERWORD

Guderian ended up in the Tyrol, with the staff of the Inspectorate-General of Armoured Troops, where they waited for the Allies to arrive. On 10 May, he was taken into captivity by the Americans. His dream of a war-winning Panzer Army had turned to ashes. After initial successes in Poland and France, the British had learnt how to fight the Panzers with anti-tank screens in North Africa, then the Russians and the Americans used their industrial might to out-produce the German Panzer manufacturers.

Although initially unco-operative with his captors, in June 1947 Guderian was told that all war-crimes charges against him had been dropped. He then co-operated in an American programme to detail the strategic history of the war and found himself defending the Panzer concept, once again, against his infantry colleagues. In 1948 he was released and went to live with his wife in a small house in Schwangau, where he gardened and wrote. His memoirs *Panzer Leader*, published in 1951, became a best-seller in the US and he was given honorary membership of the International Mark Twain Society. He died shortly afterwards in May 1954.

Panzer Leader has been translated into ten languages, including Polish, Russian and Chinese. Guderian also wrote a series of articles and pamphlets, including 'Can Western Europe Be Defended?' and 'This Cannot Be the Right Way', criticising NATO's unpreparedness for armoured conflict during the Cold War. The development during the Second World War of massive air forces, ballistic missiles and nuclear weapons made tanks almost obsolete, playing little part, for example, in the wars in Korea and Vietnam. However, tanks gave the Israelis their rapid victory in the Six-Day War of 1967 in the deserts of the Middle East: perfect country for a tank man. They were also used by the Soviets to crush the 'Prague Spring' in Czechoslovakia the following year, as they had been used in Hungary in 1956. Perhaps the most vivid image of the tank in recent history, though, is the picture of a single protester holding up an armoured column on its way to crush the demonstrations in Tiananmen Square in June 1989.

FURTHER READING.

Barker, A.J., *Panzers at War*, Ian Allen, London, 1978

Cawthorne, Nigel, *Fighting Them on the Beaches: The D-Day Landings, June 6, 1944*, Arcturus, London, 2002

Cawthorne, Nigel, *Turning the Tide – Decisive Battles of the Second World War*, Arcturus, London, 2002

Citino, Robert M., *Armed Forces – History and Sourcebook*, Greenwood Press, Westport, Connecticut, 1994

Cooper, Matthew, and Lucas, James, *Panzer – The Armoured Forces of the Third Reich*, Macdonald and Jane's, London, 1976

Davies, W.J.K., *Panzer Regiments*, Almark, London, 1978

Edwards, Roger, *Panzer – A Revolution in Warfare, 1939-1945*, Arms and Armour, London, 1989

Fletcher, David, *The Great Tank Scandal*, HMSO, London, 1989

Forty, George, *German Tanks of World War Two*, Blandford Press, London, 1987

Forty, George, *Tanks Aces from Blitzkrieg to the Gulf War*, Sutton, Gloucestershire, 1997

Fuller, John Frederick Charles, *Tanks in the Great War*, John Murray, London, 1920

Fuller, John Frederick Charles, *The Reformation of War*, Hutchinson, London, 1923

Fuller, John Frederick Charles, *On Future Warfare*, Sifton Praed & Co, London, 1928

Fuller, John Frederick Charles, *Memoirs of an Unconventional Soldier*, Nicholson & Watson, London, 1936

Guderian, Heinz, *Achtung – Panzer!*, Arms and Armour, London, 1992

Guderian, Heinz, *Panzer Leader*, Penguin, London, 1996

Liddell Hart, Basil, *Paris, or the Future of War*, Kegan Paul & Co, London, 1925

Liddell Hart, Basil, *The Decisive Wars of History*, G. Bell & Sons, London, 1929

Liddell Hart, Basil, *The British Way in Warfare*, Faber & Faber, London, 1932

Macksey, Kenneth, *Guderian – Creator of the Blitzkrieg*, Stein and Day, New York, 1976

Macksey, Kenneth, *The Tank Pioneers*, Jane's, London, 1981

MacLeod Ross, G., *The Business of Tanks 1933 to 1945*, Arthur H. Stockwell, Ilfracombe Devon, 1976

Piekalkiewicz, Janusz, *Tank War 1939-1945, Historical Times*, Harriburg, PA, 1986

Remarque, Erich Maria, *All Quiet on the Western Front*, Vintage, London, 1996

Rommel, Erwin, *The Rommel Papers*, edited by B.H. Liddell Hart, Collins, London, 1953

Schmidt, Heinz Werner, *With Rommel in the Desert*, Albatross Publishing, Durban, 1950

Smithers, A.J., The New Excalibur, Leo Cooper, 1986

Steiger, Rudolf, *Armour Tactics in the Second World War – Panzer Army Campaigns of 1939-41 in German War Diaries*, Berg, New York, 1991

Warner, Philip, *Panzer*, Weidenfeld and Nicolson, London, 1977

Wright, Patrick, *Tank: The Progress of a Monstrous War Machine*, Faber and Faber, London, 2000

PICTURE CREDITS